DISPUTES AND DEMOCRACY

DISPUTES AND DEMOCRACY

The Consequences of

Litigation in Ancient Athens

STEVEN JOHNSTONE

UNIVERSITY OF TEXAS PRESS, AUSTIN

Requests for permission to reproduce material from this work should be sent to Permissions, University of Texas Press, Box 7819, Austin, TX 78713-7819.

⊗ The paper used in this book meets the minimum requirements of ANSI/NISO Z39.48-1992 (R1997) (Permanence of Paper).

LIBRARY OF CONGRESS CATALOGING-IN-PUBLICATION DATA

Johnstone, Steven, 1959–
Disputes and democracy : the consequences of litigation in ancient
Athens / Steven Johnstone. — 1st ed.
    p.   cm.
Includes bibliographical references and index.

1. Law, Greek.   2. Law—Greece—Athens—History.   3. Procedure
(Greek law)   4. Procedure (Law)—Greece—Athens—History.   I. Title.
KL4115.A75 J64   1999
340.5'385—dc21   98-51231

ISBN: 978-0-292-74053-2

Portions of Chapter 3 were previously published in "Cracking the Code of Silence: Athenian Legal Oratory and the Histories of Slaves and Women," in *Women and Slaves in Greco-Roman Culture: Differential Equations,* edited by Sandra R. Joshel and Sheila Murnaghan (London and New York: Routledge, 1998). Reprinted by permission.

FOR ADAM, ALEX, AND JASON

REMEMBERING SAN FRANCISCO

CONTENTS

ACKNOWLEDGMENTS

The difficulty is not beginning, it is knowing where to end. Ordinarily, the boundaries seem clear. Readers think of a book as a discrete object, the product of a single author, a commodity, a physical thing, an elaborated argument. As an author, however, "my book" does not primarily describe the object you are holding but one of the principles that has organized my life for many years, a kind of ἄσκησις or discipline. I do not think first of my claims about Athenian litigation but about my writing routine: By 7 each morning I am at work at my desk, which sits in a sweeping bay window looking east over the stacked houses in Noe Valley. After at least two hours' work, about the time the fog begins to thin, I walk down 24th Street, stopping for coffee and to read the morning paper. I time the rest of my morning by the shouts of the children at recess at 10 and 12 across the street at St. Philip's School, and so on. This peculiar, sometimes even obsessive, discipline has governed not only my own life but those of the people around me as well. Thus, there are many I want to thank not only for supporting me in this project but also for acquiescing themselves to the discipline of the book.

Although sometime in the summer of 1993 I realized that my dissertation, even in a revised form, was not the book I wanted to write, the present project grew out of that earlier attempt. I cannot imagine a better place than the Department of History at the University of Chicago to have been trained in the rigor and imagination of the discipline. My understanding of history in large part comes from the many extraordinary people, both students and faculty, I met there. Dan Beaver, Mike Kugler, Dan Gordon, Emie Aronson, Bill Kunze, David Goodman, Joe McCormick, and Martin Zelder were all essential to my life as a graduate student. Antoinette Burton continues to be so brilliant and so funny that she deserves a sentence of her own. Probably more. My dissertation committee—Ian Morris, James Redfield, Charles Grey, and particularly my advisor, Richard Saller—not only oversaw that project; their comments, suggestions, and insights have continued to animate this work just as their practice as historians continues to be a model for my own. Earlier still than even all this, Carol Thomas first introduced me to the joys and potentials of Greek history when I was an undergraduate at the University of Washington. Although most of these people have not seen the present work, in small ways and large, their influence runs throughout it.

Scholarship is much more a collective than an individual endeavor, and this book is the product of many conversations over the last few years. I think immediately of Jerry Shurman, Mary James, William Diebold, Darius Rejali, Jennifer Dellner, Wally Englert, Andrew Kelley, Martin Bloomer, Leslie Kurke, and Lisa Maurizio. During most of the period when I was writing this book, the Classics Department at Stanford University provided a collegial, intellectually stimulating home. The department provided essential institutional support, both buying my computer and arranging my teaching schedule to have time off, for which I am extremely grateful. While at Stanford, I also taught in the Program in Cultures, Ideas, and Values; my colleagues in Great Works were an extraordinary group of scholars, teachers, and friends. Although it sometimes seems like there is a tradeoff between teaching and research, this book would not be as good as it is without all I have learned from my students at both Reed College and Stanford.

Many people have enriched my life and contributed to this book (in ways they may not suspect) by doing so. I owe thanks to Dave Bates, Jean Bates, Emily Bates, Einar Molver, Kermit Nies, Colm Davis, Todd Payne, Ellen Tilden, Lamar Witmer, and Erin Carlston. My parents deserve special gratitude for always supporting me, especially in my education, no matter how esoteric the choices I made must have seemed.

Several people have read all or part of this manuscript; their thoughtful comments have dramatically improved it. Ian Morris has read three different versions over the years and responded thoughtfully to each. Mark Edwards has not only read and commented on much of it but endured my disquisitions at countless dinners early on when I was trying to figure out what I was thinking—and he was always kind enough to pick up the check. Mike Jameson has focused and broadened my thinking not only by his feedback but by our many conversations over lunch about Greek history. Jon Goldberg-Hiller read the manuscript late in its development; his early insistence that I explain what I meant by "the law" echoed through my mind as I wrote every section. Margaret Imber read an early version of Chapter 3 and let me know I was on the right track. Stephen Theilke gave me many helpful comments on the Introduction. I delivered an embryonic version of Chapter 5 at the convention of the American Philological Association in 1993 and appreciated the comments of the respondent, Mogens Herman Hansen, and of the panel co-organizers, Adele Scafuro and Bob Wallace. At a critical juncture, Matt Christ scoured the manuscript, which benefited in ways both detailed and fundamental. Finally, Michael Gagarin gave me a remarkably precise, insightful, and practical set of comments, twice. There are places where we disagree, but if my arguments persuade you, it is only because he helped sharpen them.

I wrote the first draft of this book between January and September 1995. During that time and subsequent periods when I was revising it, three people made especial sacrifices to accommodate my cloistered life. Alex Robertson Textor brought me great joy with his passion, intelligence, and silliness. Jason McGraw's friendship has been a bedrock in my life for many years. The intricate workings of his mind inspire my own; he suggested that I should have a blurb on the back that says: "In the event of water landing, this book can be used as a flotation device." Jason has given considerable buoyancy to both my book and my life. Finally, what I owe to Adam Geary is difficult to express. He read the manuscript several times and often seemed to understand it better and have more faith in it (and in me) than I did. His enthusiasm for this project and love for me have made my life especially rich and wonderful.

S. J.

LIST OF

ABBREVIATIONS

The following abbreviations for ancient authors and works are used throughout this book:

Aesch.	Aeschines
Andoc.	Andocides
Ant.	Antiphon
Arist.	Aristotle
Ath. Pol.	*Constitution of Athens*
Rhet.	*Rhetoric*
Rhet. ad Alex.	*Rhetoric to Alexander*
Aristoph.	Aristophanes
Athen.	Athenaeus
Dem.	Demosthenes
ep.	epistle
D. Hal.	Dionysios of Halicarnassos
Din.	Dinarchos
Eur.	Euripides
Hdt.	Herodotos
Hyp.	Hyperides
IG	*Inscriptiones Graecae*
Isae.	Isaeos
Isoc.	Isocrates
Areop.	*Areopagitikos*

Lyc.	Lycurgos
Lys.	Lysias
Plato	
Apol.	*Apology*
Symp.	*Symposium*
SEG	*Supplementum Epigraphicum Graecum*
Thuc.	Thucydides
Xen.	Xenophon
Ath. Pol.	*Constitution of the Athenians*
Mem.	*Memorabilia*
Symp.	*Symposium*

The University of Texas Press is in the process of publishing new translations of all Athenian legal orations; meanwhile, the Loeb series contains
translations of all of them. All translations are mine, except where noted.
In citing speeches, I have used the abbreviation for the author, followed
by the standard speech number and section number. So, for example,
"Dem. 24.149" means Demosthenes speech 24, *Against Timokrates*, section 149. I have not indicated speeches wrongly attributed to a particular author by bracketing his name because, for my purposes, correct attribution is irrelevant as long as it is an authentic ancient speech (cf. Ober
1989, 48–49).

DISPUTES AND DEMOCRACY

INTRODUCTION

Athenian law was essentially rhetorical. No lawyers, no judges, no public prosecutors, just two litigants addressing several hundred jurors. This book analyzes the ways litigants tried to persuade them. Descriptive and analytical, not normative, it does not attempt to decide whether their arguments were relevant or proper. Judgments on these points are certainly possible; indeed, litigants offered them all the time. I do not, however, attempt to settle such questions, because disagreements about how the normative should be understood were themselves an integral part of Athenian litigation. Litigants wrangled repeatedly about the meaning of the law. Athenian litigation, therefore, was not so much about applying the law as about struggling over what the law was and how (or even if) it related to the dispute at hand. In Athenian litigation, the law was not opposed to, or even separable from, rhetoric. In the absence of authoritative legal specialists, the only historical sense in which the law existed in Athens was in and through the rhetoric of litigation. To treat Athenian law otherwise, as a standpoint outside litigation, misrepresents both law and litigation.

Athenian litigation was rhetorical not only because of the language that litigants used but because of the setting that shaped that language. Litigation introduced a powerful third party—the jury—that thoroughly transformed the conditions and possibilities of pursuing disputes. The relationship between litigant and jurors was fundamental but problematic. In seeking to persuade the audience, speakers attempted to appear authoritative, yet the institutional context of litigation limited the intrusion of external, social sources of authority. Laws against bribery, panels of several hundred jurors, and random assignment to the courts effectively curtailed the direct influence of wealth on trials. These features also limited the effect of social factors such as reputation. Athens was far too large to constitute a "face-to-face" society in which everyone knew everyone else.[1] When a litigant faced a jury, all but the most famous must have been largely unknown to most of the jurors. Minimizing possible sources of external authority and local knowledge made juries more impartial,[2] but it left jurors with little basis on which to trust the words of a speaker other than those words themselves. The institutional context of litigation exacerbated the problem of authority in other ways. Because of the adversarial setting, opposing speakers always attacked each other's authority. This sharp dichotomizing of conflict, moreover, seems to have entailed a belief that one of the parties spoke the truth and the other lied.[3] Far from being a precondition of speaking in the courts, then, authority was in fact the hoped-for outcome of the trial.

Because language alone established the relationship between speaker and audience, the uncertainties of this social relationship were expressed as anxieties about language. The unease Athenians felt about rhetoric in the courts stemmed from the absence of other sources of trust in the relationship between litigant and jurors. Athenians usually established trust over time through enduring interpersonal relationships. In contemporary society we routinely invest trust in what Anthony Giddens calls abstract systems through their representatives—tellers, pilots, mechanics, technicians, clerks, and many others—most of whom are usually unknown to us.[4] This form of trust, however, was largely absent from the lives of most Athenians. Athenians were disquieted when called upon to trust not people they knew but mere language.[5]

In Athenian courts, the dependability of a litigant's speech was not guaranteed by a preexisting trust in the speaker, but was created and authorized largely through this language itself. To counter this problem of self-authorizing language, speakers attempted to ground their speeches in extralinguistic sources of authority, sources of authority outside language and its uncertainties. One strand in the yarn of this book follows litigants as they sought authority for their words. Sometimes this involved telling the type of story that jurors would recognize as true. At other times, it meant appealing to written, publicly sanctioned norms, especially laws, but also the oath all jurors had sworn. It could entail referring to actions outside the court (offers to settle the dispute by torturing a slave or the speaker's public services, for example) that showed the truthfulness and good character of the speaker. It might even mean relying on ritual language and actions, the force of which was felt to be immediate and certain. The variety of strategies, however, all reveal a desire to overcome the indeterminacy of rhetorical language and to stabilize the relationship constituted through that language.

In the Athenian courts, at least, the more success rhetoric achieved, the greater its internal tensions. Scholars have often noted that litigants used artful rhetoric to deny their own rhetorical artfulness.[6] More generally, virtually all these strategies for authorizing language themselves relied on language. Litigants related accounts of their character and their actions outside the court, for example, in precisely the same way they told of their quarrels; neither had greater epistemological certainty. Thus, what this book studies were not really strategies for grounding rhetorical language in some external authority but strategies that rhetorical language used to conceal its status as rhetoric.[7] The extralinguistic authority of litigants' claims was less the cause of their persuasiveness than its effect.

This rhetorical language of litigation produced significant effects, both for individuals and for the larger society. For litigants the rhetorical resources of litigation constituted the most important endowment for pursuing their disputes in court. Thus, the language of litigation holds the key to understanding their strategic choices, whether to initiate litigation and how to pursue it. The complex system of rhetorical arguments, intimately connected to the institutional dynamics of the relationship between speaker and audience, structured the choices of individuals. The effects of the rhetorical language of litigation, however, radiated well beyond individual litigants. Indeed, the language of the courts produced significant, though unintended, systemic, social consequences as well. Significantly, this language enabled the reproduction of groups in Athens, that is, the perpetuation and re-creation through time both of the objective circumstances of the group and of its subjective awareness of its common interests.[8] To persuade a majority of several hundred jurors, litigants linked their appeals to interests they attributed to jurors. Thus, one of the most important consequences of litigation was the reproduction of various social identities: as men or women, elite or common, citizen or slave, as "Athenians." Most importantly, litigation reproduced and strengthened Athenian democracy: the equality within the citizen body and the hierarchy outside it.

These two kinds of consequences are analytically distinct, although they are also theoretically and practically interrelated. The next two sections of the Introduction separately trace each of these consequences of litigation as well as the theoretical perspectives informing my account.[9]

DISPUTES AND ATHENIAN LITIGATION

The language and institutional setting of Athenian litigation imposed unique shapes on conflict. In distinguishing between legal and nonlegal forms of conflict, I have used a concept articulated in legal anthropology, the dispute, which is, broadly, a conflict between people. Disputes can take many forms, only one of which is legal.[10] In fact, most disputants voice, pursue, and even settle their quarrels without litigation or even reference to the law.[11] Dispute theory does not just classify different forms of conflict; it also understands that the key to the course of a dispute lies in the transformations from one form to another (say from a feud to litigation). Such transformations, effected or asserted by interested parties, are both provisional and contestable. Indeed, "negotiations over what a dispute is about are a critical dimension of the disputing process."[12]

Analyzing the transformation of disputes into legal cases underscores the unique characteristics that distinguished litigation from other ways of pursuing disputes in Athens.[13] At least three features stand out: Litigation required the intervention of a powerful new third party, the jury. Litigation imposed specialized roles on previously undifferentiated disputants. Finally, litigation simplified disputes by dichotomizing both conflict and the options for settling it.

As the discussion of the problems of language in the courts has made clear, nothing so affected the contours of a litigated dispute as the presence of the jury. Legal scholars recognize the importance of the introduction of third parties to disputes;[14] at Athens, the jury's intervention made litigation radically different from other forms of disputing. It is true, of course, that in nonlegal quarrels, disputants may have appealed to "public opinion" as a way of gaining leverage. Gossip, for example, could play an important role in nonlegal quarrels.[15] Yet appealing to a public through gossip was quite different from making a speech to secure a jury's verdict.[16] The relationship between "speaker" and "audience" in gossip was much less formal and direct. Gossip, too, except in the most celebrated cases, probably remained localized within the community that knew the disputants, whereas litigation involved an audience that knew almost nothing about them. Juries also held a special power: to make a definitive, explicit, irreversible judgment. The presence of this powerful third party meant that the litigants' primary relationship, which in the nonlegal stage had been with each other, was now with the jury itself. The jury now mediated and thereby transformed their relationship to each other.[17] The extent and complexities of rhetorical language are a gauge of the fundamental nature of this transformation.

The decision to litigate transformed the dispute because the parties took on interrelated but differentiated and asymmetric roles. In a non-legal form of dispute, although various factors may have distinguished the parties, as disputants their roles were roughly equivalent. The law, however, sharply distinguished prosecutor from defendant. These novel roles altered the resources available to each party for pursuing the conflict. The transformation to the legal arena opened up new resources and foreclosed old ones. For example, although in a nonlegal dispute the ability to mobilize mutual kin, friends, or neighbors to one's side by doing them favors could prove decisive in successfully pursuing the dispute, such people could not apply the same informal pressure to a jury.[18] On the other hand, the ability to speak fluently and think quickly, essential to arguing a case before a large jury, would be of less importance in trying to win concessions from an adversary through the intervention of friends. Litigation thus bestowed particular and unique resources on litigants, but it did so asymmetrically. A prosecutor, for example, told at least a story with a specifically legal form: the story of two people, one of whom had violated the law. A defendant, however, in contesting this definition of the dispute, had more latitude to draw upon his character and previous life; so, as I argue in Chapter 4, for the most part defendants, not prosecutors, cited their services to the city as a reason to vote in their favor. One of the most important consequences of litigation, then, was that it bestowed on two disputants the roles of prosecutor and defendant, roles that were structurally asymmetrical.

The law made decisions possible by simplifying, sometimes radically, the complexity of social life.[19] In part it did this by allowing only two primary parties, prosecutor and defendant, dispersing all others to various ancillary "third party" roles. As I argue in Chapter 2, however, conflict is not invariably dyadic; frequently, more than two people are involved. Litigation also focused conflict on a single incident (a "crime") rather than on an ongoing relationship of hostility. Such simplifications operated to make a definitive judgment possible: Jurors were not (ideally, at least) confronted with several competing claimants or with the problem of inventing an outcome acceptable to all parties. Rather, they simply voted one way or the other. The kinds of legal stories that litigants, prosecutors especially, told reflected these simplifying tendencies of the law.[20]

The transformation of a dispute into a legal case was the outcome of a strategic decision of one of the parties, since at Athens only private individuals, not the state, prosecuted cases. A violation of the law may be a necessary condition of a legal case, but it is never sufficient.[21] Though the law creates the possibility of litigating, this is always contingent, and the law itself cannot dictate this choice.[22] The transformation depends, instead, on the choice of one disputant to pursue his quarrel in a different way, using the resources of the law. A potential Athenian prosecutor, therefore, considered the institutionally unique features of litigation in calculating whether to initiate a case: Would his goals in the dispute, whatever those might be, be better served by appealing to a formal body of jurors, by defining his dispute as a specific crime, by naming one individual as the defendant, by highlighting the defendant's character, by using the people on his side as witnesses and advocates, and by making the decision an either/or, winner-take-all choice? He needed to consider how litigation would affect the endowment of resources available to himself and to his opponent or opponents. It is not quite correct, therefore, to say that a prosecutor was constrained to tell a legal story (as though this were externally imposed); rather, the decision to litigate was already the decision to tell such a story.

Litigation was not the natural outcome of a violation of the law but a strategic decision of a party to a dispute to transform it in a particular way, or, perhaps better, to assert a particular transformation. Definitions of disputes, no matter how authoritative, were always interested and contestable, including the assertion that a particular dispute should be viewed as a legal case.[23] As noted above, at stake in every dispute was how to understand the dispute, including what it was about and who the relevant parties were.[24] The attempt of one party to impose a legal form did not end the conflict over how to understand the dispute: Many defendants denied that the law was relevant to the conflict. Although a prosecutor might assert that his case concerned a single act that violated the law, say, an assault, a defendant might claim, even if a fistfight took place, that the conflict was really about two gangs of young men who had drunk a bit and were just roughhousing and that it certainly did not belong in the courts.[25] From a "strictly legal" perspective, of course, such claims might be called irrelevant precisely because they deny the appropriateness of the legal perspective. But from the perspective of a dispute, the question is how each party attempts to impose a perspective in the first place. This study, therefore, treats with equal respect both the prosecutor's assertion that the dispute constituted a legal case and the defendant's challenging of the relevance of legal categories. The point is not which of these was correct but how each side made its arguments.

The concept of the dispute helps make sense not only of an individual's decision to litigate but of the simultaneous decision of what kind of case to bring. Robin Osborne has argued that Athenian law offered a procedural versatility to prosecutors: For any particular "crime" there was often more than one procedure that could be used against it.[26] Athenian law distinguished procedurally between public cases and private ones: Basically, in a private case only the wronged party could prosecute,[27] whereas in a public case, any citizen could act as accuser.[28] There were other important differences between these kinds of cases: It was easier to compromise a private case before trial, public trials were allotted more time and larger juries, many private cases went through mandatory official arbitration, and penalties were often greater in public cases. Osborne argues that potential prosecutors chose what kind of case to bring based on strategic considerations. But there is a problem. While it is true that for some events, say, an assault, there were many ways to prosecute, for others, say, not following the correct procedure for drafting a decree, there were not. From this perspective, Osborne seems to have overstated the versatility of Athenian procedures.

Nevertheless, prosecutors did face procedural choices, though not quite for the reasons Osborne suggests. Osborne predicates his argument on a legal perspective: There was a violation of the law. But from the perspective of a dispute, there is often more than one event that could serve as the basis for a legal claim. Again, it is not that "crime" leads to litigation; rather, in most enduring disputes more than one legal shape could plausibly be imposed on the conflict. In many Athenian disputes, either side could have found grounds for initiating a case and giving legal shape to the conflict. This was not (or not mostly) because different meanings could be attributed to the same event (as in assigning blame in a fistfight) but because in an ongoing dispute there were usually many "events" that could be plausibly constituted as violations of the law. The procedure chosen was not an outcome of an objective "crime"; instead, because different types of procedures bestowed different rhetorical resources on prosecutors, the choice of procedure was also a choice of what type of criminal meaning to attribute to a dispute. When considering whether to transform the dispute into a public or a private case, therefore, potential prosecutors had to consider that although defendants in both kinds of cases had relatively similar resources, those available to prosecutors were quite different in public and private cases.

In analyzing the ways in which people pursued disputes, I have made no judgment that they did or should have concluded in settlement. Traditional understandings of the role of law in society usually see it as a way of limiting or suppressing conflict. This derives from a functionalist perspective, which sees conflict as harmful to society.[29] But because dispute theory shifts the perspective from society to individuals and the choices they make, there is no supposition that disputes should end in settlement.[30] If some disputants wanted an amicable settlement, others desired a crushing victory, and some may not have had a single, specific goal. Thus I do not claim that the function of the Athenian courts was the regulation of conflict or the settlement of disputes, though this surely happened. Rather, in the courts, disputants sought to use the law to pursue their disputes, whether this ended in settlement or not.[31]

Though initially developed by legal anthropologists, the concept of the dispute seems extremely useful for classical Athens.[32] Several scholars working on Athenian law and society have recently used it.[33] Indeed, anthropologists in the 1960s (most importantly, Laura Nadar and her students) formulated the idea of the dispute as a way of discussing processes of social conflict across cultures without having to rely on the Western category of law. Later, following the work of Comaroff and Roberts, scholars began to look more at the social context of disputes, at the behavior of disputants rather than institutions, at the transformation of disputes, and at the ways in which the meaning or shape of the conflict was part of what was in dispute.[34] Reflecting the recent consensus among legal anthropologists that law and legal institutions should not be studied in isolation but within a larger cultural context, scholars have attempted to link the study of disputes to broader questions of power, ideology, and the politics of meaning.[35]

LITIGATION AND ATHENIAN DEMOCRACY

This book investigates the ways in which litigation, understood as a set of social practices, reproduced social structures and subject positions. Courts were, of course, only one of many venues in which the structures of Athenian society were reproduced; nevertheless, the effects of litigation radiated broadly. I am not so much concerned with the vision of how society should operate written into the law, the effects of which have often been overestimated,[36] as with the systemic social consequences (intended and, more often than not, unintended) of the practices associated with litigation.

The relationship between individuals and social structures (e.g., "society," "gender," or "class") has been a central problem of recent social theory. Whereas subjectivist approaches assume the existence of autonomous subjects whose agency derives from their intentions, objectivist theories bestow ontological primacy on society and other social institutions. Though diverse in character, much of the best recent work in social theory has sought a solution to this opposition. There has been no consensus on this, but several relevant tendencies are evident. First, social theorists have attempted to retain the important insights of each approach by describing some sort of reciprocity between structures and subjects. Anthony Giddens, for example, has developed a theory of "the duality of structure," in which the constitution of structures and agents are simultaneously implicated: "The structural properties of social systems are both medium and outcome of the practices they recursively organize." [37] From this perspective, subjects and structures are interrelated, and neither has primacy over the other.[38]

The second tendency of social theory has been to locate the link between subjects and structures in the quotidian: in language, in bodies, in routine, in what people ordinarily do ("practice"). Giddens suggests we study "neither the experience of the individual actor, nor the existence of any form of societal totality, but social practices ordered across space and time." [39] It is just here, in the most mundane of actions, that agents draw upon social structures in acting, simultaneously reproducing those structures. The emphasis on the quotidian has been pervasive in social theory, from Bourdieu's theory of the *habitus* to Foucault's ideas on dispersed power.[40]

Third, following from the idea that structures and subjects are reciprocally constituted, social theorists have tended to theorize agency, the ability of subjects to act, as part of understandings of power as both constraining and enabling.[41] Thus, structures not only limit subjects; they also provide resources or strategies for action. Foucault's work has inspired some of the most subtle of these theories of agency, perhaps because it has at times seemed so problematic in denying both agency and subjectivity to individuals.[42]

Parallel to these trends in social theory, many historians have moved toward studying culture. The recent rise of cultural history is, of course, complex,[43] but part of its aim has been to integrate the study of structures and of subjects. The work of E. P. Thompson, for example, mediates these through "experience," which is essentially cultural.[44] Although the idea of experience is not unproblematic,[45] Thompson's histories carefully delineate the ways structures imposed limits, but also bestowed resources, on people, and how they, in turn, appropriated and used them. He argues, for example, that in the eighteenth century, English peasants redeployed the ideology of paternalism to resist the spread of the capitalist market.[46] In studying these peasants' actions in "food riots," Thompson carefully pays attention to the ideological system that had exploited the peasants and to their ability to adapt and transform it into an instrument of resistance. Like many cultural historians, Thompson pays attention to the ways people attribute meanings and to their struggles over these.[47] In this view, the cultural does not reflect or play out the real forces of history (e.g., class relations); rather, it is only in the quotidian lives of people that historical forces are realized and contested.

In investigating the ways in which litigation effected the reproduction of Athenian democracy, I understand democracy rather more broadly than the Athenians seem to have and than modern scholars as well. Democracy is usually construed to refer to the structure of relationships between adult male citizens (i.e., political subjects). Ober has considered these relations in detail.[48] Following the insights of feminist theorists and historians, however, who argue that no account of men can be complete if it abridges women,[49] I have considered democracy as the word that describes the peculiar constitution of power relationships in all Athenian society, including those usually considered outside the political realm. Athenian democracy entailed not only a group of ideological equals but other groups that were excluded from this inner group and regarded as inferior.[50] Litigation reproduced this sense of democracy as the equality of some and the inequality of others.

One of the important consequences of litigation in Athens was the reproduction of various Athenian identities, including that of "the Athenians." To avoid both reductionism and essentialism, analyses that merely assume that people's subjective outlooks derive mechanically from their objective circumstances (so that, for example, all men think alike merely because they are biological men), many social theorists consider identities as contingent, as culturally constructed. This does not mean that a person can claim an identity willy-nilly (a purely subjectivist stance) but that the ways people define themselves and recognize their interests are culturally disposed in historically specific ways; we must, therefore, study the means by which such identities are produced and reproduced.[51] Although conditions in contemporary society may offer unique opportunities for the self-fashioning of identity,[52] fourth-century Athens was not a society in which identity simply derived from a person's position in a fixed, traditional order.[53]

Thus it is important to ask how identities (as men, as commoners, as Athenians) were invoked and reinforced, how people were induced and seduced into identifying their interests in certain ways, how these groups were, so to speak, conjured. Though some work on Athens has sought to do this,[54] most has assumed these identities as given. For example, despite its sophistication, Ober's analysis derives its classes, masses and elites, from the existence of a clear division in wealth, an instance of economic determinism.[55] But this distinction, though it depended on a difference in wealth, was only realized insofar as it became culturally relevant, and this was the result of considerable labor.[56] Ober argues that it was through cultural forms, that is, through language, especially rhetorical language, that these groups related to each other. This study goes further and argues that through this language, the groups were themselves constituted and reproduced.[57] Crucially, the discourses and practices of the Athenian courts reproduced these various Athenian identities.

This book studies the dynamics of Athenian culture within a specific institution, the courts. In the last few years, a number of scholars have studied the ways in which social practices and values impinged on the operation of the Athenian courts.[58] This book follows the lead of this important body of work in seeing Athenian legal practices as part of a larger social system. But because this recent work reacts against previous scholarship that often portrayed Athenian law as an autonomous institution that regulated social life, it has had less to say about the effects of the legal system on society. Indeed, this recent scholarship often loses a sense of the institutional uniqueness of the law, sometimes denying that there was anything unique or autonomous about it.

Autonomy, however, is always a matter of degrees and forms, and no institution is either completely autonomous or completely dependent.[59] Certainly the Athenian courts were not as autonomous as modern American courts, but they were, whatever their interdependence with the rest of society, distinct from other social practices and institutions: Prosecutor, defendant, witness, and juror were uniquely legal roles. As a result, I have based this study on speeches given before the courts at Athens and have not grouped them with those given before the Boule (the Council) and the Assembly (as, for example, Ober 1989 does).[60] Indeed, as I note several times, the evidence points to marked differences between the practices of these institutions. Even at Athens, where institutions had a lower degree of differentiation than in modern societies, a study of power and politics must take account of institutional specificity.[61] The complementary influences of law and society delineate the extent and limits of the autonomy of the legal system.

EVIDENCE: ATHENIAN LEGAL SPEECHES

As evidence for this project I have relied on the hundred or so preserved speeches delivered in the Athenian courts, assuming they record with reasonable accuracy what litigants said and did in court. This assumption is not without its uncertainties, as the processes by which these texts were written and transmitted were complex and are not entirely understood.[62] Although we cannot be sure that they were not revised after delivery to make them better literary products, in most cases, if they were, revisions were probably not significant.[63] (However much they were revised, they still attempted to sound like actual court speeches, and so nothing too foreign would have been introduced.) Actual speeches also probably contained nonscripted, extemporaneous elements that do not appear in the texts. (One can often appreciate what these elements were by noting the kinds of arguments or behaviors by their opponents that litigants expected or mentioned but that do not appear in the speeches themselves.) Neither of these, however, impairs my project, which concerns patterns manifested in differences between types of speeches; there is no reason that one type of speech (say, defense speeches) was consistently altered from its delivered form in ways that others were not.

These speeches cannot simply be assumed to tell truthful tales. Rightly approaching litigants' claims with a fair degree of skepticism,[64] scholars have realized, nonetheless, that the presence of an audience put a check on how far a speaker could distort his reports. The most sophisticated modern readings often attempt to discover the truth in the incidental (reports that the speaker would have had no reason to distort) and the typical or plausible (claims of a kind that would not have seemed unreasonable to the audience).[65] Although I focus mostly on how people made arguments and told stories (and not whether these were true), I too rely on these methods. Nevertheless, as I argue in Chapter 2, these methods also have their limits. What is plausible may have less to do with the kinds of things that actually typically happen than with the kinds of stories that are normally told in a particular context.

Finally, I have tried to make generalizations based on patterns that appear in the whole body of speeches. Generalizations based on one or two or even a handful of the most prominent speeches may, quite unintentionally, not accurately reflect the common practice of Athenian litigants. The advantage of the abundance of speeches, however, is that it permits the use of a straightforward method of generalization, one whose premises and methods can be clearly stated. I have, therefore, made a number of generalizations based on statistics, generalizations that do not supplant but ground and facilitate close readings of the texts. By providing a panorama of general patterns among all speeches, statistics provide some assurance that a particular passage is representative, not atypical. An appendix explains how I compiled the statistics and offers some help in understanding them.

PROSPECTUS

Each of the following chapters examines a kind of argument litigants made. In each case I analyze the ways the context of litigation gave a unique shape to these arguments and trace the consequences of these arguments for both individuals and Athenian society.

Athenian litigants based their speeches on the laws. Chapter 1 investigates the ways litigants made arguments about what the laws meant. In discussing laws, litigants often attributed them to an author, "the lawgiver." Though this did not constitute what we would consider a properly historical argument, it provided the basis for justifying interpretations of specific laws by linking them to other laws through the fiction of a single author. The dikastic oath, sworn by all jurors (dikasts), enjoined them to judge in accord with the laws. This was not, however, a rule that determined the use of laws in the courts; rather, since it was itself subject to interpretation, litigants deployed it to support different interpretations of the laws. Both the figure of the lawgiver and the dikastic oath provided protocols for making arguments about what the laws meant. Knowledge of these protocols, which were not recorded but remembered in the ongoing practices of the courts, differentiated male citizens from those who were excluded from participating in litigation.

The second chapter examines the ways that litigants used the laws to tell stories about disputes. Because they chose to initiate a legal case, prosecutors represented their dispute through a legal narrative; such judicial stories centered on a specific incident that supposedly violated the law, concerned a single opponent, and frequently dichotomized conflict. Defendants responded by denying the coherence of the prosecutor's story or contradicting it with a story of their own, frequently alleging that the prosecutor had initiated the case for corrupt reasons. Defendants' stories, which may seem irrelevant or diversionary, contested the prosecutor's attempt to transform the dispute into a legal case. The distribution of these narrative resources reflected the asymmetric positions of prosecutor and defendant. Litigants of all kinds, however, also drew on the law as a way of understanding and evaluating their own and their opponent's behavior. Although such stories did not necessarily accurately portray disputes, their selective portrayal of events nevertheless played an important part in the reproduction of groups within Athenian society, both those with access to litigation and those excluded.

The third chapter analyzes how litigants talked about a specific procedure, the dare or challenge. A dare was an offer to settle a dispute through another procedure, such as the torture of a slave, the taking of an oath, or arbitration. Outside the courts, dares were a way of carrying on the dispute, sometimes leading to settlement when they were accepted, sometimes exacerbating it by their effrontery. In the exchange of dares, procedural disagreements substituted for substantive ones, so that disputants could bargain truth, justice, and honor while saving face. Within the courts, however, litigants sought to find extralinguistic grounds for authority in the offer of the dare and in the dared procedure. They represented these as actions or facts (*erga*), as opposed to their opponents' mere stories (*logoi*). The anxiety over the relationship between speaker and audience in the courts gave rise to the claim of truth, the claim that words accurately represented reality. This discourse of truth, which pervaded litigants' speeches in more than their discussions of dares, thus reflects the institutional peculiarities of litigation at Athens. Under the sway of the discourse of truth, paradoxically, litigants frequently misrepresented the practice of dares in social life.

Defendants frequently reminded jurors of their public services (liturgies) and asked for reciprocal favor (*charis*), the subject of Chapter 4. Reflecting the asymmetric positions of prosecutors and defendants, these claims comported with the emphasis in legal stories on the person of the defendant. Defendants, however, frequently relied on their liturgies to undermine the prosecutor's legal narrative. In claiming that the tenor of his whole life was more certain evidence than the prosecutor's story of a single event (a "crime"), a defendant implicitly challenged the legal framework of the prosecutor's story. Defendants also relied on their public services to claim the favor of a verdict from the jury. Such claims did not merely mobilize Athenians' interests; they also instilled and reproduced them. Paradoxically, although private benefaction and *charis* often strengthened social hierarchies, in the courts, where litigants needed to mobilize a group to win their case, frequent appeals for *charis* strengthened Athenian democracy by reinforcing jurors' awareness of their collective interests.

Defendants often begged for the jurors' pity. The fifth chapter recounts how defendants not only addressed these appeals to the jurors verbally but enacted them in rituals of weeping and supplication. Searching for more certainty than representational language, defendants used performative language and gestures to relate to the jurors. However emotional these pleas for pity may have been, they had a more important cognitive function. In them, litigants, who were as often as not elites, humbled themselves before the people collectively, undercutting the social hierarchy at odds with the ideals of citizen equality. Such pleas did not merely rely on a democratic consciousness but were one of the ways it was reproduced. In them, the Athenians dramatized democracy daily.

The final chapter analyzes the relationship between litigation and Athenian culture. Athenian litigants disagreed about the degree to which litigation should take account only of the law or of other cultural considerations as well. This disagreement, however, was a structural feature of litigation, since prosecutors advocated a narrowly legal view and defendants, resisting the prosecutors' transformation of their dispute into a legal case, constantly asked jurors to consider more than just the law. Thus, the relative autonomy of litigation consisted not in a final answer to this question but in the way litigation structured and incorporated the debate over its own boundedness. Litigation, therefore, affected Athenian society because the kinds of arguments speakers made on these points depended on mobilizing groups which, in turn, required defining them and attributing interests to them. Thus, one of the crucial consequences of litigation was the reproduction of Athenian society.

The rest of this introduction briefly describes Athenian society and politics in the period under consideration and gives an account of how Athenian courts operated.[66]

THE ANCIENT CITY OF ATHENS

During the period under consideration (422–322 B.C.), Athens was intermittently but constantly at war. The pan-Hellenic Peloponnesian War (431–404), which pitted Athens against Sparta, each at the head of an alliance, had the greatest internal repercussions for Athens. Twice because of this war the democratic government at Athens was suspended. In 411 a group of oligarchs, the Four Hundred, ruled Athens for a short time before the democracy was reestablished. More significantly, with Athens' defeat at the end of the war, Sparta imposed a very restricted oligarchy, the Thirty, who ruled for several months (404–403). The Thirty's program was more extreme and was implemented further than the Four Hundred's and included, significantly, curtailing the powers of the popular courts. When they began to kill Athenians and metics, the free noncitizens, by the hundreds, however, they were finally overthrown. The restored democracy passed a general amnesty that prevented the prosecution of previous crimes and the enforcement of legal decisions rendered under the oligarchy. The deeds of the Thirty were long remembered, and they essentially discredited any public advocacy of explicit oligarchy in Athens for the next several decades. A number of other important Greek wars punctuated the fourth century, but none had such serious internal consequences for Athens. Conflict with Macedonia persisted for many years at the end of this period, and in 322 the conquering Macedonians imposed a less democratic government on the city. Democratic institutions thus seem to have been quite strong during this period, suppressed only twice, and each time by a foreign army.

Though the population fluctuated through this period, the social structure remained relatively stable.[67] There were probably between 20,000 and 40,000 adult male citizens, the same number of adult women of citizen status, and about twice as many children of citizen status. The number of slaves may have equaled those of citizen status. Athens was also home to several thousand metics. Citizens enjoyed several privileges because of their status.[68] Only citizens could own land and participate in government. In the courts, only citizens served as jurors. Women, children, and slaves could not appear themselves as litigants but required a citizen advocate. Metics could represent themselves in many kinds of cases (especially commercial cases, where they are prominent among the extant speeches), though in some kinds of prosecutions they apparently required the assistance of a citizen patron.

Among the citizens, there were several potential cleavages, especially based on differences in wealth. Even in the fourth century, certain offices were officially restricted based on property qualifications, though these were often ignored in practice. Though Athenian citizens were free from taxes, the polis required the wealthiest to undertake certain duties, including producing a chorus in a dramatic festival, sponsoring a banquet, or, most importantly, outfitting a warship (a trireme) for a year. The number of men routinely liable for these liturgies was probably between 1,000 and 1,200, less than 5 percent of the citizen body.[69] There were some 2,000 who might be called upon to pay a special war tax.[70] Elites were distinguished not only by their wealth but often as well by the styles of living their wealth enabled.[71] They also tended to occupy positions of formal and informal leadership in the democracy. Some scholars have claimed in addition that there was a substantial group of citizens of middle wealth, neither wealthy nor penurious, often identified with those who served in the infantry as *hoplites*. For the fourth century, at any rate, significant evidence for such a self-conscious middle class is lacking, unless it denotes merely the mass of ordinary Athenians who had to work for a living, usually by farming.[72] There were also many citizens who were not very well off, indeed, who owned no land, but their poverty did not constitute the basis for self-identification as a coherent class. There is little evidence for how such people lived, but it was probably through seasonal labor and farming rented land. There was no "urban mob," not even a substantial group of workers involved in handicrafts.[73]

Despite these economic stratifications of the citizens, however, the democracy was undergirded by an ideology of citizen equality, which was realized to a remarkable degree. Though generals and treasurers were elected by voting, most offices were appointed by lot. Levels of participation in the Athenian government—in the Assembly, which met at least four times a month, in the Council of Five Hundred (the Boule), which prepared its agenda, and in the hundreds of other offices—seem to have been quite high. Service in the courts, attendance at the Assembly, and filling of some other governmental posts were compensated with a stipend that made it more possible for even the poor to participate. Because of appointment by sortition, limited tenure (one year), collegiality (boards of officials undertook most responsibilities), and strict reviews of all officeholders (through the *dokimasia*, a review of formal qualifications before entering office, and the *euthyna*, an audit of official conduct after completion of the term), individuals could not amass political power through formal governmental institutions. Nor were there auxiliary organizations like political parties through which politicians could accumulate power.

Instead, the primary avenue to prominence was the ability to persuade mass audiences, in both the Assembly and the courts. It is true that there was an informal "political elite," but, lacking formal institutionalization, their power always depended upon their ability to win the assent of mass audiences composed of ordinary Athenians.[74]

The great achievement of Athenian democracy, then, was the participation and exercise of political power by the majority of citizens with only limited restrictions based on wealth. Unlike most other Greek cities, there was no minimum property qualification for full participation as a citizen.[75] From a modern perspective, however, Athenian democracy looks questionable at best: The majority of adults (women, slaves, metics) were excluded entirely from the privileges of citizenship.[76] Citizens constituted the elite of this society, whose freedom was made possible and defined by institutions of slavery and patriarchy. Even as generated in the courts, Athenians' understandings of themselves as citizens depended on the exclusion of others. I think it is important to consider how much these forms of oppression were essential to Athenian democracy, but it is not my intention to attack or defend it. Nevertheless, it is essential to note that within the body of citizens, the Athenians achieved a degree of political equality that minimized the claims of wealth to a degree unparalleled in most societies, certainly in our own.

THE ATHENIAN COURTS:
STRUCTURE AND HISTORY

The Athenian judicial system differed radically from our own. Without legal experts, the jurors were the heart of the system. All citizens over the age of 30 could serve as jurors. The courts met between 150 and 200 days a year, on days when the Assembly did not meet or there was not a religious festival. From those who showed up each morning, enough were randomly selected to fill however many juries were needed that day. Each jury (*dikasterion*) consisted of hundreds of jurors (usually 201 or 501, sometimes bigger, very rarely up to 6,000), the majority of whom determined the verdict. They voted immediately after the litigants' presentations without deliberation. There was no judge; although a magistrate presided at the trial, he did not affect its outcome. Those who served earned a day's minimum wage of a half drachma.

Litigants who faced Athenian juries did so with minimal professional help. There were no legal experts, no lawyers, in Athens. Litigants found and cited whatever laws they thought relevant, and the jury interpreted them itself. Litigants usually addressed the jury themselves, sometimes supported by friends or relatives who appeared as witnesses, added a plea for them, or showed solidarity by sitting with the litigant. Now and then, a close friend or relative might speak for a party who thought himself disadvantaged in speaking (old age or youth were the most common reasons). Women, children, and slaves had to be represented by a male. In some cases, free noncitizen males could uphold their own interests. There were no police and no public prosecutors. The aggrieved party brought suit himself, although there were many public actions in which anyone who wanted could prosecute.[77] The accused, too, had to persuade the jurors himself. Litigants might, however, commission a speechwriter to compose their oration. It is from these, about a hundred of which survive from 422–322 B.C., that I have drawn my evidence. We rarely know either what the opponent said or the verdict. In some cases, the successful prosecutor received part of the fine. Each side had only a limited amount of time in which to speak, and trials never lasted more than a day.[78]

Jurors and litigants were in all likelihood socially distinct. Juries probably approximately reflected the composition of the Athenian citizen body. Ancient writers sometimes complained that the poor controlled the juries, though by poor they probably meant those who actually had to work for a living, which is to say the mass of ordinary Athenians, mostly farmers. Modern attempts to argue that some subgroup of Athenians disproportionately dominated the juries are unconvincing, unless, of course, that means that the great majority of Athenians who were not particularly rich and had to work for a living (usually on the land) were also in the majority on the juries.[79] Nevertheless, while it is reasonable to suspect that juries reflected the whole population, litigants were undoubtedly much richer than normal. It was this social difference between litigants and jurors rather than the exact social composition of juries that was important. Several considerations operated to exclude conflicts that involved the humble from the realm of public litigation. Most immediately, small disputes (of less than ten drachmas) were settled by local judges from whom there was no appeal to the courts.[80] There were also expenses incurred by litigants, even if they were not necessarily overwhelming. Litigants in private suits had to pay the official arbitrator a drachma each, and certain types of suits required fees or deposits of one or both parties.[81] Perhaps the greatest expense would have been to hire a professional speechwriter; we cannot be sure how much this cost, but the rarity of speeches for manifestly poor people in the preserved corpus suggests a professionally written speech, if not litigation itself, was beyond the means of most.[82] It is a reasonable guess that at least half of the preserved speeches were written for Athenians in the wealthiest class, those who performed liturgies.

Because of the scarcity of contemporary sources, the development of the Athenian legal system is known only in the broadest outline down to the fifth century.[83] The usual narrative closely links the development and growing power of the courts to a more general democratization, a trend, that is, through the sixth and fifth centuries for an increasing proportion of the citizens to be involved in most aspects of ruling.[84] At least two key periods stand out in the development of Athenian legal institutions. In 594/3 Solon first constituted juries made up of the whole of the citizens and increased their oversight by specifying that all cases could be referred to this court from the magistrates who had previously given final judgments. He also established the public case, those in which any citizen (not just the victim) could bring the charge. Later, during the fifth century, as trials before citizen juries became increasingly frequent, the single body of citizen jurors (the Heliaia) was broken into smaller panels (*dikasteria*). Sometime soon afterwards (in the late 450s), Perikles sponsored the introduction of pay for service on juries. In contrast to these institutional changes, virtually nothing is known until the 420s about the specific topics of this book, the kinds of things litigants said and did in court.[85] Still, the general (though not unswerving) trend in the institutional development of the courts during these two centuries was for more citizens to have more powers to oversee more cases.

The end of the fifth century and beginning of the fourth also saw a number of important innovations in the procedures for legislating. These depended on a distinction between laws, enduring rules of general application, and decrees, specific, one-time enactments. So sometime between 427 and 415 the Athenians instituted the *graphe paranomon*, the charge against proposing a decree that contradicted the laws, which essentially gave to the courts the duty of making sure that decrees were drafted in conformity with laws. Between 410 and 399 there was a fitful but somewhat successful attempt to compile an authoritative and consistent catalogue of all the laws.[86] Finally, in the early fourth century, new procedures were introduced for the passage, review, and repeal of laws that gave final authority for this to boards of lawgivers (*nomothetai*) drawn from the pool of jurors.[87] All this represented not a retreat from the democracy of the fifth century but an increasingly complex articulation of democratic political institutions.

One

AUTHORITATIVE
READINGS

According to Ariston, he and his friend Phanostatos had been taking their customary stroll one evening through the agora, the civic and commercial center of Athens. After going up to the temple of Persephone, they doubled back and were traversing the agora again when Konon, his sons, and their friends, unprovoked but flush with wine, ambushed them. Some of the gang held Phanostatos back while the rest stripped Ariston's clothes and beat him almost to death. As he lay in the mud, naked, bleeding, his eyes swollen shut, the gang taunted and insulted him until finally Konon began to crow like a victorious fighting cock, flapping his elbows like wings. These details in the story Ariston told the jurors when he brought Konon to court were not merely picaresque elaboration but essential: The affront to Ariston's honor in Konon's crowning mockery made the difference between mere assault and the more serious charge of hubris. To support his claims, Ariston had the court official who handled documents, the *grammateus*,[1] read the laws:

> [*To the grammateus.*] Please pick up the laws, both the law of hubris and the law about clothes stealers. [*To the jurors.*] In fact you will see that these men are liable to them both. [*To the grammateus.*] Read them.
> LAWS.[2]
> Konon here is liable to both of these laws because of what he's done: He committed hubris, and he stole clothes. If we have chosen not to prosecute according to these laws, we should reasonably

seem to be easygoing and moderate, but he's just as much a low-life. Further, if anything had happened to me, he could have been subject to a charge of murder and to the most terrible penalties.[3]

It is easy enough to see instances like this, where a litigant cites a law by having the *grammateus* read it out, as equivalent to the use of laws in modern Anglo-American courts. A close examination of Ariston's use of the laws, however, confounds such an idea. Although Ariston had the *grammateus* read only these two laws, they were not, as he himself admitted, the law that authorized his charge, which was assault, but only laws under which he *could have* initiated other proceedings. His further reference to the law of murder as the basis of a possible charge was even more hypothetical. Earlier in his speech, Ariston had referred to several other laws (laws against slander, wounding, and, indeed, assault) without, however, having the *grammateus* quote them to the jurors (§§17–19). Thus, although he frequently referred to and sometimes cited laws and claimed that they were the basis of his plea, Ariston never quoted the statute under which he had initiated his case. Indeed, he had much more to say about laws other than that of assault. This common practice of Athenian litigants, adducing a variety of laws, though frequently not the law on which they based their charge, raises fundamental questions about the status and use of law in Athenian courts. These questions in turn influence how we understand the operation of the courts and their relationship to Athenian society.

LEGAL ARGUMENTS

Modern scholars' judgments about the Athenian courts have often hinged on the place they attribute to law in litigation. The censorious view that the arbitrary whim of the jurors alone determined verdicts has fallen out of fashion, but no consensus on the role of law has emerged. Some hold that Athenian jurors decided cases considering only the law, which they interpreted strictly.[4] This view rightly recognizes the preeminent importance that the law holds in litigants' rhetoric, but it fails to account for the seemingly curious ways litigants often invoked the laws and treats the application of the law as an unproblematic process. Others, attempting to allow for contingency in the interpretation of laws, have abandoned the model of a rule and its application. Stephen Todd notes that the litigant himself was entirely responsible for gathering whatever laws he wished to present. More than this, most Athenian laws did not define their terms; instead, they simply stipulated that if someone committed a crime (such as assault, hubris, or murder), the victim should seek legal redress in specific ways.[5] Following Aristotle, then, Todd sees laws not as "binding" but as pieces of evidence (*pisteis*). Thus, the laws did not provide rules to apply as much as limits within which the jurors resolved the dispute.[6] David Cohen, also attending to the lack of definitions in laws, argues that "in democratic Athens . . . cases turned not on technical definitions but on the common understandings of the ordinary citizens entrusted with the task of judgment."[7] This buttresses his view that there was little that was specifically "legal" about conflict in the courts. Both Todd's and Cohen's accounts have the great virtue of treating litigation as a contingent process of determining meaning rather than as a simple procedure of applying an objective rule. Todd nevertheless provides little explanation of how the laws set limits for judgment. Cohen, although he correctly attributes an important role to social values and understandings, underestimates the degree to which litigation expressed these in specifically legal ways. Much more can still be said about this process.

The laws provided a fundamental and essential basis for arguments in the Athenian courts. In this chapter and the next, I explore these legal bases of argument not by examining the meaning of texts (e.g., the law of assault) but by understanding the processes by which Athenians attempted to attribute meaning to them. My question is not, What does the text mean?, but, How did litigants make arguments about what the text means? I do not assume that a text had a single, objective, authoritative meaning and, consequently, that conflicts over interpretation invariably involved one party's bad faith, bad arguments, or "misinterpretation." Litigants themselves usually asserted that the law did indeed have one meaning that was objectively true, but this must be understood as a powerful rhetorical claim, not an adequate or accurate description of the practice of legal rhetoric. When scholars adopt similar assumptions, they commit themselves to substituting their own judgments of true interpretation for those of the litigants. My intention, however, is not to win or even decide the contest over meanings (by giving the "correct" interpretation) but to give an account of the contest itself. The precise text of a law, of course, matters, though as it happens, we often know more about how litigants construed laws than what the laws actually said. As will become clear, the laws could support a range of interpretations. This was a limited range, to be sure, though even the limits of acceptable interpretation were themselves open to debate. By studying the protocols of attributing legal meanings, I hope to respect litigants' interpretations but also not to be limited to them.[8]

THE MEANING OF THE LAW

Athenian litigants used a number of strategies to make arguments about the meaning of laws, as Lysias 10 shows. This prosecution speech in a private case against Theomnestos for defamation (*kakegoria*) has a complex background.[9] The case arose from a dispute between Theomnestos and, arrayed against him, Lysitheos and his supporters, one of whom was the unnamed speaker of Lysias 10. In the first case between the parties, Lysitheos had charged Theomnestos with addressing the Assembly after deserting his military post. The jury acquitted Theomnestos, who in retaliation brought a suit for defamation against Lysitheos and charged and convicted Dionysios, one of Lysitheos' witnesses, for false testimony. Next, the unnamed speaker of Lysias 10, who had also been a witness for Lysitheos in the first trial, struck back by charging Theomnestos with defamation for his remark (in that same trial) that the speaker of Lysias 10 had killed his own father. This was defamation, he claimed, because his father had been killed by the Thirty, and he had been only thirteen at the time, too young to have been complicit.

> Well then [the prosecutor continued], perhaps Theomnestos will not defend himself on these points, men of the jury, but will say to you what he dared say even to the arbitrator: that it isn't forbidden to say that someone *killed* his father because the law does not forbid those words, but only saying that someone is a *murderer*. It seems to me, men of the jury, that you must vote not based on words but their meaning, and you all know that those who've killed someone are homicides and that homicides are those who've killed someone. It was too great a task for the lawgiver to write all the words that could possibly mean the same thing, and so he indicated them all by mentioning one. I suppose, Theomnestos, that if someone called you a *father abuser* or a *mother abuser*, you would think you ought to be able to convict him. So then, if someone said that you had *hit your female or male parent*, would you think that he ought to go unpunished because he hadn't spoken a forbidden word? . . . Men of the jury, consider this further (since I doubt this man has ever gone up

to the Areopagos, because of either laziness or indolence). You all know that in that place when they judge cases of murder, they don't use this particular word in the oaths required of litigants but the one used to slander me. The prosecutor swears that his opponent *killed* and the defendant swears that he didn't *kill*. Wouldn't it be preposterous to acquit the culprit even though he admitted he was a *murderer* because the prosecutor had sworn that the defendant *killed*? How is this any different from what Theomnestos is saying? [10]

The speaker continued by citing several laws with archaic vocabulary, pointing out that different words were currently used in ordinary speech for the same objects and actions but that no one would fail to apply the laws because of this.

Though the speaker's arguments seem persuasive,[11] Theomnestos' position, as Hillgruber argues, may not have been as indefensible nor as absurd as this speaker made it out to be.[12] Though the Thirty had killed his father, the prosecutor (who was still a boy at the time) may have been inadvertently complicit, perhaps, for example, by revealing his hidden father's whereabouts. When, in a moment of anger, Theomnestos blamed him for his father's death, this may have been unfair and exaggerated, but Theomnestos seems to have replied that the defamation law did not cover this. The arbitrator, at least, who had earlier heard this case, decided in his favor. The speaker's response in the trial was to so caricature Theomnestos' defense as to make it seem absurd.

The point is not, however, to determine whether the speaker was intentionally misreading the law but rather to understand the process through which he construed its meaning. To do this, the speaker engaged in three interpretive strategies: First, he insisted that the words do not mean exactly and only what they say, that is, that their correct interpretation must be found outside the text itself; second, he sought to locate the correct interpretation in the purpose of the law; third, he attempted to bring other laws to bear in interpreting this one.[13] In general, the speaker argued, a law meant what the author, "the lawgiver," meant when he wrote it.

THE LAWGIVER

As the putative author of the laws, the lawgiver, often specified as Solon,[14] occasionally as Drakon, provided a method for specifying and debating the meaning of laws. "The lawgiver" was, however, a fiction and not merely because Solon had nothing to do with many of the laws attributed to him.[15] The idea of a singular author of a law grossly oversimplified the process of legislating at Athens, a process that, since it required popular approval, involved hundreds or even thousands of people.[16] There were, moreover, no historical records an Athenian could have used (had he ever cared to) to investigate the "legislative history" of a law. For these reasons, Hillgruber believes that the invocation of "the lawgiver" fundamentally misrepresented the actual meaning of a law: Since there was no attempt to discover the historical intent of the actual drafters of the law, the invocation aimed only at persuading a mass audience, not solving juristic problems.[17] Yet the point is not whether litigants' claims accurately represented history or conformed to a literal interpretation of the laws— often, indeed, they did not—because to insist on either historical or literal interpretations is merely to assert the superiority of some interpretive protocols over others.[18] Again, the object of this study is not to discover the "true" meaning of the laws but to ask how the Athenians themselves reasoned about this.

Modern readers of the speeches have suggested that the figure of Solon attributed traditional authority or legitimacy to particular laws,[19] reflected a tendency to ascribe inventions to a single originator,[20] or promoted a particular political program,[21] but just as importantly, it defined the limits and means for the Athenians to interpret laws. Not a person but a trope, "the lawgiver" created a context for interpretation, a context that was only ostensibly historical.[22] The Athenian lawgiver represents not (or not just) the intrusion of the "extralegal" but an Athenian form of legal reasoning.[23] "The lawgiver" allowed at least three related interpretive strategies: nonliteral reading, reading in conformity with other laws, and reading of laws as fundamentally democratic.[24]

The figure of the lawgiver provided a way to argue for interpretations of the law that were not explicitly literal. In the most extreme case, a speaker used the lawgiver's intentions to extend a law to cover a situation it did not explicitly deal with but would have (so litigants argued) if the lawgiver had suspected it would ever happen.[25] The lawgiver's purpose not only corrected oversights in the laws but allowed for the deduction of implicit meanings.[26] The intentions of the lawgiver also allowed, as the case of Theomnestos showed, the argument that even when the words differed, their similar meanings should prevail.[27]

By invoking the lawgiver's intentions, litigants were able to hone the law to support their positions more closely.[28] For example, the son of Philonides argued that he was the legal heir of Menekles because he had been adopted by him.

> I wish to show you that the adoption was carried out in accord with the laws. Please read the law that orders that a man can will his property however he wants, unless he has legitimate male children. The lawgiver, gentlemen, made this law because he saw that for men without children, being able to adopt whoever they wished was the only refuge from loneliness and the only consolation in life.[29]

The speaker's allegation of the purpose of the law, to provide emotional support for the elderly, corresponds precisely to what he had done for Menekles and to what his opponent could not claim to have done.[30] The adoption was "in accord with the laws" not merely because (as he claimed) it was technically correct but because its goal was the same as that of the law. The particular circumstances of the dispute obviously informed his reading of the law. How legitimate we may find this is not my point; rather, the speaker's argument shows the way that the notion of the lawgiver allowed the attribution of purpose to the law through the fiction of an author.[31] In this case, by attributing to the lawgiver the sentiment that the elderly should not be abandoned, the speaker interpreted the law in light of this common attitude.

More commonly, however, litigants created a context for interpreting a law by locating the lawgiver's purpose in his other writings, that is, other laws. In a dispute over the estate of Archiades, for example, Leochares had filed a *diamartyria,* a sworn statement that the estate was not open to litigation by other claimants because there was already a lawful, direct heir. The only way to challenge such a claim was to sue the man who made the statement for false testimony, and so Aristodemos' son sued Leochares, claiming the estate on his father's behalf. In his speech, the son of Aristodemos sought to rile the jurors against his opponent because he had chosen to rely on a *diamartyria* instead of a *diadikasia* (an ordinary inheritance hearing in which all claimants were on equal terms).

> The following considerations will show that *diamartyriai* are the most unjust kinds of trials and that you ought to be very angry with those who choose to undertake them. In the first place, they

aren't mandatory, like other forms of procedure, but happen only because of the deliberate choice of the person who swears. . . . If it's possible even without *diamartyriai* to get a hearing before all courts, isn't such a procedure a sign of rashness and desperation? The lawgiver did not compel parties to use this; instead, he allowed them to choose whether to undertake a *diamartyria,* as though he were testing the character of each of us, to see whether we inclined to such a reckless action.[32]

His opponent's actions, the son of Aristodemos suggested, although technically allowed by the law, in fact transgressed its spirit. He discovered this through a comparison with other laws, those that authorized ordinary hearings in inheritance cases, all of which the intentions of the lawgiver united.

The idea of the lawgiver, then, allowed Athenians to interpret one law in light of others. Because the lawgiver had authored all the laws, litigants could treat them as a consistent body informed by a uniform purpose. The figure of the lawgiver was not absolutely necessary for this manner of reading (litigants assumed the unity of the laws without invoking a single author[33]), but he was the usual sign under which the dominant mode took place. By the fourth century, the intricacy and magnitude of the laws compelled the Athenians to introduce several procedures for rectifying them,[34] procedures that themselves were said to be due to Solon's desire for a consistent code.[35] (These procedures included the *graphai* against illegal decrees and laws.) But the trope of the lawgiver went further than these measures: It was not merely that the laws were consistent but that their underlying logic or purpose was uniform as well. This universalizing of the logic of the laws was one of the most powerful ways of reading them.[36]

Many speakers relied on this strategy of interpreting one law through others by assuming a unity in the laws through the will of the lawgiver. Take the case of Epikrates, who wished to invalidate a contract he claimed was deceitful (Hyp. 3). Epikrates (as he narrated the dispute) had earlier found a young slave boy so attractive that he approached his owner and sought to buy his freedom. The owner, Athenogenes, an Egyptian, refused this offer and instead got Epikrates to agree to buy not the slave's freedom but the entire perfume business in which the boy worked. Athenogenes stipulated that Epikrates would assume the debts of the perfume shop (which the contract listed), but in his eagerness to get his new slave,

Epikrates neglected to pay attention to the details of the agreement. Soon after the purchase, one by one, creditors began to appear, each one claiming a new debt. Epikrates had paid forty minae for the enterprise, but as it turned out, after all the debts had been declared, these came to about five talents (three hundred minae). Only then did he read the contract closely, discovering a small clause that included all unitemized debts. In his arguments, Athenogenes, the seller, could cite their contract and the law that stated that agreements are binding.[37] On Epikrates' side, however, there was no law that explicitly overturned deceitful contracts, and so he referred to other laws and inferred their relevance: A law prohibited telling lies in the agora; the failure to disclose all debts, he argued, is a lie. A law allowed refunds on purchased slaves who are discovered to have physical disabilities; if physical defects are covered, monetary debts should be as well. Another law specified that only "lawful" marriages made children legitimate; this shows that not all agreements are legally binding. A final law invalidated wills made under the influence of old age, illness, insanity, coercion, or a woman; this again shows that there are limitations on contracts: Unjust agreements are invalid.[38] Epikrates then said to Athenogenes:

> I think that *you* [are responsible for the debts]. If we disagree
> about this, let's make the law the arbitrator, since it was made
> neither by lovers nor by conspirators against others but by that
> great democrat Solon. Because he knew that there are many sales
> in the city, he made a just law—and everyone agrees it's just—
> that the master at whose establishment slaves work must make
> good the losses the slaves cause and their expenses.[39] That's quite
> reasonable, because if a slave does something good or gains a
> trade, the profit goes to his owner. But you dismiss the law and
> talk about contracts that have been violated. Solon thought that
> no decree, even if it were justly drafted, should take precedence
> over a law. But *you* think that even unjust contracts should be
> supreme over all laws.[40]

It is tempting to say that Epikrates had to make all these arguments because, although his claim was just, the law was against him. This was not, however, his position: He asserted that these arguments proved that the laws supported him. Indeed, I will resist the seduction of judging the case and of pronouncing what the law really was and instead confine myself to the small pleasures of analysis. This was probably a suit for damages (δίκη βλάβης), but Epikrates chose not to interpret that law by exploring what "damages" might mean (indeed, he may never have cited the law, though the beginning of the speech is lost) but instead invoked entirely different laws. What made other statutes relevant was the unity of all laws, personified in the lawgiver, Solon.[41] The law, then, by Epikrates' argument, was not the text of a single statute but the meaning of the whole system of laws expressing the will of the lawgiver.

Litigants frequently used the trope of the lawgiver to link heterogeneous laws into a coherent code.[42] Arguments about what legal procedure a prosecutor could or ought to use, for example, depended upon how offenses were defined. Though litigants disagreed about whether definitions of offenses were exclusive and unique or multiple and overlapping, they nevertheless advocated both positions based on an assumption of the overall architecture of the laws. Diodoros, in his prosecution of Androtion (Dem. 22), expressed in detail this sense of the design of the laws. Anticipating the defendant's claim that he was being tried under the wrong procedure, Diodoros maintained that "for each offense the man who made these laws, Solon, . . . provided not merely one method to those who wished to prosecute wrongdoers but many."[43] The victim, therefore, could choose a form of prosecution suitable to his status and resources. In this view, the laws were not abutting but imbricated, shrewdly interwoven to cover all crimes and all conditions of victims. Thus, he claimed, Androtion should not complain that the prosecutors should have used a different procedure but simply show that he had not done what was charged.[44]

Yet defendants did complain that their accusers had used the wrong procedure, and they, too, based this argument on the idea that the laws composed a unified system.[45] In this case, however, they claimed that the lawgiver had made only one procedure for each kind of crime. When Euxitheos was defending himself on the charge of murdering Herodes (Ant. 5), he strenuously objected to the procedure used: Rather than use the normal *dike* for homicide, his accusers denounced him and had him arrested under the law governing common criminals (*kakourgoi*, literally, "evildoers").[46] But, Euxitheos complained, this procedure did not cover murder: "[My accusers] say that murder is a serious, evil deed. I certainly agree, most serious—as are temple robbery and treason. Yet there are separate laws established for each of these."[47] The assumption of order here is that the system of laws provided only one remedy for each kind of offense, each of which it defined exclusively. Since there was a law that explicitly concerned murderers, the law about *kakourgoi* did not cover them. When prosecutors made the claim that the laws allowed them a choice of procedures and when defendants argued that each offense was covered by only one law, they were all making self-serving analyses.[48] Despite their different conclusions, however, each claim rested on a similar understanding of the laws as a coherent, ordered system, the product (speakers often claimed) of the lawgiver's design.

The fiction of the lawgiver aided in a third, related interpretive strategy: seeing the meaning of the law as fundamentally democratic.[49] In this sense, not only was the lawgiver understood as the architect of a system of laws; this system of laws was equated with democracy itself. The lawgiver sought, litigants sometimes claimed, to make the laws accessible to and protective of simple, ordinary Athenians.[50] More broadly, he aimed to fortify the democracy that protected the interests of common folk. Speakers used this implicit democratic program to interpret meanings of the laws. When Diodoros indicted Androtion (Dem. 22) for drafting an illegal decree, one of his claims was that Androtion had moved his proposal although disqualified by the law that debarred those who had prostituted themselves from addressing the people. Solon made this law, he asserted, because

> he thought it wouldn't be safe if there were ever many men at the same time who were clever, audacious speakers but filled with disgraceful evil. The demos can be led into many errors by such men, and they will either attempt to overthrow the democracy entirely . . . or induce the people to be as bad as possible, in order to bring them down to their level.[51]

The text of the law itself, of course, mentioned nothing about such a possibility. But by attributing it to Solon, who Athenians believed strengthened the power of the demos especially by enlarging the scope of the popular courts,[52] Diodoros gave this law a very specific purpose and meaning.

Interpreting Athenian laws in this way, as the unified product of an author's design, runs at odds with modern historical accounts. A historical account would find the meaning of a law in the particular circumstances of its drafting and ratification or, more often, in the larger context of general social values. We cannot realize the former project with the evidence available, since we know very little if anything about the situations under which specific laws were "written." But even the latter historical understanding differs from the way litigants interpreted laws, as Aeschines' accusation of Timarchos shows. Aeschines indicted Timarchos, a prominent politician, because he had joined Aeschines' rival Demosthenes in attacking him in the courts. The year was 345; the charge, addressing the people although disqualified by law because he had prostituted himself. In the opening period of his speech (Aesch. 1.4–36), Aeschines insisted upon the lawgiver's concern for *sophrosyne* (moderation or self-control), a prominent theme throughout his address. This was evident, he claimed, not only in the law on which he based his charge but in others that governed "the orderly conduct of children" (§8). These included the regulation of teachers, gymnasiums, choruses of boys, laws prohibiting the prostitution of citizen boys, as well as the law of hubris.

> The *grammateus* will read you these laws so that you may know that the lawgiver believed that the boy who has been brought up morally will be a man who is useful to the city. But when the person's nature receives a bad beginning right from early training, he thought that such a corrupt upbringing would create citizens much like Timarchos here. Read these laws to them.[53]

Historians have been more likely to see a concern for *time* (honor) in these laws than for *sophrosyne;* and by this reading, the concern of the laws was less with the moral training of the boy than with his reputation and that of his father.[54] Yet, however misleading Aeschines' reading may be historically, the way it united the laws in the global intentions of the lawgiver made it rhetorically and legally persuasive.[55]

Of course, litigants sometimes insisted on what a single law explicitly (διαρρήδην) said, but even then, they often sought to justify their literal reading as conforming to the lawgiver's intentions. In part this must reflect the power of the lawgiver as an interpretive convention; in some of these cases too, the speakers were attempting to thwart their opponents' interpretations of a law that depended on seeing it in a system of laws.[56] Even Theomnestos' prosecutor (the speaker of Lys. 10) could insist that the lawgiver's purpose was to be found in the letter of the law:

> I hear, men of the jury, that he will resort to the argument that he said these things out of anger because I had given the same

testimony as Dionysios [that Theomnestos had thrown away his shield in battle]. But you must keep in mind, men of the jury, that the lawgiver gives no pardon [συγγνώμην] for anger, but punishes the speaker if he cannot demonstrate that what he said is true.[57]

Athenian litigants used the idea of the lawgiver, then, as a flexible strategy for advocating their interpretations of the law. Even in its most common form, in which other laws supplied the context for interpreting one law, litigants never presented the lawgiver's intentions as opposed to the law but instead insisted that they revealed the meaning of the law itself.[58] Claims that such interpretive strategies involved the intrusion of the extralegal are both right and wrong. They are right because the laws did not specify how they should be interpreted, so that any interpretive protocol, even a literal one, is outside the texts of the laws themselves. But they are wrong, therefore, because they depend on an untenable distinction between law and rhetoric. In litigation, Athenians determined the meaning of the law only through rhetoric. They are also wrong because this rhetoric of interpretation took on a unique shape in the courts and represented itself as specifically legal. Litigants argued for particular meanings of a law by situating it in the whole system of laws, not by invoking other contexts, even though these might be more historically accurate. Thus only one litigant, Demosthenes, quoted Solon's poetry. He did so not to establish the meaning of a law but to turn a previous argument of his opponent Aeschines (that Solon disapproved of people who behaved like Timarchos) back against him.[59] Outside the courts, however, the author of a history of Athenian politics and government quoted Solon's poetry extensively in his attempt to reconstruct the purpose of his legislation.[60] The interpretive trope of the lawgiver, therefore, precisely to the degree that it was not historical, constituted a uniquely legal mode of argumentation.

THE DIKASTIC OATH

Many scholars have rooted their accounts of the role of laws in Athenian courts in the dikastic oath, which all Athenians who might serve as jurors swore at the beginning of each year.[61] The oath, this view goes, governed how jurors used laws in making their decisions (or, at least, it should have). Despite the importance they place on the oath, however, scholars do not agree on its exact wording. It may have gone something like this:

I will vote in accord with the laws and decrees of the demos of the Athenians and of the Boule of Five Hundred. I will not vote to institute tyranny or oligarchy. If anyone tries to overthrow the demos of the Athenians or speaks or makes a proposal against these things, I will not listen. [I will allow] neither a cancellation of private debts nor a redistribution of the land and houses of Athenians. I will not recall exiles nor those sentenced to death. Those who live here I will not myself exile in violation of the established laws and the decrees of the demos of the Athenians and the Boule, nor will I allow anyone else to do this. I will not confirm the appointment to office of anyone who has yet to undergo an audit for another office, namely the nine archons, the recorder, any officer appointed on the same day as the nine archons, herald, ambassador, and councilor. [I will not allow] the same man to hold the same office twice, nor the same man to hold two offices in the same year. I will not myself accept gifts in my capacity as juror, nor with my knowledge will another man or woman accept them for me in any way whatsoever. I am at least thirty years old. I will listen equally to both prosecutor and defendant, and I will cast my vote on the matter of the prosecution. The juror will swear by Zeus, Poseidon, and Demeter and will call down deadly curses on himself and his household if he transgresses this oath in any way, but if he keeps this oath, he will prosper.[62]

I have quoted the version preserved in the manuscript of Demosthenes' speech *Against Timokrates* (Dem. 24). Modern scholars agree that this version cannot be an authentic text and that a later ancient editor reconstructed it and inserted it in the manuscript. Here, unfortunately, consensus ends: Some suggest that this version is largely correct, some reject most of its clauses, and most retreat to the safe ground of vagueness.[63] Recovering the precise wording of the oath is a difficult undertaking. No surviving source quotes a complete version (the manuscript of Dem. 24 excepted), although many litigants quoted or paraphrased snippets. Differences in these quotations show that the Athenians changed its wording during the fourth century, though when, how, and how often we cannot be sure. Such complexities can make reconstructions of a single, authentic text of the oath seem impressionistic and arbitrary. Bonner and Smith, for example, excise the provisions in the version quoted above about guarding against tyranny and the abolition of democracy because they were "especially *appropriate* in 410 and 403 B.C. but not long afterward."[64] Yet only Bonner and Smith's vision of what the oath ought to have concerned seems to justify dismissing these clauses. It is unclear that the Athenians themselves would have found these clauses inappropriate at other times; certainly the problem of tyranny concerned them enough to enact still another law against it as late as 336.[65]

In any case, an authoritative text would not guarantee a single valid meaning, if for no other reason than because the oath itself, just like the laws, was subject to debate and interpretation in the courts.[66] Instead of arguing for a single, correct meaning, then, I want to explore how Athenian litigants used the oath to make arguments about the use of law in litigation. Despite the difficulties of restoring the text, the preserved speeches provide abundant evidence for the range of contemporary interpretations the oath bore.

The dikastic oath and the law

Of all the possible implications of the oath, litigants linked it overwhelmingly with upholding the laws. A rough count of references to the oath in the speeches shows that litigants drew out this signification some 51 times, but they construed other meanings much less often: justice (30 times), religious sentiment (10), denial of *charis* (10), preservation of democracy and the *politeia* (8), overcoming deceitful language (8), denial of begging (8), mandating *eunoia* (5), requiring an equal hearing (5), voting on the prosecution's charges (5), and the jurors' using their "most just judgment" (3).[67] At least in 330 B.C. the initial clause of the dikastic oath bound the jurors to "vote in accord with the laws."[68]

Athenians thus often stressed that the oath insisted on the primacy of the law. Some scholars have therefore argued that when jurors swore to "vote in accord with the laws," they were required strictly to enforce the literal meaning of the law. Edward Harris, for example, argues that this clause meant that the courts had to "rigorously enforce the law."[69] He cites speakers who quoted the laws that authorized their suits and argues that only in rare "'hard' cases" did the law have to be interpreted.[70] Harris follows Meyer-Laurin, who argues that the oath bound the jurors strictly to the law.[71]

Certainly some litigants claimed that the meaning of the oath was exactly what Harris describes. For example, the man who used a public pro-

cedure to charge some grain merchants with buying up more than the
legal maximum of grain insisted that the oath required strict enforcement
of the law. After he questioned one of the merchants who admitted that
he had exceeded the limit but claimed that the officials who monitored
grain sales had ordered him to do so,[72] the prosecutor continued:

> Very well, men of the jury, if he can show that there is a law that
> orders the grain merchants to buy up grain when the officials tell
> him to, acquit him. Otherwise, it's only just that you convict him.
> We provided for you the law that forbids anyone in the city to
> buy up more than fifty measures of grain. So, men of the jury,
> this accusation alone ought to have been enough, since this man
> admits that he bought up the grain, and the law clearly forbids
> it—and you have sworn to vote in accord with the laws.[73]

The oath, the prosecutor claimed, required the simple and obvious application of the law.

This speaker's claim, however, far from being a neutral description
of the jurors' task, was an attempt to persuade them of what they ought
to do. He used the oath to claim authority for his interpretation of the
law, which was not as incontestable as he implied. Despite his claim to
have "provided" the law, he had done no more than paraphrase a clause.
Moreover, as Todd notes, there is enough uncertainty about the extent of
a "measure" and about the meaning of the verb I have translated "buy
up" (συνωνεῖσθαι) to suspect equivocation on the speaker's part.[74] In this
case, the speaker's demand for strict adherence to the law in conformity
with the oath attempted to render a particular interpretation of the law
inviolable. The speaker generously allowed for acquittal if the defendants could find another law authorizing their conduct, but he used the
oath to forestall any contrary interpretation of the law to which he referred. The idea that the oath required strict application of the laws, therefore, was an important rhetorical argument, but it is inadequate as a description of rhetorical practice. Litigants used the directive of the oath to
vote in accord with the laws as a way of making and claiming authority
for particular interpretations of laws.

Although the question of strict adherence to the laws has preoccupied
modern discussion of the clause in the oath to "vote in accord with the
laws," Athenian litigants frequently construed this clause in very different
ways, particularly as a demand to uphold the whole system of laws that

TABLE 1. Speakers Who Mentioned the Jurors' Oath

	Prosecution	Defense	*Diadikasia*	*Paragraphe*	Total
Private	7/26 [27%]	4/10 [40%]	3/9 [33%]	3/9 [33%]	17/54 [32%]
Public	20/29 [69%]	9/15 [60%]			29/44 [66%]
Total	27/55 [49%]	13/25 [52%]			46/98 [47%]

Private vs. Public speeches p < .001

was thought to constitute the democracy. Such rhetoric most commonly appears in public cases: Twice the proportion of public cases referred to the oath as private cases (66% vs. 32%). (See Table 1.[75]) Speakers' equation of "voting in accord with the laws" with preserving democracy seems to largely account for this difference. This suggests that the meanings Athenians assigned to the oath depended on the context. In public cases, litigants frequently construed the oath to mean something different than in private cases.[76]

One of the most important kinds of public cases, one in which speakers drew heavily on the oath to make their arguments, was the *graphe paranomon*. This procedure was part of the complex process the Athenians developed for reviewing and checking legislation. All laws (that is, permanent, general rules) and decrees (ad hoc legislation), whether proposed or passed, could be indicted by *graphe* (a public prosecution) for contradicting the established laws.[77] A regular jury court tried the case; a negative verdict would render the indicted decree or law invalid. If less than a year had elapsed since the measure had been passed, the proposer was simultaneously on trial and was punished if convicted. Though such cases had become common in the second half of the period of this study, they were not in all ways typical. Because the "crime" involved the contradiction of texts, litigants highlighted questions of interpretation and the role of the oath in this much more than in other kinds of cases.

In the course of his ongoing political battle with Demosthenes, Aeschines prosecuted Ktesiphon in 330 B.C. for proposing a decree that had conferred an honorary golden crown on Demosthenes, contravening, he claimed, some laws. Though Aeschines' speech against Ktesiphon (Aesch. 3) deploys arguments about the oath in unusual detail, they fairly represent the types of claims litigants made, particularly prosecutors in public speeches. Aeschines insisted that especially in such a case the jurors must obey the directives of the oath:

> You know, men of Athens, that there are three kinds of constitutions in the world: tyranny, oligarchy, and democracy. Tyrannies and oligarchies are administered according to the moods of those in power, but democratic states are administered according to established laws. Don't any of you forget this, but keep clearly in mind that on the day you enter a courtroom to judge a *graphe paranomon* you will vote on your own freedom of speech. This is why the lawgiver put the words "I will vote in accord with the laws" at the very beginning of the dikastic oath, because he knew quite well that when the laws are carefully guarded in the interests of the city, the democracy is safe. Remember this, hate those who propose decrees that are contrary to the laws, never think that any such violations are trivial—they are not, they are very serious—and do not allow your rights to be taken away by anyone, not by generals acting as advocates (the same generals who by cooperating with some of the politicians have long been abusing our system of government) and not by those foreigners, either, who some defendants (you know the ones, the ones whose conduct as citizens has insulted the constitution) march up here to beg and so escape from the courts. No, just as each of you would be ashamed to desert his position in battle, so you must now be ashamed to abandon the post assigned by the laws today: guardians of the democracy.[78]

When Aeschines asked the jurors to vote in accord with the laws he did not (or not primarily) mean "vote in accord with the law that authorized this case" (the law against illegal decrees, that is) but rather "vote for the laws that this decree [supposedly] contradicts." The difference is crucial and points to an endemic feature of these kinds of cases. In a *graphe paranomon*, the "crime" was that the decree contradicted established laws. The abundant citation of these laws by prosecutors, therefore, was equivalent to the testimony of witnesses in other cases: They established what we would call the facts of the case, namely, that there was a contradiction between two texts. They did not, however, address what we would term the law, and, in fact, no prosecutor in an extant *graphe paranomon* ever cited the authorizing law.[79] This was the logic of the argument Demosthenes addressed to the jurors in his prosecution of Leptines for his law that canceled the exemptions from performing liturgies, exemptions that the Athenians had granted as honors to public benefactors:

> Moreover, men of Athens, you must keep this in mind and see that you have come sworn to give judgment today in accord with the laws not the laws of Sparta or of Thebes or those used by our earliest ancestors, but in accord with those under which these men obtained the immunities from liturgies which Leptines now seeks to take away with his law.[80]

Here κατὰ τοὺς νόμους, "in accord with the laws," did not refer to the law that Leptines' proposal may have *violated* (that is, the law that prohibited contradictory laws) but to the laws it may have *contradicted*.[81] Speakers in other *graphai paranomon* gave the phrase a similar meaning.[82] The citation of the oath in these public cases (especially by prosecutors) had less to do with how to construe the law that authorized the case than with upholding the whole system of laws that was thought to constitute the democracy.

Prosecutors in public cases used the oath to attribute a particular gravity to the defendant's "crime." They commonly construed the provision of the oath that the jurors decide "in accord with the laws" to mean that they should uphold the laws as a whole, the basis of the democracy, which the defendant's actions threatened.[83] This was true in other public prosecutions[84] but was especially linked with the *graphe paranomon* and the *graphe* against an inexpedient law. In reviewing decrees and laws, these cases could be said to make sure that the process of lawmaking had been properly followed and to preserve the purity of the laws as a whole.

This threat to the laws, however, was less an objective quality of the "crime" than one of the resources available to prosecutors in public cases. Significantly, both speeches just quoted (Aesch. 3 and Dem. 20) indicted decrees and laws that conferred or revoked honors, hardly, one might suspect, the most fundamental constitutional or political issue. Yet both speeches were typical. The majority of such cases we know of were exactly of this type: indictments of decrees that conferred honors on an individual. Of the thirty-three *graphai paranomon* where we know the

content of the indicted law, twenty of them (61%) were honorary decrees.[85] Hansen takes this to mean that it was not the decree but the proposer or person honored who was the real target of the indictment.[86] It
indicates as well that the threat to the democracy was not an objective
feature of the act subject to indictment. Rather, by bringing a public case,
and by exploiting the rhetorical resources associated with this, a prosecutor hoped to persuade the jurors to attribute a particular meaning to
the proposing of the decree: that it threatened the foundations of Athenian democracy.

Many litigants, especially prosecutors in public cases, argued that
the emphasis of the oath on upholding the law preeminently denoted
the preservation of the Athenian *politeia* and democracy.[87] That jurors
played a fundamental role in Athenian politics in both the fifth and fourth
centuries sanctioned the interpretation.[88] In the process of Athenian
lawmaking in the fourth century, jurors sometimes functioned as lawgivers (*nomothetai*) who ratified all laws[89] as well as reviewing legislation through the *graphe paranomon*. Speakers in public cases, therefore,
appealed to jurors to think of themselves not only as those who enforced
the laws but, indeed, as Dinarchos put it, as "the guardians of the democracy and the laws."[90]

The dikastic oath and justice

Scholars have suggested that one other aspect of the dikastic oath affected the role of law in Athenian courts, its emphasis on justice. As I
noted above, speakers frequently linked the oath to justice. One prosecutor, Epichares, said: "It is best . . . to distinguish those who speak well
and clearly from those who say what's just. After all, you have sworn
to vote about this."[91] Or Andocides, a defendant: "You who will vote
about me have sworn great oaths and vowed with great curses on both
yourselves and your children that you will vote justly regarding me."[92]
Aristotle, therefore, advised litigants who found the written law against
them to appeal to the oath and to urge jurors to ignore the law in the interests of justice.[93] More recently, Ruschenbusch used the oath as the basis of theory of legal "gaps," a theory Sealey has expanded upon.[94] This
theory claims that Athenian laws were not comprehensive; because the
laws did not cover every possible case, the jurors' most just judgment
filled these gaps. "As the oath shows," Sealey writes, "the Athenians believed that there were laws but there were also gaps between the laws;
occurrences not foreseen in the laws fell in the gaps."[95]

There are, however, a number of problems with the idea that the oath sanctioned appeals to justice independently of the law. Significantly, it does not conform to the ways litigants actually spoke about the question. We might imagine that a law or its application in a particular instance could conflict with justice or that the written laws might not cover every possibility. In both tragedy and philosophy the Athenians themselves contemplated the sometimes conflicting relationship between law and justice. Yet in court, litigants never used the oath to make a claim based on justice against or opposed to the law. Often, when speakers warranted their appeals to justice by reference to the oath, they simultaneously claimed that both justice and the oath were consonant with the laws. One speaker, for example, as he concluded his speech, urged the jurors to "remember the law, the oath that you've sworn, and what I've said about the topic; then with justice and in keeping with your oath vote in accord with the laws." [96] Speakers did not urge the jurors to disregard the law in the interests of justice, did not suggest that justice alone should inform their decision, did not oppose justice to the law, did not even argue that justice was a necessary supplement to areas not covered by the law.[97] In the courts, at least, litigants treated justice and the law as though they were entirely consonant.[98] Even litigants who relied explicitly and extensively on appeals to fairness sought to ground their appeals in the law. Epikrates, for example, who sought to nullify a contract with Athenogenes because he thought it was unfair, claimed that unjust agreements are invalid not merely because they are unjust but because this is what the law stipulates.[99] Athenian litigants usually claimed the law vindicated their claims.[100] They did not use the oath to suggest otherwise.

The theory that the jurors' judgment supplemented gaps in the laws depends upon the stipulation in the oath that jurors should vote with their "most just judgment" (γνώμη τῇ δικαιοτάτη).[101] The text of this clause may well have also specified that the jurors were to use their most just judgment "concerning matters on which there are no laws" (περὶ ὧν ἂν νόμοι μὴ ὦσι).[102] Athenian litigants, however, paid very little attention to this clause, certainly far less than to the other aspects of the oath catalogued above.[103] Only two litigants supported their case with this clause, though a third also mentioned it.[104] Even when they invoked it, litigants imagined the complete harmony of the laws and the jurors' most just judgment. The two speakers who said that the oath directed the jurors to use their most just judgment on matters where there were no laws both also claimed that the law and the most just judgment of the jurors simultaneously supported their claims. Mantitheos, for example, who

sued his stepbrother Boiotos to stop him from also using the name Mantitheos, quoted no law that explicitly prohibited two people from having
the same name or that gave him a legal right to sue on this point.[105] He
did claim, however, that their father had named his stepbrother Boiotos
and that "the law, which you all know as well as I do" gave to the parents
the right to bestow and revoke children's names.[106] Mantitheos plainly
claimed the sanction of law for his suit, though he added that the provision in the oath that the jurors exercise their most just judgment meant
that they would justly vote for him "even if there were no law on these
matters," a situation he presented as entirely hypothetical.[107]

Because Athenian litigants represented the jurors' most just judgment
as complementing, not supplementing, the law, the theory of gaps, despite its supposed ancient pedigree,[108] does not correspond to what these
litigants claimed they were doing.[109] Among the extant speeches, no litigant ever urged the jurors to apply their own most just opinion because
there was no law authorizing the case. Indeed, in a case where the prosecutor, Lycourgos, admitted (extraordinarily) that no law explicitly prohibited the defendant's conduct, he made no reference to the oath at all
but rather insisted that the jurors become lawmakers.[110]

Fairness and justice played an important role in Athenian litigation,
but the law circumscribed and shaped such arguments. Although some
claim that litigants "call[ed] on their hearers to bring in a verdict on the
basis of more general considerations of justice, in circumstances where
(we may suspect) the letter of the law is against them," [111] litigants still
presented their appeals to justice, as this consideration of the dikastic oath has shown, as consonant with and supported by the laws. The
arguments litigants made about justice with the oath demonstrate the
openness of the Athenian legal system to common social values, but they
show as well that these values were limited and inflected in specifically
legal ways.

ATHENIAN DEMOCRACY
AND THE INTERPRETATION OF LAW

The particular ways Athenian litigants made arguments about the meaning of the laws account for the peculiarities of Ariston's citations of laws
in his prosecution of Konon (Dem. 54, referred to at the beginning of
this chapter). Ariston's invocation of several laws other than the statute

against assault was, in fact, part of an argument about what constituted assault. He adduced these laws in a section in which he anticipated part of Konon's defense (§§13–25). Ariston imagined that Konon would say that the brawl was not an assault but a youthful revel fueled by erotic rivalry and wine. Ariston's reply suggests that the meaning of "assault" is to be found in the systematic relationship between the law of assault and other laws. There are suits for slander, Ariston claimed, so that words do not lead to blows, suits for assault so that fists do not lead to weapons, and actions for wounding so that murder does not result. "The least of these, abusive language, has been provided for [by the laws], I think, to prevent the final and most serious, murder, from happening, so that things don't gradually escalate from abusive language to blows, from blows to wounds, and from wounds to murder." [112] Situating assault in the context of a system of laws allowed Ariston to argue that its seriousness and meaning were not to be found in the result of the fight, nor in the intentions or dispositions of those involved, but in its most serious possible outcome: "Assault" is only two short steps from murder.

Ariston also invoked the laws of hubris and cloak stealing, saying that Konon was liable to these as well (§§24–25, quoted at the beginning of this chapter). Here, too, Ariston attempted to give meaning to the idea of assault by situating it in a legal design. Whereas his first account of the system of the laws defined assault as a part of a progressive escalation of violence, here he defined it by the number and relationship of overlapping remedies the laws allowed for it. That he could have initiated cases for hubris or clothes stealing, charges that entailed much more serious penalties, showed the seriousness of what Konon did. That he did not bring such grave charges showed his own moderation and reasonableness. [113] The meaning of "assault," in this view, was substantively the same as the offenses named in other laws that merely provided different procedural remedies. [114] This argument depended on the idea that the laws orchestrated different kinds of trials for the same offense, the choice for the prosecutor depending upon his resources and status, those of the person he accused, and the risk he wished to undertake.

To participate in litigation, as a disputant or as a juror, required specialized knowledge not so much of the law but of how to make arguments about the law. The laws themselves offered no specifically legal definitions, as scholars who see little autonomy in the legal system point out. Yet, as this chapter has shown, litigants argued in particular and refined ways about what the law meant. The specialized knowledge of the courts consisted not in a knowledge of a body of substantive law but, in part, in an ability to understand and use certain protocols of interpretation. The laws themselves no more specified how they should be interpreted than they defined their terms: No law suggested that its meaning was to be found in the intentions of the "lawgiver" or of Solon; no law excluded Solon's poetry as irrelevant to this task; no law directed an uncertain reader to consult other laws to fathom its meaning. Even the one text that briefly directed how jurors should judge (the dikastic oath and its charge to judge "in accord with the laws") was itself subject to methods of interpretation it did not specify. The unique knowledge to be found in the courts was not a knowledge of the laws but of how to make arguments with and about the laws.

The relative autonomy of the courts, then, must first be understood as an aspect of its institutional practices. Those who deny the autonomy of the courts usually note that there were no specialized professional personnel: no lawyers, jurists, or judges. This was certainly true, and the presence of such specialized roles is one of the ways that many legal systems (from the Roman to the modern American) distinguish themselves from other aspects of society. Such professional personnel can also contribute to the development of an institutionally unique discourse, for example, "legal" definitions of crimes. Yet even without specialized personnel, Athenian litigation gave rise to insular traditions of legal practice. Although there were no objective and specifically legal definitions of crimes, there was an objective and (in some senses) legal set of interpretive methods for making arguments about what terms meant. The practices of litigation mark the autonomy of the courts.

Understanding how these practices of litigation contributed to the autonomy of the courts is important because of their contribution to Athenian democracy. The interpretation of the laws in litigation did not merely reflect a democratic consciousness; it also constituted it. Litigants urged jurors to think of themselves as a group with collective interests: They had taken their oath, Demosthenes asserted, on behalf of the city.[115] When litigants insisted that jurors interpret both the oath and the laws in ways that upheld democracy, they implicitly asked the jurors to think of themselves as a group, the demos. This shared identity of the jurors could thus be contrasted to other groups, tyrannies and oligarchies, that exercised power in their own interests.[116] But the practices of litigation constituted the jurors as a group in more subtle ways as well. Through their knowledge of the conventional methods of interpreting laws, Athenian jurors made up what Brian Stock has called, in another context, a community of readers. This does not mean that jurors were literate in the narrow sense; indeed, half of them or more probably were not. Rather, Athenian citizens shared the ability to interpret a specific kind of text, laws, in specific ways. As Stock has noted about medieval Christianity: "Through the text, or, more accurately, through the interpretation of it, individuals who previously had little else in common were united around common goals."[117] Because such a community was linked by shared interpretive protocols applied to texts that were read orally, its members did not have to be literate in the strict sense.[118] Moreover, the texts themselves did not explain or record these interpretive protocols. Rather, these protocols resided in the traditional and unwritten practices of the group. Those who did not go to the courts or the Assembly (women, slaves, and metics) were excluded from this community not (or not primarily) by their lack of literacy in the narrow sense but by absence from the collective activity of interpretation. In this sense, a woman would not "know" what a law meant (from a male citizen's perspective, of course) not because she could not decipher its letters but because she was inexperienced in the interpretive protocols customary in litigation. The methods of legal interpretation practiced in litigation thus contributed to the generation of a differentiated and privileged body of adult male citizens.

Two

LAW AND

NARRATIVE

Sometime in the middle of the fourth century, a man whose name we do not know (his father's name was Teisias) was sued by his neighbor Kallikles for damage resulting from a flood. Between their farms ran a road, a portion of which was also an arroyo. Kallikles alleged that the dry wash followed the road for a distance but then naturally ran off through the land of the son of Teisias. Many years before the suit, however, Teisias had dammed off the channel so that the water, instead of flowing through his own property, would continue to flow down the road. Years later, after a particularly heavy storm, that is exactly what happened: The water rushed down the road and onto Kallikles' land. Kallikles then sued the son of Teisias in a suit with a fixed thousand-drachma penalty.

In his defense speech (Dem. 55), the son of Teisias admitted many of these facts: There had been a flood that damaged Kallikles' belongings. His father Teisias had built a wall to keep out the water. But he asserted others as well: The arroyo did not run naturally through his land but had only been allowed to do so by a neglectful previous owner. Kallikles' father, Kallippides, had never complained about Teisias' wall. The damage had been so minor that a thousand-drachma penalty was exorbitant. And—the point he emphasized the most, beginning and ending his speech with it—Kallikles, his brother, and his cousin were engaged in an ongoing conspiracy to harass him with lawsuits, get control of his land, and drive him out of the neighborhood.[1]

Kallikles and the son of Teisias thus presented the jurors with two competing stories. Kallikles told a narrowly legal story: An unlawful act (Teisias blocking off the natural arroyo and diverting the water back into the road) had eventually resulted in a legal claim against Teisias' heir. The son of Teisias, however, related a broader social panorama: Kallikles and his brother and cousin, plotting against him, unjustly harassed him with lawsuits (even going so far as to sue his valued slave Kallaros), thus destroying the neighborliness that had existed between their fathers and, until very recently, between their mothers.[2] The insignificant damage from the flood was only an excuse for Kallikles' cabal to continue its persecution. The primary task of the jurors in this case, then, was not to decide disputed facts[3] but to choose between two different narrative frames that gave significance and meaning to facts. In Kallikles' story the law determined the relevant facts and their meaning: The son of Teisias was liable because what his father had done was prohibited by the law. Neither the prosecutor's motives in pressing this charge nor the social consequences of doing so were relevant to this story. The defendant's story, however, focused centrally on these and, in fact, invoked values outside the law (neighborly harmony) to question the legitimacy of using the law at all.

Although jurors had to decide between these two stories, the same necessity does not govern us. This case illustrates a point made in the Introduction, that in any dispute, what the dispute is about and, frequently, the narrative perspective that determines this are themselves at stake. This chapter explores the parameters of these disputes about disputes as they took shape in the courts in the competing stories of prosecutors and defendants. It analyzes the essential elements of the legal narratives of prosecutors, for whom the choice to transform the dispute into a legal case was also a decision to tell a story from a legal perspective. It also investigates the stories typically told by defendants who, like the son of Teisias, frequently challenged the appropriateness of the prosecutor's legal perspective.

DEFINING JUDICIAL NARRATIVES

Systems of litigation promote certain kinds of stories. To a degree, these judicial or legal stories differ from those told in other contexts. In some societies, the difference may not be that great. Natalie Zemon Davis argues that in sixteenth-century letters addressed to the French king requesting pardon in homicide cases, the specifically legal elements of the narrative (for example, an assertion that the deed happened in a moment of passion, without premeditation) can be recognized and isolated and that they do not substantially distort the authentic narratives of the accused killers.[4] In modern American courts, on the other hand, Conley and O'Barr suggest that rules of legal narration (like the rule against hearsay) create a deep chasm between a narrative that conforms to legal rules and nonlegal stories.

> Perhaps the most common complaints of litigants at all levels of the legal process are that they did not get a proper opportunity to tell their story and that the judge did not get the real facts in their case. This troublesome situation arises in formal courts as a result of the rules of evidence and the management of account-giving by lawyers. . . . This suggests that lay and legal conceptions of adequate accounts differ in ways that have practical as well as theoretical significance.[5]

The difference between a judicial or legal story and a nonlegal story in part derives from their content. Conley and O'Barr define the substantive difference in American law by the role of rules or laws in the narrative: "Many litigants speak of their place in a network of social relations and emphasize the social context of their legal problems. . . . By contrast, the official discourse of the law is oriented to rules."[6] Litigants and witnesses, then, tell stories where acts take on their meaning from the social relationships in which they happen, whereas judges and lawyers tend to define them in reference to laws. In making a similar distinction between the lay concept of a "problem" and a legal idea of a "case," Merry suggests that broad ideas like "a bad character" define "problems," while "cases" are much more narrowly defined around specific incidents.[7] Many Athenian prosecutors' stories show similar substantive features, emphasizing the law as the framework that bestows meanings on actions.

These scholars define specifically legal stories not only by their content, however, but also by the institutionally specialized personnel who tell them. They contrast the discourse of legal professionals (lawyers and judges) with the ways laypeople talk. Such an analysis seems limited for Athens, since here litigation did not introduce specialized professionals who might change a litigant's story because of their own institutionally determined interests and training.[8] Yet these contemporary professional roles should perhaps be seen as the expression of the characteristic institutional context that influences the telling of stories. Athenian litigation likewise took place in a defined institution, the courts, and at least three aspects of this context influenced the stories told: the distinctive role of the prosecutor, the sharply adversarial context, and the presence of a mass audience of jurors. Thus a prosecutor's assertion that events should be understood within the framework of the law represented a specifically legal kind of story, one inseparable from the institutional role of the prosecutor.

THE ELEMENTS OF A JUDICIAL NARRATIVE

In initiating a legal case, a prosecutor chose to tell a story in a legal form. Prosecutors often gave accounts that included more than this,[9] but their stories nevertheless had to contain certain elements to qualify as a legal case.[10] Three stand out: A legal story had to recount a "crime," a specific action that violated the laws.[11] A legal narration had to dichotomize the conflict: To go to law, one person had to bring charges against another, the defendant, the perpetrator. Finally, there were limits on the kinds of people who could appear as primary characters in a legal story, because litigants had to be legally competent. By emphasizing these elements, the stories of the law consistently suppressed (but did not eliminate) other possible narratives.

A legal story first demanded a "crime," an act that contravened a law.[12] Prosecutors often suggested that it was the illegality of an action that motivated the prosecution.[13] Here is how the son of Aristodemos opened his accusation of Leochares for perjury: "The blame rests squarely on Leochares here, men of the jury, both for his being put on trial and for me having to address you even though I'm so young: He thinks he has a right to inherit what doesn't belong to him, and he swore a false statement about these matters before the archon." [14] In suggesting that the "crime" caused the litigation, however, prosecutors concealed their own choice to initiate the case. In fact, litigation was less the outcome of a "crime" than a certain event was defined as a "crime" by the decision to litigate. More specifically, "crime" was the outcome of describing events with uniquely legal narrative conventions. Certainly, events actually happened, but their meaning was not inherent and objective.[15] Many actions that could be said to have violated a law were never litigated, never accorded a criminal interpretation. In many cases, litigation resulted from continuing, complex relationships of hostility.[16]

A legal story required the reduction of these complex relationships to a simple act. Sometimes prosecutors expressed some unease with this abridgment. For instance Ariston, in his accusation of Konon for assault (Dem. 54, discussed in Chapter 1), insisted on explaining the larger context of his dispute. Two years before the assault, when he was a young soldier on border duty in the same camp as the sons of Konon, they had humiliated and attacked his slaves and had even beaten him. Instead of taking them to law, however, at this point in the dispute, he and the others who had been assailed simply chose to endure their behavior, even though these actions had, by his account, violated the law.[17] Though he represented his decision to charge Konon for the later assault as due to its objective seriousness, he derived that seriousness in part from his linking it with these previous incidents. As his narrative makes clear, Ariston's sense of being wronged was ongoing and not simply a result of the one incident on which the legal story hinged. Ariston attached his sense of injustice not exclusively to a specific action, a crime, but to the whole relationship of which that action was part. But because Ariston was telling a legal story, he had to give primacy to a single event and to call it a crime.[18]

A legal narrative also dichotomized conflict by focusing on the prosecutor (often the supposed victim) and the defendant (the alleged perpetrator). Disputes, however, were often much more complex than this, involving several parties with quite different relationships to each other. Consider Chrysippos' suit against Phormio (Dem. 34).[19] Neither of them was a citizen, but Athenian law allowed suits by noncitizens on mercantile matters. This was Chrysippos' story: In Athens he had lent the merchant Phormio money to buy goods to be shipped to the Bosporos and sold. Their contract allowed Phormio either to ship a cargo back to Athens and repay the loan there to him personally or to discharge it in the Bosporos by repaying the money to Lampis, the captain of the ship, acting as Chrysippos' proxy. Chrysippos suggested that Phormio was intent on fraud from the beginning, taking duplicate loans on the same cargo.[20] When the ship arrived at its outbound destination, Phormio was unable to sell the goods, and so he could not ship a cargo back to Athens. He stayed behind to try to dispose of them while Lampis left with the ship. Disaster struck. The ship sank, though Lampis and some other slaves managed to escape in the dinghy. When he arrived back in Athens, Lampis denied receiving the payment. Chrysippos later confronted Phormio when he returned, demanding his money. Initially, Chrysippos alleged, Phormio agreed that he still owed the debt, but he subsequently claimed he had paid Lampis in the Bosporos. The money would then have been on the ship that foundered. Since it would have been formally repaid to Chrysippos' agent, the loss would be Chrysippos' alone. Since this directly contradicted Lampis' story, Chrysippos sought the ship captain's help and sued Phormio. They referred the case to an arbitrator before whom Lampis suddenly, unexpectedly confirmed Phormio's version of events. Now he said that he had received the loan repayment in the Bosporos and that it had gone down with the ship. The only way Lampis could account for his earlier statement was to say that when he made it, he must have been out of his mind. When the arbitrator refused to make a decision, Chrysippos took his suit to court.

There is a very good likelihood that Chrysippos' legal story, complicated as it is, oversimplifies the dispute leading to this case by casting it as a dyadic conflict between himself and Phormio. In reality, both Lampis and Phormio were probably victimizing him. Chrysippos never himself received his money, but it is unclear whether it was still rightfully due him and if so, whether from Phormio or Lampis. Isager and Hansen, in their analysis of this difficult speech, account for four possible scenarios: (1) The money was repaid but lost in the wreck; (2) the money was repaid, rescued from the wreck, and embezzled by Lampis; (3) after the wreck, Phormio repaid the money to Lampis, who stole it; and (4) Phormio never repaid the money.[21] The first possibility (which is what Phormio seems to have claimed) would absolve Phormio and Lampis of responsibility. In the others, someone defrauded Chrysippos. Chrysippos' narrative, based on the fourth plot, makes Phormio the mastermind of the fraud. Isager and Hansen, however, seem to believe that Lampis had bilked both parties. If there was such a fraud (as seems possible, given Lampis' starkly contradictory statements), both scenarios require Lampis and Phormio to have been in cahoots: Either they had agreed to divvy up the money (as Chrysippos claimed), or Lampis, exploiting his position as Phormio's key witness in his defense against Chrysippos' charge, blackmailed or bribed Phormio into remaining quiet.[22] The dispute thus begins to look like an unstable network of alliances and oppositions based on fear, interest, and expediency. Chrysippos' decision to sue Phormio, however, cast the case as a dichotomized conflict between the two of them, with Lampis as a third party (a witness for Phormio). Chrysippos may have decided to do this based on its strategic consequences: In suing Phormio, he created a legal opponent whose sole witness was, at best, unreliable.[23] Chrysippos' decision to litigate (and the incumbent dichotomizing of the conflict) also seems to have solidified the alliance between Lampis and Phormio, who now presented a united front against him. The legal story may have failed to encapsulate the dispute, but it had real consequences.[24]

If a prosecutor chose to bring a public case, he could tell a story that defined the pertinent parties along a different polar axis. In private suits like Chrysippos' against Phormio (or Ariston's against Konon), the prosecutor usually told a story in which he and the defendant were the opposing parties. In a public suit, however, instead of (or, occasionally, besides) presenting himself as the victim, a prosecutor bifurcated his story between the defendant (the perpetrator) and the city or the jurors (who, he claimed, had been wronged). Public prosecutors spoke, for example, of the "polis" more than three times as often as speakers in other kinds of cases and invoked the jurors directly (using the plural "you") about twice as often.[25] In constituting the jurors as the wronged party in the conflict, such speakers married the language of the courts (with its insistence on bilateral conflict) with the language of the Assembly, which asserted the collective identity and interests of the variegated citizenry of Athens.[26]

Predictably, public prosecutors usually did not represent a bilateral conflict with themselves as victims; in the stories they told, they minimized their role. On average, they used first-person pronouns less than a third as often as speakers in most other kinds of cases.[27] This lower average for public prosecutors was about the same as for Demosthenes' Assembly speeches, indicating the use of a similar kind of political discourse, which did not focus on the person of the speaker.[28] Nevertheless, Robin Osborne has shown that behind many seemingly disinterested public prosecutions, there was a history of enmity between the parties, even if this was not the story they usually emphasized.[29] The insignificance of personal hostility in these stories does not necessarily reflect, therefore, an objective feature of the dispute so much as an outcome of the kinds of stories they promoted; their political nature was as much an effect of the use of a public procedure as an objective quality of the dispute. The stories that particular people told (and that were told about them) marked them as politicians and particular conflicts as political. The choice of the type of case to bring against another, which was also a choice of the type of language to use and story to tell, attributed a particular meaning to the conflict and to the participants as much as it derived from it. More than its objective nature, what made a particular dispute political was the way one party chose to epitomize it as a public crime, the specific way he bifurcated it, particularly his assertion that the jurors were the victims of the crime.

The third requirement of a legal narrative was that the parties to the case be legally competent. Whereas disputes could take place between all kinds of people, legal cases largely concerned adult male citizens.[30] Euphiletos' defense (Lys. 1) on a charge of murdering Eratosthenes demonstrates how a legal narrative represented conflict in a particular, selective way by insisting on legally competent parties.[31] As Euphiletos told the jury, he and his young wife were living a happily married life, made even more intimate and trusting by the birth of a child. But then one day an old woman lurking near his house accosted Euphiletos. Sent by a spurned lover of a certain Eratosthenes, she warned him to watch out for this man: "He's seduced not only your wife but many others as well. He's a real professional."[32] Stunned, Euphiletos interrogated his housemaid. She disclaimed knowledge; he threatened torture. She persisted in her denial; he mentioned the name Eratosthenes and said he knew everything. The servant broke down, begged Euphiletos not to harm her, and revealed a continuing liaison between Eratosthenes and Euphiletos' wife. Euphiletos then demanded she help him catch Eratosthenes in the act. Days passed. Then, one night, the servant awoke Euphiletos to tell him that Eratosthenes was in the house, in his wife's room. Euphiletos went out and rounded up some friends who lived nearby, returned home, and burst into the room. Naked, Eratosthenes jumped up, but Euphiletos knocked him to the ground and pinned his arms behind his back. Eratosthenes implored Euphiletos, he begged him to let him pay compensation, but Euphiletos told him he had broken the law. "Thus," Euphiletos told the jury, circumspectly omitting the name of the act and its agent, "that man got what the laws prescribe for people who do such things."[33]

The traditional analysis of this case closely follows Euphiletos' perspective: This legal case arose from a conflict between two men over adultery. David Cohen has argued that adultery figured in contests of honor between men, that the male adulterer gained honor at the cuckolded husband's expense.[34] There is much to recommend Cohen's understanding, but it does make adultery essentially a transaction between men through a woman. Cohen, it is true, admits that wives must have had reasons for taking lovers,[35] but it is necessary to go further: Within the Athenian courts at least, it was impossible to tell the story of adultery as a conflict between a husband and a wife. The very decision to litigate had crystallized the dispute, focusing it on two men. The reasons Cohen suggests for wives taking lovers (loneliness, dissatisfaction) were not merely structural features of women's lives in Athenian society; they are also ways of describing wives' disputes with their husbands. Thus adultery may have been not only the *cause* of a dispute between two men, from another perspective, unspeakable in legal terms, it may have been the *result* of a dispute between a wife and a husband.

Euphiletos' legal narrative failed to relate fully the stories that other parties to this dispute might have told, but in this case, enough traces of them remain to begin to see how they may have understood the dispute differently. From these suppressed perspectives, the conflict was less about a contest of male honor as trouble between women and men. Euphiletos first learned of Eratosthenes' activities through a messenger sent by one of Eratosthenes' previous lovers, the older woman who was evidently jealous that he was neglecting her. From one perspective, then, the whole affair was the outcome of the discord between Eratosthenes and his earlier lover, which, however, could be told in a legal venue only as a footnote to the subsequent conflict between male citizens. Moreover, Euphiletos himself admitted to trouble with his wife: He revealed that she was angry because he had been forcing their maid to have sex with him.[36] It is reasonable to understand Euphiletos' wife's involvement with a paramour as a stage in a dispute between wife and husband, but such a conflict could not take legal form. Thus the conditions of legal discourse, in which male citizens faced off against each other, mandated that their stories make each other the primary, even exclusive, disputants. Other possible narratives, other possible understandings of the events, were elided. The problem with our evidence, then, is not merely that women could not represent themselves but that due to the structural demands of the courts, citizens' narratives had to make other citizens the prime actors. Figuring adultery as primarily about men and their honor repeats the systematic silence of the sources.[37]

THE DEFENDANT'S PROBLEM: ATTACKING A LEGAL NARRATIVE

However much he may have supplemented it, every prosecutor told a legal story. A defendant had to respond, and here he faced a quandary: What kind of story should he tell? He might claim that the prosecutor's story was wrong, illogical, or without evidence, providing what I will call an *antinarrative*. An antinarrative was not a story but an assertion that there was no story. On the other hand, the defendant might choose to present a competing story of his own, a *counternarrative* to the prosecutor's account.[38]

An antinarrative denied the coherence or foundations of the prosecutor's story. Such was the main argument of a man who was accused of
sacrilege (Lys. 7). Throughout Attica, on both public and private land,
grew hundreds of sacred olive trees, which the city protected from harm.
Even when they died, their stumps were still inviolable. This man found
himself accused of uprooting the stump of one of these trees, which had
supposedly been on his land. His defense was to deny that there ever had
been such a stump on his property; his speech consisted largely of refu-
tations of the facts of what he claimed was the prosecutor's story.[39]

Though such a strategy may seem reasonable to us, particularly since
in the American legal system a defendant in a criminal case is supposed to
need to show only reasonable doubt, Athenian defendants seem to have
been quite reluctant to rely on antinarratives alone.[40] Jurors may have
found an unelaborated refutation of the prosecution's story less than persuasive, as the speech of Euxitheos, who was charged with the murder of
Herodes, suggests (Ant. 5). Both men had been passengers on the same
ship, but one morning, after general drinking the night before, Herodes
was mysteriously gone, never to be seen again. After some investigating,
the dead man's relatives charged Euxitheos with murder. During the trial,
Euxitheos spent most of his speech arguing that various of the prosecution's contentions were wrong or unlikely. Then he continued:

> The prosecutors make the most of the argument that the man
> disappeared, and perhaps you want to hear about this. If I must
> make guesses about this, you are as competent to do so as I am.
> After all, you're not responsible for this crime, and neither am I.
> On the other hand, if the truth is to be discerned, let the prose-
> cutors ask one of the culprits. They would learn it best from him.
> . . . I think that each of you, if someone asked about something
> you didn't happen to know about, would say this much: that he
> didn't know. If the person demanded you say more, I think you
> would find yourself in great difficulty. So don't present me with
> this difficulty which you yourselves could not easily solve. Don't
> make my acquittal depend on whether I can present likely guesses,
> but let it suffice that I show that I had nothing to do with the
> deed.[41]

Euxitheos related some events: While on a voyage, Herodes disap-
peared. But this was, at best, a defective story, a story without closure,

one that did not make sense. That Euxitheos defended in such detail and so vehemently his failure to supply a competing story suggests that there were strong pressures for a defendant not simply to refute the narrative of the prosecutor but to provide one of his own.

General structural features of Athenian litigation seem to have prompted defendants to offer counternarratives. There was no questioning of witnesses or litigants by third parties (as a judge at an inquisitional hearing) to find evidence for an alternative narrative independent of either party's version. Since jurors voted immediately at the conclusion of the litigants' presentations, there were no collective deliberations in which they might have thought up and evaluated stories that had not been offered to them. Because Athenian litigation was starkly adversarial, jurors judged between competing presentations. More than this, although the events of life do not always, perhaps not even often, obey the logic of stories, accounts of events may be most persuasive, most accepted as true, when they follow familiar narrative lines.[42] Athenian defendants, like many American defendants, found that providing a competing narrative increased their chances of persuading the jurors.

Rather than simply denying the story of the prosecutor, then, most Athenian defendants provided an alternative story of their own, a counternarrative. Two varieties of defendants' counternarratives stand out. The first accepted the prosecutor's definition of a particular event as a "crime" but reversed the polarity of responsibility, asserting that the prosecutor was the guilty party. The defendant in Lysias 3, for example, was charged with attempted murder by Simon for an assault stemming from a rivalry over a slave boy, Theodotos, who seems to have worked as a prostitute.[43] Each of the men was in love with Theodotos and sought to woo him. After earlier tussles over the boy, the defendant took him abroad to get away from Simon. When they eventually returned, the rivalry reignited. In his prosecution, Simon apparently asserted that he had paid Theodotos for his company but that the defendant had lured him away.[44] Later, Simon seems to have claimed, the defendant and Theodotos came to his house with pottery fragments in their hands, threatened to kill him, and attacked him. In this case, the defendant admitted there had been a brawl, and he did not deny that he had struck Simon. He claimed, however, that the fight had started when Simon and his drunken friends tried to kidnap Theodotos. They attacked those bystanders who tried to protect Theodotos, and when the speaker tried to rescue Theodotos, they pursued and attacked him too. For the general riot that ensued, the prosecutor, Simon, was responsible. Defendants in cases of assault often seem to have used this counternarrative, but other defendants did as well.[45]

The second variety of counternarrative, rather than mimic and invert the legal story of the prosecutor, asserted that the dispute should not be understood as the story of a crime. Like an antinarrative, this counternarrative denied that there had been a "crime," but it also provided a competing story of its own: It explained why the prosecutor decided to initiate a case even though the defendant had not violated the law and no crime had been committed. Such a counternarrative, which defendants frequently used, suggested that a violation of the law had not spurred litigation, but other factors had: The prosecutor's suspect motives were at the center of this plot. Defendants who mounted such counternarratives explained the "crime" not as an objective feature of the world but as the result of the prosecutor's decision to litigate for reasons having nothing to do with the commission of the "crime." Constructing a narrative about that decision became the key to dismantling the idea of a "crime" and contesting the appropriateness of a judicial narrative.

One strategy defendants used to present a counternarrative to the "crime" was to assert that the prosecutor was a sykophant, a person who unfairly or dishonestly exploited the legal system for his own benefit.[46] Another such counternarrative made the "crime" an effect of ongoing personal or political hostilities.[47] The argument of the defendant Polyainos shows this (Lys. 9). He was indicted by some of his enemies (as he called them) as a debtor to the state for owing a fine. A board of generals had imposed this fine on him for slandering them in public. He had been upbraiding them to Philios in his bank because he thought that they had enrolled him for military service even when he should have been exempt. Polyainos claimed at trial that this situation did not fit the requirement of the law that the abuse be uttered in court. Polyainos said that the treasury clerks had in fact canceled the fine for this reason, although the prosecutors seem to have denied that they had the authority to do this. Thus part of Polyainos' defense was a technical antinarrative: He denied that his utterance fit the law's definition of a crime and that he legally owed the fine. Beyond this, he explained that some of the generals had become hostile to him when he allied himself with Sostratos, a prominent Athenian and political opponent of the generals and through whose power he had risen in importance.[48] Polyainos' counternarrative explained why there was a trial even though there had not been a crime:

because the generals had abused the legal process to further their own private, political feud.[49]

Such counternarratives contested the claim that there had been a "crime" by redefining the context in which actions were understood. Often this involved thinking of the dispute much more broadly than confined to the dyad of prosecutor and defendant, the core of a legal story. As the case of Ariston versus Konon suggests, disputes often took place between groups: groups of kin, groups of neighbors, groups of political allies. While prosecutors might use this broader context to supplement their judicial narrative, defendants sometimes used it to contest a legal story by redefining the meaning of the act in question. Ariston anticipated Konon would respond to his indictment for assault in just this way:

> I want to tell you beforehand what I have learned he is preparing
> to say. By changing the subject from hubris and what actually
> happened, he will try to turn it into a lighthearted joke. He will
> say that there are many men in this city, the sons of respectable
> people, who play like young people and have named themselves
> Ithyphalloi and Autolekuthoi[50] and that some of these are in love
> with mistresses. His own son is one of these, and he's often been
> on both ends of fights about girls. This, he will say, is typical
> of young men. About me and all my brothers he is inventing a
> story that we are not only drunken, violent, and hubristic but
> unreasonable and vindictive.[51]

Ariston may have been caricaturing the tone if not the facts of Konon's story. Yet the force of his proleptic rebuttal depends on discrediting the type of argument a defendant in Konon's position might well have made: that the act in question should be understood not as a crime but in the context of ongoing social relationships.[52]

In public cases, defendants frequently sought to reframe the case as a political dispute with or between political groups, suggesting that the decision to litigate was not the outcome of any act of wrongdoing but simply a tactic in a larger political struggle.[53] They usually also insinuated that the political goal of their opponents was illegitimate. When Euxitheos had been expelled from the citizen register by his local deme assembly, he appealed to the courts.[54] As part of his defense, he blamed the president of the deme, Eubulides (who brought the prosecution), and his minions, who had abused the citizenship-review process by illegally introducing foreigners into the deme as citizens. Such countercharges, from a legal perspective, were not to the point, but Euxitheos thought they were essential to understanding the case. About the insinuation of foreigners as citizens he said:

> These conspirators have done the most terrible thing. (By Zeus and the gods, do not be upset with me if I show you that these men who have wronged me are wicked. I think in showing you their wickedness I am speaking to the matter itself, at least as far as I experienced it.)[55]

Anticipating such a defense, prosecutors often insisted that the case should concern only the act that was the basis of the charge.[56] So Epichares, who had charged Theokrines with owing money to the state:

> You shouldn't expect that Theokrines himself will admit that he owes money to your treasury and say he has been indicted justly, but he will say exactly the opposite. He will make all sorts of charges. He will say he is the victim of a political conspiracy. He will say he has been put into this situation because he has brought indictments for illegal proposals. This is all that's left to someone convicted by the facts themselves—to invent charges and excuses that will make you forget the matter at hand and think about arguments beyond the scope of the accusation.[57]

The prosecutor's framing of the case as about a specific instance of wrongdoing also entailed definitions of what the dispute was and of who the relevant parties were. Aeschines' prosecution of Timarchos, which modern scholars understand as a maneuver in his policy dispute with Demosthenes over relations with Macedon, said almost nothing about this political controversy, though he anticipated that Demosthenes (who defended Timarchos) would introduce such "irrelevant" considerations; but Aeschines insisted the jurors vote only on the question of whether Timarchos had done what was charged.[58] What the dispute was "really" about was part of the debate of the case itself, and each side could muster reasonable arguments for its definition. The range of arguments, however, reflected the structural tension between the legal definition of a specific act of wrongdoing, a definition inherent in a prosecutor's narrative, and the nonlegal understanding of a specific action as part of a larger context, one of the main resources of a defendant's counternarrative. Litigants argued over how to understand their disputes by using these competing narratives.

THE DIKASTIC OATH
AND LEGAL NARRATIVES

Prosecutors and defendants invoked the dikastic oath to buttress the kinds of stories they told.[59] By invoking some of the procedural implications of the oath (that jurors vote on the prosecution's charges, for example, or that they listen equally to each side) both prosecutors and defendants found rhetorical resources for reinforcing the different stories they each told about the defendant's status: a criminal, the villain in a legal narrative, or a citizen wrongly imperiled by the legal process, the victim in a common counternarrative.

Prosecutors relied on the oath to insist that the jurors consider the defendant's conduct in a strictly legal narrative and that any of the defendant's attempts to portray himself in any other terms were attempts to pervert the legal process. Several prosecutors suggested that the oath required jurors to vote based on the prosecutor's charge.[60] This was Aeschines:

> What do I say against Timarchos? What is it I've charged him
> with? That he addresses the Assembly even though he's sold
> himself as a prostitute and consumed his inheritance. And what
> have you sworn? To vote on the matters that the prosecution
> charges.[61]

Similar claims by accusers relied, apparently, on interpretations of the vow to vote "according to the laws." This meant, prosecutors claimed, that the oath ruled out counternarratives by the defendant.[62] Epichares argued the following about Theokrines' expected defense:

> He will presently say that this indictment was brought against
> him so that he could not follow through on the case he brought
> against Demosthenes, and the case against Thucydides. . . . But it
> isn't just to offer such a defense to those who have sworn to judge
> according to the laws.[63]

Prosecutors attempted to use the oath to delineate their dispute as a narrow legal case, to define the defendant exclusively in terms of a legal narrative. For similar reasons, prosecutors also claimed that the oath nullified defendants' begging,[64] weeping,[65] or asking for *charis*.[66] As the prosecutor of Alcibiades on a charge of desertion said: "Since you believe this man to be a hereditary enemy of the city, you ought to convict him, and you should consider neither pity nor pardon nor any *charis* whatsoever as more valuable than the established laws and the oaths you have sworn."[67] As subsequent chapters will show, such defendants' strategies attempted to construct particular relationships between themselves and the jurors, relationships that entailed the defendant's identity as someone deserving or requiring the jurors' aid. Prosecutors, on the other hand, applied the dikastic oath as an antidote, trying to deny the legitimacy of attributing to the dispute any other interpretive framework except a narrowly legal one and trying to position the defendant exclusively in relationship to the law he was charged with breaking.

Defendants, too, found in the oath resources to define their identities and relationships to the jurors. They used the procedural stipulations of the oath to tell stories not about an act that may have violated the law (as prosecutors did) but rather about the trial itself. In relying on the oath for procedural fairness, defendants represented themselves as citizens whose status had been unjustly jeopardized by the prosecutor's decision to litigate. They reminded jurors that the oath obliged them to listen to both sides equally.[68] More than this, they said it allowed, even required the jurors to listen to them with *eunoia* (which might mean anything from "goodwill" to "partisanship").[69] This is how one defendant put it: "In every way possible I request that when you have listened to us all the way through with *eunoia*, you vote for what you think is both best for you and most in keeping with your oath."[70] The request for *eunoia* (which litigants also made without reference to the oath) was a procedural claim. *Eunoia* was thought to equalize the trial; it was claimed by those who represented themselves as at a disadvantage because they were young or inexperienced[71] or by defendants who were at a disadvantage because of speaking second or because of the great danger facing them if they lost.[72] *Eunoia* was not a recompense for any previous benefit but restored the equality that was part of the Athenian ideology of citizenship. *Eunoia* was a procedural safeguard that was due every litigant simply out of fairness, but many defendants requested special *eunoia* because they were disadvantaged simply by being the defendant. As one defendant claimed:

By necessity the defendant is in an inferior position, even if you listen to him impartially. Prosecutors have had a long time to hatch their plots, and they make their accusation without any danger to themselves. But we face trial surrounded by fear and slander and the greatest danger. So it's reasonable that you have more *eunoia* for defendants.[73]

The claim for *eunoia* asserted a defendant's primary identification as being a citizen whose status was wrongly imperiled by both the prosecutor and the legal process. In contesting the prosecutor's judicial narrative, which defined him as a person who had violated the law, a defendant could thus invoke the dikastic oath to buttress his counternarrative.

ORIENTATION TO THE LAW

The presence of the law influenced litigants' stories in more than these specific ways.[74] In the courts, litigants used the law as a comprehensive model for human action. Recasting the history of a dispute in legal terms, speakers not only offered the law as an excuse for their actions, they also retrojected it as their motivation. This was especially the case with defendants who sought to show that the law did more than excuse their actions; instead, they claimed, the law demanded that they act as they did.[75] Of preserved speeches, the story of Euphiletos, who had found Eratosthenes in bed with his wife, stands out (Lys. 1). Overpowered, bound, and naked, Eratosthenes begged for his life, offering compensation.

But I said: "It's not me that's going to kill you, but the law of the city. By violating it, you considered it of less account than your pleasures. You chose rather to commit this crime against my wife and children than to obey the laws and live as a decent citizen." Thus, gentlemen, that man got what the laws prescribe for people who do such things.[76]

Euphiletos then proceeded to have the laws on adultery and murder read out (though perhaps only in part). Though these excused a husband's slaying an adulterer on the spot, however, they certainly did not require it. Other remedies were available: He could formally charge him in court, physically abuse the man (explicitly allowed by the law), or even accept some compensation. Yet Euphiletos repeatedly insisted that he had done what the laws required:

The laws, gentlemen, have not only acquitted me of any wrong-doing but in fact ordered me to inflict this penalty. . . . I think every city lays down its laws so that when we're at a loss, we can go to them and consider what we must do. So it's the laws that prescribe in cases like this that the victims of the crime exact such a penalty.[77]

These arguments were certainly self-serving, but they exhibited at least two characteristics common to the ways other litigants talked about the laws. First, Athenians sometimes spoke of laws as mandating or prohibiting behaviors, not structuring choices; they said the laws "ordered" (κελεύειν) actions. Some laws of course did create and structure possibilities of action, but the Athenians often represented them as foreclosing choices.[78] Second, the laws were imputed as motivations, and exclusive ones at that. This undoubtedly overestimates the general knowledge of the laws and underestimates both the range of reasons people do things and the effectiveness of other means of social control. But, especially for defendants like Euphiletos, it absolved them of personal responsibility.

Many stories told in court oriented human action by the law. My point is not that speakers distorted or misrepresented the history of their troubles—that, for example, Euphiletos was disingenuous in failing to describe himself as a jealous husband or a dishonored citizen (or, for that matter, as a greedy schemer or even as a calculating murderer)—but that litigation provided a ready template that described and made sense of behavior: the law. Such a model failed to encompass the full complexity and indeterminacy of life, but stories are like that. They inevitably select, emphasize, and omit. Stories built around an orientation to the law seem to have been persuasive, however, perhaps not only because they corresponded to some extent to people's experience of life but also because they were a kind of story people knew well.

The idea that human action is oriented toward the law provided litigants a way of narrating the events leading up to the case and of characterizing and evaluating themselves and their opponents. Frequent charges and countercharges of illegal behavior (beyond the question of the indicted crime itself) fill the speeches.[79] Take the case of Kallistratos against his wife's brother Olympiodoros (Dem. 48). When a relative, Komon, died, the two of them conspired to divide his estate and exclude other relatives, drawing up a written contract to this effect. These other relatives, however, sued, and in the subsequent legal battles, the courts awarded the entire estate to Olympiodoros, who kept the whole thing for himself.

Kallistratos then sued him, alleging that Olympiodoros had agreed to split the estate between them. Near the conclusion of his speech, Kallistratos explained why Olympiodoros refused to honor his agreement:

> But he's gone crazy, men of the jury, he's lost his mind. It hurts me and I'm ashamed, men of the jury, at what I'm about to tell you, but I'm absolutely compelled to. I want to make sure that you who will vote will have heard everything when you decide what seems best about us. But this man is to blame for what I'm about to say because he wouldn't settle these matters with me among our relatives; no, he chose this shameless course. Well, Olympiodoros here, men of the jury, never married an Athenian woman in conformity with your laws, nor has he ever had children. Instead, he bought the freedom of a mistress and keeps her at home. She's the one who insults us all and makes Olympiodoros more and more deranged.[80]

From the perspective of the law, whether Olympiodoros married an Athenian was irrelevant to whether he agreed to this contract. Two factors, however, seem to have been at work in Kallistratos telling this story. First, he was characterizing his opponent by his orientation to the law. More than this, however, he was indicating that his understanding of the disagreement was broader than the bare terms of the case, involving as it did Olympiodoros' mistress, whom Kallistratos blamed for the trouble. But there was more. Kallistratos then began speaking of his wife (Olympiodoros' sister) and daughter, who were apparently implicated in the dispute more than the legal case alone revealed:

> Aren't they being wronged, aren't they suffering terribly when they see this rich man's mistress in gold jewelry and fancy clothes parading around like royalty and insulting us [ὑβρίζουσαν] with our own money—meanwhile my wife and daughter are worse off in every way—aren't they being wronged even more than I am? And he, isn't he obviously crazy and out of his mind in devising such things for himself? So that he cannot allege, men of the jury, that I am saying these things out of slander because of this suit, I will read to you a deposition from his relatives and mine. DEPOSITIONS.[81]

Of course this was slanderous, but to note this does not explain Kallistratos' statements so much as push the question back one level: Why were these specific slanders effective in this particular venue?[82] Kallistratos wanted to portray the dispute as something larger than a specific incident under the scrutiny of the law. Yet this narrative of the extralegal aspects of the case, as told in the courts, took on a legalistic form; that is, it recast much of the rest of the dispute in terms of orientation to the law. He hoped the slander would be effective not just because Olympiodoros' actions were scandalous but because they were illegal.

Kallistratos' repeated assertions that Olympiodoros was out of his mind, curious and hyperbolic as they seem, were in fact the ultimate step in portraying his opponent in reference to the law. Immediately after the words I just quoted, he reminded the jurors: "This man is deranged (as the lawgiver Solon calls it) like no one ever has been because he's under the influence of a woman who's a prostitute. Solon established the law that whatever someone does under the influence of a woman is invalid—especially a woman like this."[83] Solon's law actually specified that a will made while insane or under a woman's influence was invalid.[84] Kallistratos' interpretation of this law, that it covered Olympiodoros' failure to follow through on their agreement because his mistress had urged him to and he was insane because he listened to her, may be problematic,[85] but the important point is that he attempted to portray these familial disagreements as fundamentally legal. Olympiodoros' mistress seems to have been a significant source of hostility with both his sister and her husband (Kallistratos). However important such antipathy was to the dispute, though, it could not lead to litigation in that form and had to be subordinated to the "crime" in a legalistic narrative. Nevertheless, when it was recounted, it, too, was retold not so much as a tale of family jealousy and envy but as an account of a person's orientation to the law: a man who was legally insane because he was under the influence of a woman.

The idea that behavior was oriented toward and in fact determined by the law, a common way of telling a story in court, intersected with the rhetorical context in one further way. It provided material for an argument from probability.[86] Speakers sometimes asserted that the actions attributed to them by their opponent were inconsistent with the law and that it was improbable, therefore, that they happened as alleged.[87] Theopompos' speech over the estate of Hagnias provides an interesting example of such argumentation, in part because (like Kallistratos above) his opponent, representing Theopompos' nephew, had said that there had been a private agreement to split the estate between Theopompos and his brother Stratokles and, after Stratokles' death, with his son.[88] After a court initially awarded the estate to Theopompos, however, he denied such an agreement ever existed. When his nephew sued him for breaking the agreement, he said to the jurors:

> My opponent has alleged the most contradictory thing, which you must pay attention to, gentlemen. He says that I agreed to share half the inheritance with my nephew if I won my legal case against the previous holders of the estate. But if my nephew had a legitimate claim based on his relationship, as my opponent says, what was the point of this agreement between them and me? . . . On the other hand, if he has no rights to inherit by closeness of kinship, why did I agree to share it, since the laws gave the whole inheritance to me?[89]

It is possible to imagine that Theopompos might have agreed to share the estate with his brother and, after his death, with his nephew as part of their plot to get it from the other relatives,[90] or even, in addition, out of fraternal affection, even if the law did not require it. Theopompos, however, told a story in which only the demands and requirements of the law, nothing more, motivated both his actions and theirs. In such a story, a criminal conspiracy was as unlikely as love between brothers. The point is not that his story misrepresented reality (to a certain extent, every story does) but that the legal context of the telling imposed certain narrative patterns.

THE CONSEQUENCES
OF THE LAW'S STORIES

The narrative resources provided by the law offer one way of analyzing the autonomy of the Athenian legal system and its effects on society. Comparatively, American law constructs legal narratives with some more highly differentiated characteristics than Athenian law did. In American courts, rules of evidence and of procedure significantly shape stories. For example, because they are constructed through the questioning of witnesses, stories are fragmented and multiple.[91] The transformation of a dispute into a legal case in the American system also decisively introduces powerful third parties (lawyers, judges, police, therapists, and other professionals) with interests of their own who may coopt and change the stories of victims, accused people, and witnesses.[92] Neither factor operated as strongly in Athens. The two systems of law, however, impose some similar narrative conventions. Like any legal system that defines violations as discrete incidents, they insist that the prosecutor's or plaintiff's story describe a single act that contravenes the law. Through their adversarial nature, both also generate competing stories that take account of and respond to (or at least purport to respond to) each other. This is especially noticeable in the way Athenian defendants offered antinarratives and counternarratives, each of which aimed, in the first place, to undermine a rival story. Beyond this, litigants at Athens drew upon some more characteristic narrative resources. The broad way in which law was considered relevant and the rhetorical context allowed for not only arguments from probability but the extensive portrayal of human action as oriented to law. In the absence of disinterested public prosecutors, Athenian law may have more strongly emphasized dichotomized narratives. Finally, the restrictions on legal competence meant that at Athens legal stories largely concerned adult male citizens.

Athenian legal stories thus described conflict in particular, characteristic ways. The implications of these narrative conventions, however, go well beyond simply understanding how litigants tried to persuade jurors. The authority of stories fabricated with the law carried real consequences for contemporary Athenians. Litigation affected not only prosecutor and defendant through the verdict; the influence of the law seeped outward from the courts through the whole society—even to the lives of those whom the law neglected.[93]

An episode in the life of Neaira illustrates the effects of the stories of the law. In the late 370s, when Neaira, a former slave who lived as a courtesan, felt abused by her lover Phrynion, who had helped her buy her freedom, she fled Athens, taking some of their household goods. After a couple of years, she wanted to return to Athens but was fearful of Phrynion, and so she enrolled her subsequent lover Stephanos as her patron and went to Athens to live with him. There, when Phrynion tried to seize her, Stephanos asserted her freedom ("in accordance with the law," as the narrative states), and bond was posted with a magistrate, pending adjudication. Phrynion brought charges against Stephanos for wrongly claiming Neaira was free and for holding property stolen from him. Here friends intervened and persuaded both men to submit their quarrel to a group of three arbitrators, one chosen by each man and a neutral third. These reconciled the men, affirmed Neaira's freedom, returned the goods to Phrynion, allowed Neaira to keep her own, and stipulated that Neaira should be shared between them.[94]

The invocation of the law fundamentally transformed the shape of this dispute. It allowed for only two disputants, it insisted each be a legally competent male, and it focused on specific acts defined by the law (a formal assertion of freedom and the theft of property). Even in the settlement, the aim of the arbitrators (chosen because of their relationships to the men) was to reconcile Stephanos and Phrynion, who were, after all, the legal opponents. Neaira's future became just another condition stipulated for their reconciliation. The language of the law formulated the dispute (and its resolution) as a dyadic conflict between male citizens about a wrong one did to the other.

Legal narratives not only represented social life, they also affected it. As this case shows, the law was unable to construct a legal narrative with a woman, Neaira, as its subject. Nevertheless, Neaira did not appear as an impotent pawn in these events. Indeed, she enrolled Stephanos as her protector precisely to stand up to Phrynion more effectively. In seeking the leverage of the law against Phrynion, however, Neaira had to displace her interests because a legal narrative could express them only insofar as they were subsumed by a male citizen's. To invoke the law, she had to effect this displacement herself. Neaira did not merely require a patron to champion her interests; more importantly, she had to sublimate those interests into someone else's, she had to mediate her relationship with her own interests through a male citizen. Stephanos was not her representative or advocate in a direct sense: He did not bring a suit against Phrynion on her behalf for legal wrongs she had suffered. Rather, Stephanos' formal legal intervention, actively sought by Neaira, decisively transformed the dispute: He now spoke for himself in his dispute with Phrynion, which was partially (but only partially) about Neaira. His interests subsumed hers. A legal narrative, which dichotomized conflict between two competent legal actors on the question of a crime, could not capture Neaira's perspective in this dispute, though she could certainly take account of this in her actions.

The narratives of Athenian litigants, even when they include more than the minimum requirements of a legal story, fall well short of providing a full account of a dispute. This is in part because they insisted on certain elements (a crime, dichotomized conflict, legally competent parties) and portrayed human action as oriented toward and determined by the law; it is, however, also because some of what was at stake in a dispute was precisely how to describe it. Disputants' stories, though they often provide hints of other perspectives, offer totalizing, hegemonic narratives; indeed, suppressing other perspectives, other narratives was an essential strategic element in telling the story of conflict, whether in court or out. A complete account of a dispute, however, should be contrapuntal: It should recognize that there were not only competing narratives but opposed narrative frameworks and that disputants sought to further their interests precisely by presenting an interested (and, often, interesting) account as though it were objective. The important point is not locating the truth behind the distortions of a litigant's speech (though this is certainly valuable) but accounting for the narrative resources available to different parties, the ways they strategically deployed these in pursuing a dispute, and the broad social effects of legal storytelling. Athenian legal narratives attributed meaning to events through simplification; the problem modern historians face is precisely the opposite: to write a story of complexity.

Three

DARE, OR TRUTH

In the late 340s, the ex-slave and former courtesan Neaira found herself facing the charge of pretending to be the wife of an Athenian, Stephanos.[1] So that only the offspring of citizen parents could inherit citizenship, Athenian law reserved marriage strictly for those of citizen status, and it punished with enslavement and confiscation of property any noncitizen who lived with an Athenian in the pretense of marriage. In practice, the false claim that the two individuals were validly married meant that they were attempting to insinuate the children of the noncitizen parent into the citizen body as though they had been born of parents of citizen status. Though Theomnestos formally charged Neaira, Apollodoros delivered the main prosecution speech; his feud, he claimed, was with Stephanos, Neaira's partner, who spoke in her defense.[2] At the conclusion of his address, Apollodoros attempted to block Stephanos' expected claim that his children were of legitimate citizen status because his former wife was their mother, not Neaira. Apollodoros argued: "In response to the obscene contempt of his argument and his contrived defense (as well as the suborned witnesses who support it), I offered him a precise and reasonable dare by which you could have known the entire truth."[3] In lieu of a trial, Apollodoros dared Stephanos to hand over some slaves to be tortured: If they admitted that Neaira had borne Stephanos' children, Neaira was to be enslaved and the children disenfranchised. If they denied this, Apollodoros would drop his suit. A document in the text preserves the conditions of this proposed wager:[4]

Apollodoros made this dare to Stephanos concerning the charge
on which he has indicted Neaira, that she is living in marriage
with a citizen although she is a foreigner. Apollodoros was ready
to take for questioning under torture Neaira's maidservants whom
she brought with her from Megara, Thratta and Kokkaline, and
those whom she acquired later when living with Stephanos, Xen-
nis and Drosis, who possess accurate knowledge about Stephanos'
children, namely, that Neaira is their mother. The children in
question are Proxenos who is dead and Ariston who is still alive
and Antidorides the sprinter and Phano. And if they should admit
that these are the children of Stephanos and Neaira, Neaira is to
be sold in accordance with the laws, and the children were to be
aliens; but if they did not admit that these children were by this
woman but by another wife of citizen birth, I was ready to with-
draw from the case against Neaira and, if the slaves had suffered
any damage from the examination under torture, to pay for any
damage suffered.[5]

Apollodoros himself then continued:

When I had made this dare, men of the jury, Stephanos here
refused to accept it. Doesn't it seem therefore that Stephanos
himself, men of the jury, has given a verdict in this case, a verdict
that Neaira is guilty of the charge I brought against her and that
I have told the truth to you and provided truthful depositions,
but whatever this man says is a complete lie, and he convicts himself of lacking a sound case because he refused to hand over for
torture the servants I demanded?[6]

This section of Apollodoros' speech goes to the heart of the problem of
understanding the many references to dares in Athenian legal speeches.
On the one hand, Apollodoros' dare set out a procedure (in this case, the
torture of some slaves) that would forestall, and substitute for, a trial. Had
Stephanos accepted the dare, the case would not have come before the jurors. On the other hand, Apollodoros explicitly linked the dare to the revelation of truth. He not only claimed that Stephanos' rejection of his dare
had shown the truth of his own statements; he also said that the jurors
"could have known the entire truth," but only, he implied, if Stephanos
had accepted his dare. There is clearly a contradiction here: The accep-

tance of the dare could not have both precluded a trial and informed the jurors of the truth.

This contradiction, whether the dared procedure substituted for the trial or established truth for it, runs throughout the body of evidence about dares, especially dares to torture slaves and to have someone swear an oath. Indeed, despite litigants' repeated claims that these procedures establish an incontrovertible proof, remarkably, in no known legal case was the truth of any fact determined by these means, as will be discussed later in this chapter. All modern scholarship on dares attempts to address this paradox: Some claim that because disputants offered dares as an alternative to trial for settling their quarrels, in the court speeches we hear only of those that have been rejected; others (in fact, the majority) argue that people formulated dares in order to be rejected and then used that rejection as the basis of a rhetorical argument in court.[7] Both perspectives offer important insights: The former points to the ways disputants used dares outside the courts or before trial; the latter attends more scrupulously to the kinds of arguments made before jurors. The problem is that each of these positions replicates one of the two sides of the contradiction in the evidence itself without giving full weight to the other. My analysis of dares, however, aims not to resolve the contradiction but to elaborate and understand it.

Dares functioned in two contexts: outside the courts, they were a flexible means of pursuing a dispute. Litigants used dares to negotiate their relationship with each other. Their function was much broader than their ostensible form, an offer to end a dispute; litigants sometimes used them, in fact, to exacerbate a quarrel. In court, however, dares (or, rather, accounts of dares) functioned as a way of establishing and securing the relationship between a litigant and the audience of jurors. The link between these two functions, indeed, the linchpin of the contradiction, was the way litigation transformed disputes. The previous two chapters have shown some of the features of Athenian legal discourse and how these related to the institutional context. This chapter extends that argument. Litigants' claims that dares fundamentally concern truth derived from the problematic and insecure relationship between a pleader and a mass audience. This discourse of truth, which flourished in the courts, misrepresented the function of dares outside litigation. I do not intend, however, to accord greater importance to either the function of dares in pursuing disputes or their rhetorical function in court as the authentic and primary one; rather, I hope to show how legal discourse systematically transformed the use, and therefore the representation, of dares.

THE DOUBLE CONTINGENCY OF DARES

As people pursued their disputes, with a view towards victory or reconciliation or just escaping the trouble or even, perhaps, without a single, determinate goal, they might confront their opponents with a πρόκλησις, a dare or challenge. The movement of a dispute, whether towards resolution or escalation, often took place through dares and counterdares. A dare was a conventional offer, often made with bravado, to settle all or part of a dispute, depending on the outcome of a specified, formally contingent procedure. The dare consisted of two contingencies: first, whether the other party accepted it, and, second, if he did, the outcome of the specified secondary procedure.[8]

The secondary contingency commonly consisted of one of three procedures: First, a slave, who presumably knew something about at least some of the facts at issue, was tortured and asked to assent to or deny a particular statement; the slave's answer determined the winner. This torture (*basanos*), when it was the result of a dare, was a private transaction between citizens inflicted on a slave who was (usually) accused of no wrongdoing. Accused citizens were not tortured, nor did the state itself sponsor or carry out the torture of the slaves. This torture was, thus, a form neither of trial by ordeal nor of punishment.[9] Second, a disputant offered to swear an oath or to have his opponent or one of their supporters swear; whether they took or refused the oath determined the outcome. Third, the dispute could be referred to arbitrators, whose decision was binding on both parties.[10] (This form of arbitration, voluntarily initiated by the disputants, differed from the official arbitration required in most private suits.[11]) Importantly, a litigant could always appeal the decision of an official arbitrator to a court. Dares always offered secondary procedures that were, formally at least, uncertain. Speakers rarely called a simple offer to settle a dispute on specific terms, which happened often enough, a dare.[12] Though there was considerable leeway in composing the specific terms of each procedure, they generally took limited, traditional forms. They operated almost as rituals that guaranteed and finalized the agreement reached in the acceptance of the dare.

The first contingency, the dare itself, usually took the form of an offer to settle the dispute.[13] Several speakers said that an accepted dare would have prevented threatened litigation.[14] A litigant who wished to blame his opponent for their quarrel escalating to litigation might say that he had tried to end it with dares, as Demosthenes did: "Although I thought it so important, men of the jury, to avert the previous disagreement between Aphobos and me as well as the present one with the defendant Onetor, his brother-in-law, that I made many fair dares to them both, I have encountered a complete lack of reasonableness."[15] Headlam argued a century ago that dares were an alternative to a jury trial, and his views have recently found some support.[16] Nevertheless, many scholars argue that although there are some cases in which the dare was an offer to settle, most cannot be so considered because litigants did not explicitly say they were.

There are, however, strong reasons for believing most dares did take the form of a proposal of settlement. Scholars who deny this have usually looked only at challenges to torture slaves. This, however, ends up focusing the investigation on the question of torture instead of on the dare itself. Though these were the most commonly mentioned type of dare, a survey of all dares (irrespective of their secondary contingency) suggests that dares generally offered to end the quarrel. Challenges to arbitrate the dispute invariably did this. Though the sources certainly speak of challenges to arbitration,[17] and though all cases of arbitration fit the definition of a dare,[18] scholars have usually not treated arbitration with oaths and torture because they have seen the latter two as procedures for introducing evidence into court, whereas everyone admits that private arbitration forestalled litigation.[19] Athenians, however, treated them all as functionally interchangeable secondary contingencies in dares. In some dares, too, a disputant challenged his opponent to swear an oath or to be allowed to swear one himself.[20] In the latter case, the secondary contingency was what might be called self-judgment.[21] It makes no sense, however, to think that this was a way of introducing otherwise unavailable information to the jurors; the man who would swear the oath was, after all, one of the litigants.

The existence of challenges to arbitration and self-judgment, therefore, seriously undermines the idea that litigants used dares to produce information. In fact, even many dares to torture explicitly took the form of an offer to settle, such as Apollodoros', quoted at the beginning of this chapter.[22] Most litigants' accounts of their dares to torture, it is true, did not specify them as an offer of settlement. Yet litigants described dares in such highly abridged ways—even Apollodoros' report of his dare to Stephanos, perhaps the most detailed account of a dare, fails to enumerate some of the features that it must have contained—that the argument from silence is suspect. Thus, though there was no rule or law that a torture or an oath legally terminated a quarrel, the point of a challenge was usually to use it this way.[23] The idea that the acceptance of a dare terminated a legal claim most economically accounts for the complete absence of the evidence from any completed oaths or tortures introduced as the result of a dare.

TURNING SUBSTANTIVE
INTO PROCEDURAL CONFLICTS

Dares worked by transforming a dispute from a conflict over substantive issues into a conflict over procedural details. In doing so, they created a relationship between two contingent events: first, whether the opponent accepted the dare itself and second (if he did), what the outcome of the dared procedure would be. The issues negotiated in dares and counter-dares were not (or not directly) who was wrong or right or who had done what, but what specific secondary procedures would be used: who would swear an oath and what its exact wording would be, which slaves were to be tortured and exactly how much, and related issues. The key to understanding how dares functioned lies in the relationships between these two contingencies.

The quarrel between Mantias and his son Boiotos illustrates how these two contingencies worked. Mantitheos, in two suits against his half-brother Boiotos, told the following story about an earlier dispute between Boiotos and their father:[24] Mantias, a politician of some note, though legally married to Mantitheos' mother, had had another relationship with Plangon, who had two sons, Boiotos and Pamphilios. After he had come of age, Plangon's son Boiotos, supported by some men who knew how to use the legal system, initiated a suit against Mantias, demanding that he formally recognize Boiotos as his son. Afraid that his political enemies might take advantage of him, Mantias was reluctant to contest the case in court. After many meetings and much disagreement, both sides agreed that before the arbitrator, Mantias would dare Boiotos to let Plangon swear an oath affirming his paternity of Boiotos and Pamphilios. They further agreed that Boiotos would accept the dare, but Plangon would decline to swear the oath, thus freeing Mantias of the paternity claim. Mantias would give Plangon thirty minae when she had done this, and her brothers would adopt her two sons. Unexpectedly, however, Plangon swore the oath. Mantias had no alternative but to acknowledge Boiotos and Pamphilios as his own and see them formally registered.[25]

This case shows how the two contingent procedures (first, the dare; second, the action dared) functioned in practice. First, the oath ceremony was not what would have caused the intended settlement but was itself a result of the agreement of both sides. The oath may be seen as a way of determining a "winner," but this itself was (or was supposed to have been) the result of the agreement of the disputants on procedures. The oath was not a way of gathering or evaluating evidence but of formalizing the compromise the parties had reached. It was also a formal procedure that, once completed, was absolutely binding on both sides. Thus, though Mantias intended it to forestall future claims by Boiotos, when things went awry, it left him without any recourse.[26]

Not the oath but the consent of both sides to the dare was decisive in ending this case. Mantitheos' language, however, obscures this by leaving some of the details uncertain. Though at one time he said that Plangon was supposed to decline the dare (οὐ δέξεσθαι τὴν πρόκλησιν), at another he claimed that she was supposed to decline the oath (οὐ δεξαμένης τὸν ὅρκον). In the first instance his phrasing must be imprecise: If the challenge had been refused, there would have been no oath to decline. It was not unusual for litigants in speaking to conflate the dare itself with the secondary procedure,[27] the very metonymy that allowed the secondary contingency to overshadow the first. But this still leaves the question of which Plangon was supposed to refuse. Although Mantitheos says in the second speech that his father challenged Plangon, in the first he says only that he tendered her an oath. It is curious that he would have challenged her when it was her son Boiotos who was suing him. If the concern of Mantias was, as Mantitheos represents it, to forestall Boiotos' litigation, he should have challenged him, because only his acceptance of the dare would have settled the case. It seems more likely, then, that Mantias challenged Boiotos to settle by offering an oath to Plangon and that she was supposed to decline to swear the oath. Under the terms of the challenge, this refusal of the oath would be decisive. Merely declining a challenge, however, was never decisive. Even if it might be reason for an official arbitrator to give a verdict against the person who declined the oath challenge,[28] the point here was to prevent future litigation, and it would not have had this effect. (The loser could always appeal the official arbitrator's verdict to a jury court.) The point in this case cannot be, as Todd claims, that the evidence of the oath itself was practically decisive (either to the arbitrator or in court).[29] This cannot be the case because the challenge was intended to result in no oath at all, and the failure to swear was supposed to be decisive. Since the refusal to take an oath imposed only a rhetorical disadvantage in court, there must have been an agreement that this would be construed as decisive by these parties, an agreement that was the dare. Mantitheos simply conflated the two contingencies in his second speech.

Although a dare was an offer to settle a dispute through a secondary contingent procedure,[30] the first contingency alone determined whether the dispute would be settled. Although litigants consistently represented the outcome of the challenge as dependent on the procedure that was dared, in fact the acceptance of the dare itself, not its outcome, produced the settlement. In accepting a dare, both parties had agreed to reconcile, no matter what the outcome of the challenged procedure was. It is important to keep these two contingencies distinct, since one of the reasons dares worked was that the second contingency masked the first: That is, the settlement of the dispute was represented as dependent upon the outcome of the secondary contingency, as though what the slave said or whether a person took an oath determined whether the parties ended their dispute. But the acceptance of the dare had already made its outcome essentially irrelevant to whether the dispute terminated, even if it prescribed the terms of the settlement.

Although Athenian litigants frequently represented it as decisive, the secondary contingency in daring (the torture, the oath, the arbitration) was merely formal. In fact, dares worked as a tactic in disputing precisely because of this misrepresentation of their logic, by exchanging disagreements over the formal aspects of a challenge for substantive issues. Just as antagonists often focused an ongoing relationship of hostility on a specific incident or episode, so too the details of a challenge might bear the weight of the substantive disagreement. In making a dare or in deciding whether to accept or decline it, the details of the procedure mediated issues of who was right or what had truly happened. With a dare, negotiations about the specific forms of the torture, the oath, or the arbitration would supplant the substantive issues of the dispute.

With each of the three forms of secondary contingency, a number of issues routinely arose, and for each, historians have reconstructed their generic forms. Regarding torture,[31] before witnesses, during a mediation, or during the appealable official arbitration required of some cases, a person offered their own slaves or demanded their opponent's for torture in public. The details were committed to writing: which slaves were required, who would do the torturing, how they would do this, to what degree, what exact question the slave would be asked to assent to or to deny, what penalty would hinge on the outcome, what damages would be paid if the slave were injured, and who would assess these. With oaths, the most important issues were who was to take it, how exactly it was worded, and what the outcome of taking it or declining it would be. In arbitration, the most important questions were who was to arbitrate and what powers they were to be granted. The arbitrators formalized their decision with an oath.[32] When accepted, challenges were guaranteed by pledges and sureties,[33] deposits,[34] or oaths.[35] Parties may have come together with their initial dares already prepared, but in the negotiations that transpired through dares and counterdares, they added new terms or dropped old ones.[36]

Even though the acceptance or refusal of a dare would obviously depend on its exact procedural terms, one of the greatest obstacles to understanding the use of dares in disputes is that we usually have only a general idea of what these were in any specific case. For example, although Apollodoros characterized his dare to Stephanos (quoted in the introduction to this chapter) as "precise," it must have been much more specific than Apollodoros' report and than the document included in the speech.[37] He did not repeat the exact wording of the question posed to the slaves, nor did he tell whether the assent of a single slave would have been sufficient to convict Neaira—or if a majority was required, or even all four. The challenge must have specified these and many other procedural details, but Apollodoros did not report them. Other litigants reported fewer details still. As a result, it is often difficult to tell why one party issued a dare or why the other declined it.

NEGOTIATING A DISPUTE WITH DARES

Disputants used dares primarily to pursue their quarrels, not to gather information for presentation to the jurors. During a dispute, a dare frequently provoked a counterdare, and so the disputants negotiated their hostility through procedural dares.[38] Instead of refusing a dare to torture slaves outright, sometimes a disputant parried with another dare, to torture other slaves[39] or to choose different torturers.[40] A demand to hazard the case to arbitration could provoke a different formulation of the arbitration rather than a refusal.[41] With oaths, too, a challenge could elicit a responding challenge, which specified different conditions or a different person to swear.[42] Even the outright refusal of a dare could provoke the challenger to revise his dare.[43] As noted before, in the process of issuing dares, it was expected that terms could be altered,[44] an expectation that casts doubt on the theory that challenges were issued solely with the intent that they be refused. The parties' interests were, of course, at stake in these negotiations, but these interests (and therefore "truth" and "justice") were mediated through the procedural considerations of the dare.

A dare could escalate or pacify the conflict. Some scholars have argued that disputants formulated dares just to be refused and that they only provided a rhetorical advantage in court for the one who issued them.[45] Though litigants certainly tried to show themselves as reasonable in offering and accepting dares, to consider only the ways in which they provided rhetorical advantages ignores their social functions. In the prelegal stage of the quarrel, even dares that were meant to be refused could be ways of pursuing the dispute. Disputants sometimes accosted their opponents with outrageous dares that seem to have been intended to insult and anger, to signal the challenger's hostility (whether real or a ruse), or to move the opponent toward settlement through fear of escalated conflict. Apollodoros' dare to Stephanos, for example, was an outright affront. This dare specified more severe consequences for the defendant than conviction in court without, however, the same risks to the prosecutor.[46] Apollodoros could hardly have intended it as an offer of settlement (though it took that form); it seems rather to have been an insult and a sign of Apollodoros' adamant hostility.[47] Apollodoros was the master of the inflammatory dare: In his legal battles with his stepfather Phormio, Apollodoros said he demanded that slaves be tortured and asked whether Phormio had seduced or corrupted (διεφθαρκέναι) Archippe (Apollodoros' mother) before he married her.[48] Such a challenge did not indicate Apollodoros' willingness to compromise but rather showed his intent to do anything, including bringing a charge of seduction, to attack Phormio.

The majority of dares, however (at least as the speeches report them), were not so obviously and singularly antagonistic. In fact, the great flexibility of the dare was that the very same one might provide resources both for exacerbating the conflict and for pursuing a reconciliation, depending on the opponent's reaction.[49] To refuse a challenge gave potential rhetorical material to one's adversary, but it also created an incentive to issue a challenge in turn. The exchange of dares moved the conflict forward in ways that might result in aggravated hostility and litigation or might, slowly or suddenly, achieve pacification. It is a mistake, therefore, to think that antagonists invariably formulated challenges to be refused (although it seems that way since from the perspective of a trial, and therefore our evidence, they all were refused). Such a view erroneously suggests that a kind of intransigence inhered in the conflict from the beginning and fails to recognize the supple character of challenges.

Dares and counterdares, then, were not necessarily a means of escalating a conflict, nor were they only meaningless ploys to give a litigant a rhetorical advantage in the court; they could also be part of a movement toward settlement.

When dares effected a settlement, they did so through a logic of misrecognition: They let people say one thing and do another. One of the most important ways disputants used challenges was to balance competing claims of honor. Those that allowed a reconciliation seem to have been formulated so that the "victor" gave something to the "loser" or perhaps even to blur the line between the two. This often seems to have been the case with arbitration. In the dispute, for example, over Menekles' estate between his adopted son and his brother, the arbitrators insisted on deciding not what was right (τὰ δίκαια) but rather what was advantageous to all (τὰ συμφέροντα πᾶσιν).[50] (A decision on τὰ δίκαια would probably have given everything to one party or the other.) Their decision was that the adopted son should give the brother what he claimed, not as his right but as a gift. They also arranged for each to swear oaths of amicability.[51] Similarly, the first time that Apollodoros sued Phormio, they agreed on arbitrators who had Phormio give Apollodoros the amount of his claim, but as a gift, to preserve their relationship.[52] In these cases, the compromise consisted of giving the one party the money he claimed and making the other out not as a wrongdoer but as a magnanimous friend. Although it is harder to see in other kinds of procedures because the accounts of them are so sketchy, the same principles seem to have been at work. In the case of the conflict between Mantias and Boiotos, for example, the ostensibly intended settlement by oath did not require Mantias to acknowledge his children, but it also left Boiotos and his brother free of the stigma of being publicly disowned (because a refusal of an oath, not a negative oath, was to decide the dispute) and gave them some compensation. (The thirty minae that their mother was to get was a large amount of money, though perhaps less than they inherited as legitimate sons.) Similarly, the dares to torture slaves on issues ancillary or even irrelevant to the legal case may reflect not only a contest to define the relevant issues but an attempt to defuse and end the conflict by displacing it onto potentially less contentious questions.[53]

The very "irrationality" of oaths and torture was part of what made them effective methods of settling. Modern scholars sometimes react with embarrassment or shock because the outcome of these methods had so little to do with the merits of the case at hand and so much with factors extraneous to justice or truth.[54] But that is precisely why challenges were so supple, so useful, to Athenians, who, although they sometimes praised the irrefutable certainty of testimony given under torture, clearly recognized how arbitrary it was.[55] This ambivalence was essential. Because the specific procedural details of the dare so closely prescribed the result, the parties could predict and control the outcome while still leaving an arbitrary procedure to blame. Since the claims of justice and of truth were decoupled from the outcome, they could be bargained in a realm where they were overtly misrecognized.[56] It also meant that there might be no clear winner or loser or that at least the loser could blame the irrational procedure for his loss. Thus those who had agreed to a dare could always complain like Nikobulos that he had consented to it

> although I didn't think it was fair. I mean, how is it fair either that I have to pay two talents or that this sykophant doesn't suffer a thing based on the body and the life of a slave? But I gave in because I wanted to prevail with a thorough sense of fairness.[57]

In a highly competitive society, dares allowed a way out without the loss of honor a decisive defeat would bring. Dares permitted compromise without disgrace and gave room for public posturing. Adversaries needed the seeming irrationality of challenges precisely to veil their logic so that both could haggle for their honor without appearing to do so.

The case that the litigious Apollodoros brought against Nikostratos (Dem. 53) shows some of the ways that the specific details of a dare could implicate points of honor.[58] This case and the dispute behind it, for Apollodoros at least, was about one thing: a humiliating, public victory over Nikostratos. He broadcast his motives as he began his speech: He repeatedly drew the jurors' attention to the fact that he himself had filed the charge. Although this was a public case and anyone could have undertaken the prosecution, Apollodoros insisted that it would be the most terrible thing imaginable if he had suffered a wrong from Nikostratos but someone else won the victory. He even renounced the portion of the fine he might win; "vengeance," he swaggered, "is enough for me."[59]

According to Apollodoros, the trouble had begun sometime before. He and Nikostratos, his neighbor, had been friends until they came into dispute over a loan. In a subsequent lawsuit, Nikostratos convicted Apollodoros in part based on the testimony of Arethousios, Nikostratos' brother. Apollodoros then sued and convicted Arethousios for false testimony; a fine was imposed as penalty. Next, Apollodoros sued Nikostratos (this is the speech preserved for us) for the forfeiture of two slaves he claimed were really Arethousios' property, which was owed to the state for his fine. At the preliminary hearing, the two brothers dared Apollodoros to torture the slaves himself and interrogate them on the question of their ownership. Apollodoros reveals no more details about this dare, but it may well have been tantamount to conceding the case; Apollodoros himself would have applied the violence. Apollodoros, however, was in no mood for a compromise, unless it entailed the disgrace of his opponent. So Apollodoros demanded that the torture be conducted publicly, by state officials, under supervision of the Council.[60] Whether Apollodoros' response was actually a dare is unclear.[61] What is obvious is that if Nikostratos and Arethousios hoped to settle quietly, conceding the case to Apollodoros through the details of the dare, Apollodoros demanded nothing less than a public victory that allowed no room for excuses or salvaged honor. Both the privacy and the seeming irrationality of the process would have allowed the brothers to save face. Apollodoros worried that "if I had tortured the slaves privately, the defendants could have denied everything."[62] He insisted on defeating them publicly.

Although disputants did not use dares to produce evidence for the courts, they could nevertheless use them to communicate information between themselves. Through the exchange of dares, those in conflict could indicate the points on which they were willing (or not willing) to compromise. Apollodoros, for example, both with his stepfather Phormio, whom he threatened to charge with seduction, and with his neighbor Nikostratos, whom he insisted on defeating publicly, signaled his belligerence by the way he formulated his dares. On the other hand, a dare might concern only some of the matters at issue and thus attempt to narrow the dispute.[63] So, in a dispute over a shipping loan, Dareios dared Dionysodoros to repay the money they both agreed was owed (the principal of the loan and some of the interest) and to let arbitrators decide about the smaller amount in disagreement, the balance of the interest. Dionysodoros, however, refused to narrow the dispute because he was withholding the whole debt as leverage against the amount in contention.[64] Through an exchange of information, the dispute itself might be transformed, either broadened or narrowed, either of which might exacerbate or pacify the trouble.

The secondary procedure of the dare worked by providing a ritual as the sign and guarantee of settlement. The rhetoric of Athenian litigants combined with the history of the Roman canon-law tradition in continental Europe[65] have influenced the understanding of torture in Athens: that it was a form of gathering information. But this was not its primary function. It was, from the disputing perspective, a solemn action that guaranteed the settlement. Similarly, the swearing of an oath or the pronouncement of the arbitrators' verdict (also accompanied by an oath) were rituals that formalized an agreement to settle as irreversible. These procedures could be purely formal: The parties could stipulate ahead of time whether the person would accept the oath or what the judgment of the arbitrators would be.[66] In these cases, the preservation of the secondary contingency, even if purely formal, would be important because the ritual actions of the secondary contingency finalized the agreement inherent in the primary one. Until the challenged procedure had been completed, the settlement was not secure. Several of the known accepted challenges show it was possible to back out just until the secondary contingency had been completed. It was possible to renege on an agreement to arbitrate and forbid a pronouncement of the decision,[67] or, just as the slave was about to be tied to the rack, for at least the person who had accepted the challenge to reconsider.[68] Only this final ritual made the settlement binding.

Because the acceptance of the first contingency (the challenge itself) was the product of agreement, it was more likely to effect a lasting reconciliation. In Athens, the state did not guarantee the security of a settlement or enforce terms on an unwilling party. Though it is impossible to tell with certainty, the number of cases we have that follow a previous case by the same parties suggests that an outcome determined through litigation was not always very secure. Though a judicial verdict would render an unappealable decision about a particular incident, it would not necessarily end a hostile relationship. A judicial judgment might well further polarize the parties and exacerbate the sense of hostility between them, especially since one of them (the defendant) had not agreed to the procedure. The virtue of dares, from this perspective, was that, unlike litigation, both parties agreed ahead of time to settle, whatever the outcome of the secondary contingency.[69]

CONDUCTING LITIGATION WITH DARES

Outside the courts, then, disputants used dares to negotiate their relationships with each other. Before the jurors, however, they used dares (or, more accurately, accounts of dares) to establish their relationship with the jurors. The distinction is fundamental, because a different set of institutional problems confronted a litigant before a mass audience. These problems of the rhetorical context fundamentally shaped litigants' discourse, especially (in this case) their claim to be speaking the truth.

In the courts, litigants repeatedly linked dares with truth, but they did so in complex ways that suggested that not only the dared procedure (especially the torture of slaves) could reveal the truth but even the dare itself did. The defense offered by a man charged with unintentional homicide demonstrates these multiform relationships (Ant. 6). The city appointed this man as *choregos,* producer of a chorus of boys for a religious festival. During the training of the chorus, which his son-in-law oversaw, one of the boys drank a potion meant to improve his voice. It killed him. When the boy's brother indicted the *choregos,* he responded with a dare that the prosecutor question the free men and slaves who had been present, a dare he declined. In his speech before the court, the defendant remarked:

> You know, gentlemen, that the strongest and greatest human compulsions are these and that proofs based on these are the clearest and most trustworthy when there are many free men onlookers and slaves too, and it is possible to compel the free people with oaths and pledges (which are the greatest things and most important to free people), and it is possible to use other compulsions on the slaves by which, even if they will die by making their declarations, they are nonetheless compelled to speak the truth. I dared the prosecution, therefore, to do all these things; they had the opportunity to use the methods by which it is humanly possible to learn the truth and justice.[70]

The defendant claimed that the dared procedures (oaths and torture) would have revealed the truth. Yet he went further and claimed that the prosecutor's rejection of the dare had disclosed the truth anyway:

> If they had made the dare and I refused to point out who was there [when the boy died], or if I refused to hand over the servant women to those who demanded them, or if I evaded any other dare, they would take these things as the strongest proofs [τεκμήρια] against me that the charge was true. But since I made

the dare and they evaded the test, this same situation is justly a proof [τεκμήριον] for me and against them, that the charge they made against me is untrue.[71]

By the defendant's argument, even the absence of the truth was itself a sign (τεκμήριον) of the truth. (τεκμήρια usually denoted inferences drawn from circumstances or actions.) Litigants commonly spoke of dares as well as dared procedures as revealing the truth.[72] Litigants seem to have fervently sought to claim truth as their own, though of course it had a much wider resonance in legal speeches than just with dares. But what, precisely, did "truth" mean? Or, to reformulate the question, in what ways could "truth" be said to attach to these procedures?

Page duBois offers one possible answer. She argues that for the Greeks, truth was inherently bound up with the torture of slaves: The Athenians believed that by inflicting pain on the body of a slave, a spontaneous and authentic truth issued forth.[73] DuBois makes much of the original meaning of *basanos,* the touchstone by which the purity of gold was assessed. Etymologies, however, neither explain nor analyze social practices. In this case, the essential question, which duBois neglects, is why it was only in the judicial context that purity became equated with truth. As she shows, in other contexts purity stood as a metaphor for different qualities (in Theognis, for example, for nobility). Although duBois rightly draws attention to the violence with which Athenians treated their slaves, the idea of truth did not originate in torture.[74] In disputes, dares did not aim at revealing information; instead, they mediated the relationship between two parties at odds. The torture of slaves, like oaths and arbitration, did not fundamentally aim at revealing truth but at sealing and guaranteeing a negotiated settlement. The attachment of "truth" to this process was an effect of its discussion in the rhetorical context of litigation, a context in which truth was attached to much else besides torture, including both offering and declining dares.

Traditionally, legal scholars have understood dares as a way of introducing evidence into the formal setting of the court, especially the evidence of slaves (with torture) and of women (with an oath), neither of whom could testify as witnesses.[75] Thus the truth of these procedures is the information they made available to the jurors. Todd's recent account of the role of witnesses in courts is a sophisticated version of this theory.[76] Beginning with Aristotle's five kinds of raw material for proof (laws, witnesses, agreements or contracts, torture, and oaths) he regards the first

three of these as "risk procedures," against which there was legal recourse if they were introduced falsely, whereas the final two he regards
as "consent procedures" because they could not be introduced as evidence without the consent of the opposing party, and, once introduced,
their legal validity could not be impeached.[77] Although these two categories were formally different, in Todd's account their purpose was still
the same: to provide the jury with information. In treating challenges as
a form of evidence, modern scholars follow not only the analysis of Aristotle but the implications of the speeches as well. In court, litigants sometimes referred to challenges as a way of getting information that they
thought would be decisive in determining the verdict.[78]

Nevertheless, there is an embarrassing problem with this account of
dares: Despite the frequency with which disputants made dares, and despite some litigants' insistence on the decisive and irrefutable value of
their proof, in none of the extant speeches was a piece of evidence introduced by a fulfilled dare. The evidence that challenges should have
yielded is conspicuous only by its absence.[79] This curious gap has led
scholars to the paradoxical conclusion that a process for introducing evidence was never (or almost never) used for this purpose at all. Todd, for
example, argues that everyone intentionally formulated their challenges
to be rejected because no one wanted the outcome of their case to depend
on an arbitrary procedure like torture.[80]

Michael Gagarin takes the disparity between the ancient praise of the
truthfulness of torture and the modern condemnation of it (as in Todd's
account) as the launching point for his more innovative approach in trying to understand the use of torture.[81] Gagarin suggests that a challenge
to torture a slave was a legal fiction, not a way of discovering the truth
but a way of indirectly introducing as evidence to the court what the
slave would have said through the reading of the declined challenge. Litigants would issue dares on points important to their presentation of their
cases, points that they knew their opponents would concede; the actual torturing of a slave hardly ever occurred. There are, however, problems with Gagarin's account.[82] Most significantly, it fails to account for
repeated attribution of truth to torture. Gagarin suggests that litigants
commonly conflated the dare and the dared procedure,[83] so that we
should understand their praise of torture as a praise of the evidence introduced through the reading of a dare to torture. But while some litigants clearly did conflate the dare and the secondary contingency, others,
like the *choregos* quoted above, explicitly distinguished the two. This

account, moreover, does not explain why litigants praised torture as revealing truth.

There is, though, much to recommend Gagarin's account in its attention to the rhetorical deployment of dares. In shifting attention away from their use as a means of gathering evidence and the concomitant question of whether this evidence really was "true" (that is, whether slaves' tortured words accurately represented what had historically happened), Gagarin sees dares as one of the ways that a litigant could emphasize the points that supported his case: "βάσανος was designed . . . as a procedure for introducing the evidence of slaves in court by means of a rejected challenge." [84] The quality of a dare as "evidence," however, cannot refer to its informational content. If "evidence" means simply what the slave might have said, there was no need for a dare: Any litigant could give in his own speech an account of what a slave (or woman) had seen, as indeed they sometimes did.[85] Litigants did not use dares to introduce otherwise unknown or unavailable information (to take "evidence" in this sense would be to revert to the traditional theory). Rather, litigants used dares to confer a certain evidentiary authority on a claim. The specific need for that authority derived from the rhetorical context of litigation. The name for the authority was "truth."

DARES AND THE JUDICIAL
DISCOURSE OF TRUTH

The body of legal speeches reveals a consistently articulated theory of truth: the revelation of what actually happened. By whatever means they used, by arguments or witnesses, by inferences or documents, litigants claimed that their purpose was to reveal the truth, to show, that is, that their statements corresponded to or accurately represented reality. This notion of truth depended on an express distinction between language and reality, which is found, for example, in litigants' discussions of the relationship of *logoi* (words or stories) to *erga* (facts or deeds).[86] By radically divorcing *erga* from *logoi,* and by claiming to convey reality itself, litigants often ended up devaluing the medium of speech (the *logoi*). Consider the argument of one speaker in a suit against Spudias, the husband of his wife's sister, over various alleged debts. The speaker claimed that Spudias had bought a slave from their father-in-law, Polyeuktos, for twenty minae but that he had never paid for his purchase. After Polyeuktos' death, his wife had recorded this debt in her papers, and after her death Spudias attempted to hide the debt by not entering it into the account of the estate. The speaker addressed the jurors:

> Now consider as well the twenty minae that he has not entered into the account. In this matter again the defendant himself will be my strongest witness, not with words [λόγῳ], by god, such as he now uses to contest my suit (for this is no proof [τεκμήριον]), but by manifest fact [ἔργῳ περιφανεῖ]. What has he done to show this, men of the jury? Pay careful attention. That way, if he has the nerve to denounce the mother of our wives or the documents, he cannot deceive you by his talk because you will know the facts [εἰδόντας].[87]

The speaker then related that Spudias' wife and his own had opened the sealed documents of their late mother, made copies, and resealed them. At that time Spudias had not questioned their authenticity, thus implicitly admitting, the speaker reasoned, the validity of the debts they mentioned. The speaker, in opposing Spudias' (previous) actions to his (present) claims, followed a common line of argument. In this outlook, *logos* was often opposed to truth.[88] Indeed, litigants often valued *erga* as worth more than *logoi*.[89] Litigants frequently said that jurors should pay no attention to mere arguments[90] and that rhetorical language was itself the opposite of truth.[91] In his suit against Onetor, Demosthenes admonished the jurors: "Look to the truth, not to the crafty preparations someone makes in order to say something plausible—as you, Onetor, are doing."[92] Litigants explicitly devalued the *logoi* of their opponents, but in insisting that they themselves offered *erga*, not merely *logoi*, they implicitly devalued all statements in favor of an extralinguistic truth. Demosthenes, for example, demanded that the jurors judge Aeschines in light of the certain knowledge of what they already knew: "Do not be misguided today by any [evasions]. Rather, judge the affairs based on what you know. Do not consider either my speeches [*logoi*] or his, nor even his witnesses. . . ."[93]

Commonly, speakers claimed that the truth lay outside the legal oration. This extralinguistic truth grounded or legitimated the plea. Truth, therefore, might be found in a person's character,[94] in their behavior,[95] or in witnesses or documents. The common formula for introducing a deposition or document went something like this: "I will provide witnesses that I am speaking the truth."[96] Variations of this phrase appear just over 200 times in the speeches, usually invoking verification by witnesses' testimony, sometimes by documents, occasionally by common knowledge, but hardly ever did a speaker claim that a logical argument would show that he was speaking truly.[97] The model of truth in play here seems to have been the verification of a statement by appeal to an external reality. As Humphreys argues, the presence of witnesses was not only about impartially relating facts but also about enacting the litigant's good social standing.[98] Thus the truth of a pleader's claim was felt to be verified in part by the witness' statement (this was certainly not irrelevant[99]) but also by his act of support in being a witness.

The theory of rhetorical practice consistently articulated by speakers in the courts was at odds with the usual modern accounts of how this practice actually proceeded. It is commonly said that rhetoric at Athens did not aim to provide truth but rather to effectively employ language to persuade.[100] Detienne argues that although philosophers claimed truth as their goal, sophists and rhetoricians left truth by the wayside and sought only to develop a potent technique of persuasion.[101] The sophist Gorgias exemplifies this approach: On the one hand he argued that nothing exists, that if it did exist it was unknowable, and that if it was knowable it could not be communicated.[102] On the other hand he suggested that language was like a drug or magic because it influenced people in powerful but inexplicable ways.[103] Rhetorical language, then, for Gorgias, was not about representing reality but about affecting people. This may be an adequate description of the sophists' program, it may correspond to what speakers in the Athenian courts actually did, it certainly forms the basis of philosophers' criticisms of rhetoric, but it does not match litigants' own statements about what they were doing: They said they offered the truth. It does, however, conform to litigants' criticisms of what they said their opponents were doing. The adversarial context therefore created a schizophrenic theory: While speakers argued that in the case of their opponents the gap between *logos* and *ergon* was unbridgeably wide, for themselves they asserted the essential unity of these two. Indeed, like the prosecutor of Spudias, who called his own narrative "manifest fact" (as against the *logos* of Spudias, which was no "proof"), litigants strained to make the veil of their own language seem as sheer as possible. The basis of both the attack on an opponent's arguments and the defense of one's own shows that language (*logos*) held a problematic status in Athenian courts.

The rhetorical context of Athenian litigation lay behind the persistent alarm at the instability of language and of the idea of truth. To some extent, of course, language is always unstable, but this danger was felt especially acutely in this particular context and not so much in others. The problem was less language in the abstract than the specific relationship between speaker and audience in the courts. Between litigant and jurors there was no relationship except that constituted by the litigant's speech. No litigant could speak with authority because the trial itself was to decide who spoke authoritatively. Authority, in other words, was not the precondition of the trial but its outcome. As suggested in the Introduction, the relationship between litigant and audience was extremely problematic for Athenians since it required a trust in an abstract system more than in a specific known individual.

Because the litigant and the jurors were usually unknown to each other, the only relationship between them was the one established in the courtroom and established, significantly, largely through language. This contrasts with most other public speaking situations in Athens where the speaker, even before he began, was invested with authority. Poets, as Detienne notes, relied on a divine sanction;[104] sophists like Gorgias were preceded by their reputations as sophists;[105] those who gave the public funeral orations at Athens, who also confronted the dissonance between *logos* and *ergon,* had been elected to the position by the Assembly.[106] Litigants, however, addressed the jury not by virtue of some previous license to speak but in order that their account might be licensed as true. Their relationship to the audience was constructed entirely through their speech, but because of the sharply adversarial context, their opponent was likely to expose its precarious foundations (as mere *logoi,* not *erga*). Thus litigants constantly sought a bedrock outside the rhetorical language of the courts in which to anchor that language. The claim to truth, then, was not merely about language accurately representing reality but language assuming the authority of reality.[107]

Litigants' general hankering after an incontestable, extralinguistic truth, their desire to overcome the indeterminacy of their rhetorical relationship with the audience, fundamentally affected their representation of dares in court. Speakers hoped to confer authority on their claims, and indeed on themselves in general, by referring to actions outside the rhetorical context. Litigants thus represented secondary procedures like torture or oaths as actions having a certainty or a reality that rhetorical language lacked. Since accepted challenges forestalled litigation, only dares

that had been refused were brought to the jury's attention. Dared procedures, therefore, were doubly free of rhetorical pollution because they
were always absent. Demosthenes again: "How could he have better
proven that we're lying than by stretching my slave on the rack? But more
than anyone else, he knew that the witness spoke the truth, and so he
avoided the test of torture." [108] Litigants could likewise claim that torture
revealed an incontestable truth because it was unimplicated in the slipperiness of rhetorical language. Lycurgos asked:

> Who is it impossible to mislead with cunning and carefully laid
> arguments? The male and female slaves, of course, who would
> naturally tell the whole truth about every offense if they were tor-
> tured. . . . But who does the defendant seem to be able to delude
> with arguments? Whose easy disposition can he move to pity with
> his tears? The jurors.[109]

Likewise, speakers praised the veracity of oaths: "Aphobos refused to
give an oath either to these witnesses or to me. Instead," claimed Demosthenes, "he builds his case on contrived arguments and witnesses who
routinely lie. That's how he hopes to easily bamboozle you." [110] Thus it
was possible to argue that the dared procedure would have been (always
counterfactual) a clearer path to truth than the litigants' speeches. It was
easy to represent the outcome of the dared procedure (an oath, arbitration, or torture) as unambiguously clear, as indeed it would have been if
both parties, by accepting the dare and precluding a trial, had agreed to
treat it as such.

While the discourse of truth infected the representation of the function
of secondary procedures like torture, it also influenced accounts of dares
themselves. Litigants could portray issuing a challenge, after all, as an action, the certainty of which could be invoked to provide authority for
the speaker's words. Likewise, a litigant could represent his opponent's
refusal to accept a dare as an unimpeachable proof: "Although I have
so many just claims, men of the jury, I think that the greatest proof
(τεκμήριον) that Pasion cheated me of the money is that he refused to
hand over for torture the slave who knew about the deposit." [111] In light
of this, dares issued before the jurors (as they entered the court or even
during the trial) may have functioned not only as final offers of settlement, but also as dramatic enactments—before the jurors' very eyes—of
the truthfulness of the speaker.[112]

To have issued a dare might well have thus been an advantage in court, but dares were a much more supple, complex tool in negotiating disputes than just this. The ways litigants used dares in court to establish their authority with the audience involved a fundamental reinterpretation of their use to pursue disputes outside the courts. Litigants talked about their disputes from the perspective of litigation and with the aim of persuading the jurors, not rendering a historically accurate account of previous events. Paradoxically, the courts' discourse of truth falsified litigants' representations of their uses of dares in disputing. Instead, the truth of dares was not that they produced statements that accurately described some external reality but rather that they brought an external reality into existence: in the case of disputants, settlement or hostility; in the case of litigants, authority. With dares, disputants could communicate, bully, bargain, give ground, save face, and, indeed, speak authoritatively during trial.

Four

CONJURING

CHARACTER

Only a few years after the expulsion of the Thirty, an Athenian who had been appointed by lot to a public office under the restored democracy was accused at his preliminary examination (*dokimasia*) of having supported the oligarchs.[1] During his defense before a jury, he argued:

> No misfortune whatsoever, men of the jury, neither private nor public, happened to me during the time [of the democracy before the Thirty], certainly nothing that would have made me eager to be released from wretched circumstances and desire a different form of government. For I have been trierarch five times, fought in four sea battles, paid many special taxes during the war, and performed other liturgies better than anyone. Further I spent more than the city ordered just so that you would think better of me and so that if some misfortune ever happened to me,[2] I could defend myself against it better. Under the oligarchy I lost all this, since they didn't think that those who had done anything good for the people were worthy of *charis* (gratitude) from themselves; rather they placed in positions of honor those who had done the greatest harm to you. . . . Considering all of these things, you shouldn't trust the stories [λόγοις] of my accusers but rather consider the actions [ἔργων] each person has done.[3]

This litigant, like many others, drew the jurors' attention to his public services, especially his liturgies. The Athenian polis, rather than imposing taxes on its citizens, each year assigned specific public burdens, liturgies, to a number of the richest individuals. They could be required to act as trierarch, that is, to outfit (and often command) a trireme (a warship), to sponsor and train a dramatic chorus, or to oversee and pay for a number of other civic activities. Though always an ancillary plea in court cases, usually confined to a few sentences at the end of the speech, these evocations of liturgies nevertheless reveal a number of important features of litigation in Athens. They were part of the complex competition of litigants to represent their own speech as more authoritative: Defendants recalled such "actions" both to erode the authority of the prosecutor's story and to construct a relationship between themselves and the jurors that did not depend on the vagaries of rhetorical language. The specific institutional forms of Athenian litigation thus deeply affected the citation of liturgies. Indeed, in such claims the asymmetric judicial positions of prosecutor and defendant emerge again: More than twice as many defendants as prosecutors adduced their liturgies. (See Table 2.)[4] More than this, appeals to liturgies would have been impossible without the presence of the jurors as a powerful third party to the dispute. Yet defendants did not merely exploit the preexisting interests of this audience because the idea that the jurors owed gratitude for citizens' public services was problematic and contestable. Rather, such arguments succeeded when they called these interests, and, therefore, the group's consciousness of itself, into existence. A significant unintended consequence of such appeals was the reproduction of the Athenians' corporate identity.

T A B L E 2. Speakers Who Cited Their Liturgies

	Prosecution	Defense	*Diadikasia*	*Paragraphe*	Total
Private	6/26 [23%]	5/10 [50%]	2/9 [22%]	2/9 [22%]	15/54 [28%]
Public	5/29 [11%]	8/15 [53%]			13/44 [30%]
Total	11/55 [20%]	13/25 [52%]			28/98 [29%]

Prosecution vs. Defense p = .004

DEFENDANTS' LITURGIES
AND PROSECUTORS' STORIES

Defendants frequently cited their liturgies as proof of their good character. The kinds of legal stories prosecutors told, as noted in Chapter 2, focused on the defendant much more than on the prosecutor. The prosecutor's character became an issue only because a defendant could call into
question the prosecutor's decision to litigate (especially with counternarratives of sykophancy and conspiracy). As a result, the personal or public
life of the defendant, insofar as it might reveal his motives, proclivities,
or previous crimes, was central to the stories of the law as the accuser's
was not. Turning this to their advantage, defendants often relied on their
liturgies to undercut the legal story the prosecutor had told.[5] The speaker
of Lysias 25, for example (quoted at the beginning of this chapter), said
that his services proved he was not the type of man to support oligarchy,
as the prosecutor had charged. Defendants presented their services to the
state as actions (*erga*) that confounded the stories (*logoi*) told by the
prosecutor. For example, a man accused of sacrilege for uprooting from
his field the stump of one of the sacred olive trees that grew around Attica said to the jurors:

> I therefore beg you not to believe that such stories [λόγους] are
> more believable than actions [ἔργων], nor to allow my oppo-
> nents to speak on matters you all know about. Rather keep in
> mind what I have said and the rest of my conduct as a citizen.
> I have performed all the duties assigned to me with greater enthu-
> siasm than the polis required: I acted as trierarch, paid the war
> tax, financed a chorus, and executed other liturgies more lavishly
> than any other citizen. Further, if I had done these things only
> moderately and without enthusiasm, I would not now be on trial
> facing exile and the loss of my property as well, but I would pos-
> sess even more without committing any injustice or putting my
> life at risk. But if I had done what this man charges, I would
> not likely have made any profit but only put myself in danger.
> Moreover, you would all agree that it is more just to use weighty
> proofs [τεκμηρίοις] in weighty matters and to believe more readily
> what the entire city testifies to than what this lone individual
> charges.[6]

In citing their liturgies in this way, defendants attacked the consistency and plausibility of the accuser's narrative, undermining it with an antinarrative. Defendants did not use liturgies to construct or validate a counternarrative of their own; instead, they sought to destabilize the prosecutor's story by invalidating the narrow legal framework on which it depended. They suggested that the legal framework itself, which focused on a "crime," a single act of wrongdoing, conflicted with reality. The reality it contradicted, however, was not a set of facts about the world but a particular belief about human behavior: the assumption that character remains stable over time. Relying on this assumption, defendants offered their services to the state as a refutation of the prosecutor's story. The speaker of Lysias 19, for example, whose father was charged with helping conceal the wealth of another whose property had been confiscated by the state, itemized his fathers' liturgies, private benefactions, and other public services. "I'm doing this not because of ambition [φιλοτιμίας] but as a proof [τεκμήριον] that it is not the nature of the same man to spend a lot of money of his own free will while coveting public property at great risk."[7] He argued that his father's repeated public services showed his authentic character, one incapable of committing the crime: "Someone might be able to disguise their true character for a short time, but no one who was wicked could escape notice for seventy years. . . . It's not appropriate, therefore, to trust the stories [λόγοις] of his accusers more than the actions [ἔργοις] that marked his entire life— and more than time itself, which you must consider as the clearest test of truth."[8]

Although defendants claimed that liturgies were facts instead of mere stories, this polemical assertion misrepresents the matter. Statements about liturgies were not objectively more factual or known in a different way than other kinds of claims a litigant might make.[9] The defendant in the case of impiety (Lys. 7), who claimed his liturgies were "what the entire city testifies to [rather] than what this lone individual charges," asserted that service to the city had a special epistemological status: It was known directly, unmediated by the slippery language of the courts. This assertion, however, although it attempted to rely on an extralinguistic authority, was, in fact, itself a conventional rhetorical way of buttressing arguments in the courts.[10] Litigants often asserted "common knowledge" as a more trustworthy authority, particularly when (as with the speaker of Lys. 7) they provided no witnesses to their assertion. Indeed, arguments about liturgies were *logoi* twice over: first, because they were related in words; second, because they were meaningful for the case at hand because they had already been fit into an account of human behavior. Indeed, the power of this account made such claims seem unaffected by the rhetorical context of their representation. As noted in Chapter 2, people often judge the plausibility—the truthfulness—of stories less by their veracity in relating facts than by their correspondence to known and accepted understandings and narrative conventions. Defendants linked liturgies, character, and innocence through a conventional argument from probability: A person who habitually behaved one way was unlikely to act to the contrary. If defendants were able to contend that liturgies were *erga* that overthrew the *logoi* of the prosecutor, it was only because as *logoi* themselves the defendants' claims had successfully masked their own character.

STRUCTURAL ASYMMETRIES: PROSECUTOR V. DEFENDANT

Appeals to liturgies illustrate one of the unique features of litigation: the asymmetric roles of prosecutor and defendant. One of the most important and fundamental of the transformations caused by the decision to litigate was that the defendant's character was "on trial" (as it were) as the prosecutor's was not. In part this derived from the very nature of a legal narrative, but there were other reasons as well. Different consequences of the verdict for each party probably motivated defendants to talk more about their characters and their services to the city. As noted in more detail in Chapter 5, defendants stood to lose much more by an adverse verdict than prosecutors. The consequences were different not only for the parties but for society. In cases where conviction might result in execution, disenfranchisement, or the imposition of a very large fine, the city risked losing one of the households that had undertaken public services. The speaker of Lysias 19 (mentioned above), whose property was at risk because his father was accused of having acquired it illegally, recounted his father's public services as evidence of his character, but also noted that

> not only from the perspective of reputation but also from a financial standpoint it's more to your benefit to vote for acquittal: You'll get a much greater advantage if we keep the property. Consider how much in the past has been obviously lavished on the city.

Right now, from what has been left to me, I am acting as a trier-arch. My father was serving as trierarch when he died, and I will try to provide small amounts, little by little, for the public good, just as I saw him doing. The result is that the property really belongs to the polis already, and, though I won't feel wronged if it's taken away from me, the present situation benefits you much more than if you confiscate it.[11]

As one prosecutor noted, sometimes juries acquit men who they think will be useful in the future (though he hastened to add that the record of the defendant in his case, the younger Alcibiades, and of his father, showed this would not happen).[12]

As a rule, then, defendants relied on the citation of liturgies and of character more than prosecutors did. Despite the pattern, however, there were exceptions: prosecutors who adduced their own liturgies or high-lighted their character. These exceptions do not invalidate the pattern of asymmetrical positions. The logic behind them, though, shows that pros-ecutors could choose to tell certain stories whose narratives implicated the prosecutor and his public character as well as the defendant's. The first of these stories was one where the trial would determine the control of an *oikos* or household; the second was when the prosecutor defined the "crime" as an attack on his honor.

In cases concerning the preservation or disposition of an *oikos,* the performance of liturgies was especially an issue. Just when the *oikos* was most vulnerable (when the women and children had lost their male guardian or when there was no immediate heir), the state intervened.[13] In those cases where the jury was to decide the disposition of inheritance, therefore, speakers argued that they deserved it because they would use it in a more socially responsible manner. Such cases seem to correspond more closely to Cohen's model of a symmetrical competition; in these cases, unlike most others, several litigants openly compared their litur-gies, and prosecutors cited their own.[14] Parties claiming an estate often used past services as a significant indicator of future usefulness to the city.[15] One speaker, for example, representing the claims of a young man in an inheritance dispute, recounted the public services performed by the youth and his father. "If this young man is awarded Philoktemon's estate, he will hold it in trust for you and perform the liturgies you assign with even more eagerness than he does now. But if these other men get their hands on it, they will squander it and plot to get others."[16]

The preservation of the *oikos* was at issue not only in determining the proper heir but also in seeing that, when an estate was left to a minor, the guardians administered it conscientiously. When Demosthenes sued Aphobos, one of his guardians, for defrauding him of his inheritance, he contrasted his estate, which had supported liturgies when his father was alive but which amounted to almost nothing now, with others that had grown considerably while being well administered.[17]

> Keeping this in mind [he concluded], you should take some thought for us, knowing that if I recover my property because of you, I will reasonably want to undertake liturgies, since I will owe you gratitude [*charis*] because you justly gave back my estate to me. This man, however, if you give him ownership of my property, will do nothing of the kind.[18]

In such cases, the Athenians took a particular interest in the preservation of *oikoi,* especially those that could support liturgies. Given the claims of the demos on the property of *oikoi,* it would be wrong to think of it as purely private; in some senses, the Athenians considered it to be held in trust. Thus it is not surprising that litigants should discuss liturgies, which represent the obligations of the household to the city, since the interests of the demos were at stake as well.[19]

Prosecutors also emphasized their character and honor in cases concerned with the conduct of liturgies (Dem. 21 and 50) and in cases of assault (Dem. 21 and 54). In both types of cases, the prosecutor chose to tell the story of a "crime" that was an inappropriate slight to his honor. Thus, questions about his character fit into a legal narrative. In Demosthenes 21 and 50, both prosecutors, Demosthenes and Apollodoros, portrayed the "crime" as part of a blatant and ongoing refusal of the defendant to recognize the honor their liturgy deserved. The cases of assault show prosecutors telling stories in which the perpetrator assaulted not only the victim's body but also his reputation. In Demosthenes 21 and 54, both Demosthenes and Ariston sought to represent the attack on them as hubris (even if the technical charges were, respectively, violating the rules of a festival and assault). To sustain this insinuation, it was essential to prove not only that they had been hit but that their honor had been violated; this was what distinguished hubris from assault.[20] Unlike most other cases, then, the status, honor, and character of the prosecutor was one of the central issues of these cases. In contrast, in two other cases arising from brawls (Lys. 3 and 4), the prosecutors took a different tack. Rather than turn a fistfight into a question of affronted honor (hubris), they charged their opponents with attempted murder. Each kind of story augmented the seriousness of the fight by attributing a deeper motive to the perpetrator, but only the story of hubris drew in the honor of the prosecutor (the victim) as a salient consideration. Except in such cases, the honor or reputation of a prosecutor mattered much less than that of the defendant.[21]

CHARIS, RECIPROCITY, AND CONJURING THE ATHENIANS

Like the speaker of Lysias 25 (quoted at the opening of this chapter), litigants sometimes suggested that their liturgies deserved *charis,* gratitude. Some defendants quite explicitly said that their services to the state should be a sufficient basis for acquittal. The defendant of Lysias 21, for example, held forth on his services and the zeal with which he performed them. He continued:

> In exchange for these I'm now asking you to reciprocate with
> *charis.* Since I held you in such regard even in times of danger,
> now that you are enjoying such confidence, I expect you will rate
> me and these children of mine highly. I'm sure that you think that
> it would be both terrible for us and disgraceful for you if we lose
> our citizenship because of such charges, or if we are impoverished
> by being deprived of our possessions and have to wander around
> in dire straits, suffering things unworthy of ourselves but also
> unworthy of what we have done for you.[22]

Charis was an important structuring principle in ancient Greek social relationships. The ideology of *charis* insisted that a gift obligated the recipient until they returned the favor. *Charis* could mean an initial gift (a boon or benefaction), a reciprocal gift to repay the debt from a previous gift, or the idealized state of mind that motivated either of these (favor, kindness, gratitude). Various reciprocal social relationships operated on principles of *charis.*[23] Enduring relationships of reciprocity outside the market, sometimes called "gift economies," organized the distribution of many goods both in the archaic period and in classical Athens.[24] The exchange of gifts, moreover, not only took place within enduring social relationships, but was one of the ways, through a sense of indebtedness, people constituted and maintained social relationships.

Scholars have understood the Athenian system of liturgies by such a model of reciprocal exchanges. Liturgies were like the many gifts that wealthy citizens made to the polis because they largely remained in-kind contributions, not converted to cash payments like taxes. The polis often formally rewarded liturgists (and, indeed, other, voluntary benefactors) with crowns, public proclamations, honorary inscriptions or monuments, and other tokens of honor, as well as a general good reputation. Davies has argued that until the end of the fifth century, such honor was a powerful form of political capital and that politicians often achieved their success by engaging in both public and private benefaction. By the fourth century, however, Davies believes that other forms of political power had supplanted benefaction, except in the courts. There, he argues, litigants frequently invoked their liturgies and benefactions to secure a favorable verdict, which they were able to demand because of the debt the demos owed them for their gifts.[25] Many other scholars have agreed that the litigants' requests for *charis* in the courts show the city and its citizens engaged in an exchange of gifts and gratitude.[26]

Although this account of litigants' requests for *charis* is substantially correct, it requires some qualifications and modifications. The link between liturgies and *charis* was somewhat loose. As I have already shown, many speakers who referred to their liturgies did so to prove their good character and thereby undermine the prosecutor's narrative, not to ask for *charis*. Of the litigants who reminded the jurors of their liturgies, only a few explicitly demanded *charis* for them.[27] On the other hand, defendants offered many other grounds for *charis* besides liturgies: military service,[28] holding office,[29] a moderate life,[30] conducting themselves as good citizens,[31] devotion to democracy,[32] useful public speeches, or a good family.[33] Though similar in some respects, appeals for *charis* based on liturgies operated quite differently than arguments about the defendant's character: Rather than discrediting the prosecutor's story, the claim of *charis* sought to create a relationship with the jurors independent of litigation.[34] The process of attempting to induce the jurors' gratitude reflects again litigants' desires to circumvent the uncertainties of rhetorical language by appealing to a seemingly extralinguistic reality. Like all such appeals, however, this one relied on the power of language both to effect the reality it claimed to represent and to erase its own power in doing so.

TABLE 3. Speakers Who Asked for *Charis*

	Prosecution	Defense	*Diadikasia*	*Paragraphe*	Total
Private	1/26 [4%]	2/10 [20%]	1/9 [11%]	1/9 [11%]	5/54 [9%]
Public	2/29 [7%]	5/15 [33%]			7/44 [16%]
Total	3/55 [5%]	7/25 [28%]			12/98 [12%]

Prosecution vs. Defense p = .008

Most significantly, such claims did not merely rely on the presence of the Athenians as a group and their conscious recognition of their interests; reciprocally, these arguments also engendered Athenian identity and interests. Such appeals reproduced the Athenian democracy.

Litigants' use of *charis* depended upon a trick of the social imagination, an act of conjuring, which was no less real for that, so that individual jurors identified themselves with a group. If this identification seems unproblematic to us, this reflects the extent to which a contingent and complex process was naturalized to the Athenians themselves. Attempting to persuade juries, litigants relied on a discourse of reciprocity that, in establishing a relationship between themselves and the jury, constituted and defined the jurors' role and identity.

In requesting *charis*, a defendant made a claim upon a jury for its verdict. Just as defendants invoked their liturgies more frequently than prosecutors, so, too, defendants asked for *charis* more than five times as often as prosecutors.[35] (See Table 3.) In ordinary usage, *charis* might denote either a reciprocated gift or the feeling of kindliness that motivated this. In court, however, speakers' requests for *charis* sought to motivate a collective action—a verdict—not an emotional state in individuals.[36] Although sometimes defendants did not specify the meaning of *charis*, when applied to the jury, in almost no case did it clearly mean anything other than a favorable verdict. For example, Thrasyllos, defending his right to inherit the property of Apollodoros, recounted both Apollodoros' father's and Apollodoros' own generous public services. "This is the kind of man he was. In consideration of these things you would justly pay back this *charis* to him if you made authoritative his intentions regarding his property," which could only mean voting for the speaker.[37] Similarly, when applied to the Athenians in the Assembly, *charis* meant concrete collective actions (votes of thanks, election to office, tokens of honor like crowns), not the feelings of individuals.[38] The claim of *charis,* then, may have induced an emotional state, but this was always in the service of a cognitive state: a recognition by the juror that the interests of the polis were his own.[39]

A speaker's claim of *charis* from the jury, however, did not simply describe an objectively true state of the world; rather, it attempted to impose and naturalize a self-interested, contestable interpretation on certain events. The performance of liturgies might bear a range of meanings: They might be intended to magnify the contributor's reputation or humiliate an enemy,[40] they might be the simple outgrowth of the speaker's natural character, they might be the minimum requirements from a rich citizen required by the law, or they might be an honor in themselves.[41] But the problem speakers faced was more complex than merely displacing competing interpretations: *Charis* was a way of describing a relationship between two people. Yet no liturgist had actually given their liturgy to a particular individual, nor, for that matter, had any specific person received this gift or felt obliged because of it. Litigants, therefore, conjured a "person" who was obligated: "the polis" or "the Athenians." Then jurors had to be induced to identify their interests with this imaginary collective.[42] Thus "the polis" mediated the relationship between a public benefactor and individual citizens; litigants aimed to elide the artificiality of this mediating term by instigating the jurors' identification with it, thereby naturalizing it. Speakers were not (or not mainly) attempting to get individual jurors to feel an emotion of gratitude but to motivate the collective action of a group, which involved creating a group consciousness. Speakers addressed their appeals to them in the second-person plural. In this context, then, *charis* was a metaphor based on intimate personal relationships that actually described collective action based on a recognition of common interests.

The few prosecutors' claims for gratitude also depended, like those of defendants, on constituting the jurors as the polis and attributing certain interests to them. The single explicit reason prosecutors ever offered for deserving the jury's *charis* was the act of bringing the case itself.[43] They coupled this with a claim that they had brought the case in the public interest, not from any private motive. The defendant in Antiphon 6, charged with murder, made it clear that his opponents claimed *charis* for avenging an injustice to the state, but he argued that they did not deserve it because they had brought only a private suit: "If in fact the polis is being wronged," he said, apparently repeating the prosecutors' claim, "they are offering accusation, not real help; at the same time they are demanding to exact a penalty personally for alleged injustices against the polis. Indeed these charges are worthy of neither *charis* nor credence."[44] As a prosecutor, Demosthenes anticipated Meidias' claim that he should have brought a private suit: "But if I have waived the profit of a private suit, left his punishment to the polis, and chosen this action that offers me no gains, this choice ought reasonably to secure me *charis* from you, not prejudice."[45] Prosecutors' requests for *charis* thus reflected their judicial identity, which was defined predominantly by their decision to start litigation.

This act of conjuring a collective—convincing individual jurors that they were a group with singular interests in relationship to the defendant —which made an economy of *charis* possible, came most clearly into focus when prosecutors sought to undo it.[46] Prosecutors attempted to disenchant the economy of *charis* by suggesting that it depended on a direct, unmediated relationship between the defendant and individual jurors. They then opposed the motives attributable to these individuals to the collective interests of the city:

> Each one of you fails to realize that the man who benefits the polis benefits him and that the man who harms it harms him.[47] Instead, other things are of more consequence to each of you, by which you [plural] are often misled: pity, jealousy, anger, giving *charis* to one who begs, and a thousand more. . . . Little by little the error toward each of these collectively erodes the foundation, and the polis itself is undermined. Do not feel any of these today, men of Athens, do not acquit this man who has committed such great injustice against you [plural].[48]

Demosthenes did not attempt to completely dissolve the collective identity of the jury in this passage. Instead, by defining the traditional responses of juries (such as pity, anger, and *charis*) as attributes, indeed, emotions, of individual jurors rather than as ways of describing collective action, he was able to oppose them to the aggregate interests of the citizens and the city. He accomplished this, in part, by the sly movement from addressing the jurors as individuals ("each of you"), to the collective, plural "you," and then to their assembled name, "men of Athens."

A few prosecutors, then, tried to undercut *charis* between defendant and jury by asserting jurors' identity as mere individuals. Here is what Demosthenes said a little later about Aeschines' brothers pleading for him by invoking their services to the state:

> Though the ballot is secret, the gods still know. The lawgiver perceptively understood that none of those who beg for the defendant will know the one of you who bestowed *charis* on him, but the gods and the divine spirit will know the man who voted contrary to justice. For this reason, it's better for each man to preserve for himself good prospects both for his children and for himself by deciding justly and properly than to try to store up an unseen and unknown *charis* with these men.[49]

At least three other speakers made similar arguments, though more briefly.[50] Taken together, two points stand out. First, unlike the positive appeals to *charis* by defendants and by some prosecutors who almost invariably addressed the jury in the second-person plural, these speakers sought to disintegrate a collective identity by positioning each juror as an individual. They thus grammatically described jurors in the third-person singular.[51] The prosecutor of Andocides asked: "What kind of friend, what kind of relative, what kind of demesman finds it necessary to be openly hated by the gods by secretly giving *charis* to this man?"[52] By eroding the collective interests of the jurors, they sought to nullify the *charis* the defendants sought. Second, all these speakers recognized the importance of the secret ballot in rendering impotent forms of reciprocity between litigants and individual jurors. As Aeschines said: "The *charis* [of the juror] to the one who is benefited is unknown, since the ballot is cast secretly."[53]

The corporate identity of people as "Athenians" or as "jurors" was not effected purely through language but was also assisted institutionally. One of the most important ways this was done was through secret voting in the courts.[54] The Athenians probably first used ballots (as opposed to voting by hand) in order to count votes accurately, but by the end of the fifth century they were well aware of the social effects of anonymity. As Aristophanes' character Philokleon says, he is free to vote however he wants despite what he may have promised the begging litigant.[55] Obviously, such a system could help equalize the positions of richer and poorer litigants.[56] But even more importantly, it neutralized ways in which elites might dominate (through gifts or threats) the ordinary Athenians of the jury. Those who opposed democracy understood this well enough, and they also opposed secret voting.[57] By the fourth century the Athenians insisted on secret voting on any question concerning an individual, including in the Assembly and the Boule.[58] They also moved, sometime probably before 389, to strengthen the secrecy of the jury vote.[59]

The secret ballot undermined elite claims on common people (jurors). By creating a sphere of anonymity it made impossible the responsibility necessary for reciprocity between individuals: No juror could ever be linked to his *charis,* his vote. Wealthy Athenians, however, rather than abandoning the economy of *charis,* sought to exploit their wealth by reconstituting the other party in this reciprocity as the Athenians as a whole whose collective vote they could know and hold accountable. By insisting on the effectiveness of their generosity to the city and in defining the jurors' interests collectively, elites ended up reproducing and strengthening the consciousness of the Athenians as a group. In turn, paradoxically, this corporate identity of the Athenians counteracted elite attempts to isolate common Athenians from each other and subordinate them through private relationships of patronage based on *charis.*[60] The anonymity of the courts helped create not only the conditions for *charis* to the Athenians as a group but also "the Athenians" themselves.

PROVOKING DEMOCRATIC INTERESTS

Litigants' appeals to liturgies and claims for *charis* demonstrate the complex reciprocity between litigation and Athenian culture. Many historians have told the story of the ways that cultural values affected and were manifested in Athenian litigation.[61] Yet although Athenian litigation may have been more open to the influence of nonlegal factors than modern American courts, litigants nevertheless treated these values in an institutionally unique setting. The characteristic ways litigants deployed these appeals reveal an aspect of the law's autonomy. When defendants brought up their liturgies as evidence of their good character, they not only used a form of argument typical of the courts (the argument from probability) but used it for a distinctively judicial end: to undermine the prosecutor's legal narrative. The power of the argument from liturgies also depended on the especially unstable relationship between litigant and jurors and the ways this corrupted language. If liturgies were so authoritative in court, it was because they seemed to offer a ground more solid than rhetorical language. Similarly, the distribution of such appeals reveals differentiated roles that could not describe parties to a dispute before the law had been invoked: prosecutor, defendant, and juror. No law or rule, of course, allowed only defendants to recite their services and ask for gratitude, but neither was the pattern of predominantly defendants doing this merely the result of random individual choices. Instead, it reveals a structural property[62] of Athenian litigation, both a constraint on and a resource for action. An immediate effect of one disputant's decision to invoke the law was that he told a story that emphasized his opponent, the defendant, as a person. This constrained the defendant's options, but it also enabled him to use his reputation against his accuser as he could not have before he had invoked the law. But the clever prosecutor, too, should he choose to form his story in a way that made his reputation relevant, could use his own services and character as leverage. Thus he might choose to narrate a tale of hubris, not attempted murder.

The legal context also affected and transformed the cultural values litigants invoked. In asking for *charis,* defendants drew upon a value long at work in many aspects of Athenian society. Elites had used *charis* to obligate poorer Athenians through a sense of gratitude for private gifts; the introduction of widespread pay for state service by Perikles is often said to have decisively curtailed such practices.[63] The financial independence of poorer Athenians made possible by state pay was certainly important, but the operation of the courts suggests a different process as well. *Charis,* which had been a mode of elite domination of ordinary Athenians, became instead a democratic mechanism: The more elites sought to distinguish themselves and advance their positions through benefaction, the stronger the demos became. This reversal depended crucially on the introduction of the mediating term, the polis. While private *charis* created vertical, isolating links, public *charis* created horizontal links among ordinary Athenians. This was not, however, an automatic effect of the gifts themselves; instead, to be effective, the claims of elites for reciprocal favor had to mobilize and reproduce this sense of shared interests. Thus rewards for generosity to the city (whether an honorary inscription bestowed by the Assembly or consideration when on trial in the courts) encouraged elite submission to the polis not only by giving incentives to contribute wealth to the city[64] but also by reproducing and strengthening Athenian democratic identity. This process, of course, was not confined to the courts—other institutions also contributed to it— but the pleas of litigants before the jurors reveal it particularly well. The effect, the reproduction of Athenian democracy, was an unintended consequence twice over: It is unlikely that anyone designed all the institutional features of litigation to achieve this result. No supremely wise lawgiver, no Solon, conceived and built the edifice of fourth-century Athenian democracy.[65] Nor when individual litigants made their pleas did they intend to strengthen the demos by reproducing its group consciousness. From the perspective of individual actors, this consequence was accidental and, perhaps, unnoticed. Yet in the particular institutional dynamics of Athenian litigation lay a wellspring of democracy.

Five

CERTAIN RITUALS

In the summer of 343, two of Athens' leading politicians collided in court when Demosthenes prosecuted Aeschines for treasonous conduct as an envoy to Philip II of Macedon. They had both served on two embassies to Philip but had disagreed on what to report back to the Athenians. Later, at the formal review of Aeschines' tenure, Demosthenes accused him of selling his loyalty to Philip. Near the end of his defense, after finishing with substantive issues, Aeschines addressed the following appeal to the jury:

> There are people here who will plead with you for me. First,
> my father. Do not take away the hopes of his old age. Then, my
> brothers. They would not wish to live if they were separated from
> me. Then, my inlaws. And finally, these little children of mine.
> They do not yet understand these perils but would deserve pity if
> we should suffer anything. For their sake I beg and supplicate that
> you carefully consider the future and not give them over to our
> enemies.[1]

For his part, the prosecutor Demosthenes had anticipated such an appeal and warned the jury to turn it aside when it came:

> But the man who as ambassador negotiated these things will weep
> for himself, and perhaps he will bring in his children and march

them up on the platform. Men of the jury, on the subject of his children, keep in mind that the children of many of your allies and friends are refugees and wander around as beggars since they have suffered terribly through this man. They deserve pity much more than the children of a criminal and a traitor. . . . But about his own tears, keep in mind that you now have in your power the man who [betrayed your interests].[2]

These two passages point to three important points I will argue in this chapter about appeals for pity (ἔλεος). First, prosecutors and defendants occupied distinct and asymmetric positions regarding this rhetorical resource. Usually, only defendants made such pleas. This fact shows one of the ways litigation gave a unique shape to a dispute. Second, litigants enacted as well as spoke their appeals for pity. Speakers did not just make verbal requests for pity; they also wept, supplicated, and paraded their families. While reading legal speeches, it is sometimes difficult to appreciate the degree to which litigation was a spectacle. Appeals for pity provide a unique opportunity to assess the dramatization of legal rhetoric. Third, appeals for pity in the Athenian courts, though often understood as "emotional" attempts to derail the operation of "rational" law,[3] are better understood in terms of their cognitive (though unspoken) content. When speakers made such claims, far from intended to inspire an irrational psychological state, they were attempting to establish a relationship with the jurors that depended upon their own submission to the power of the demos. Petitions for pity continually reinforced Athenian democracy.

The argument of this chapter requires a brief epistemological preface. Although the words of defendants themselves provide ample direct testimony for spoken appeals for pity, the evidence for the enactment of such appeals is more indirect.[4] A few defendants (like Aeschines above) briefly described what they did, but for the most part the argument about the performance of pleas depends on representations of litigation in nonforensic texts and on prosecutors' anticipatory arguments about what their opponents might do. Both sources of evidence introduce new complications and uncertainties: Using Aristophanes' comedies as historical evidence is notoriously precarious,[5] and a prosecutor's warning against what a defendant might do does not prove that he actually did it.[6] Although this means that the conclusions about the dramatization of appeals are less certain than the argument about verbal appeals, they seem to me nevertheless sufficiently probable.

TABLE 4. Speakers Who Asked for Pity

	Prosecution	Defense	*Diadikasia*	*Paragraphe*	Total
Private	5/26 [19%]	5/10 [50%]	0/9 [0%]	1/9 [11%]	11/54 [20%]
Public	1/29 [3%]	7/15 [47%]			8/44 [18%]
Total	6/55 [11%]	12/25 [48%]			19/98 [19%]

Prosecution vs. Defense p < .001

DEFENDANTS' VERBAL APPEALS FOR PITY

Many more defendants than prosecutors petitioned for pity for themselves: Almost half of the defense speeches called for pity, whereas only one out of every ten prosecution speeches did.[7] (See Table 4.) The difference is striking and requires some explanation, especially since Athenian prosecutors were not (as they are in the American system) an impersonal representative of the state but frequently the very person who claimed to have been victimized by a criminal act. Yet, curiously, those who suffered from a violation of the law did not often request the jurors' pity for this.

The predominance of defendants' appeals for pity reflects the legally institutionalized differences between prosecutors and defendants. Whatever their relative positions had been in the prelegal stage of the dispute, because the choice to litigate had been the prosecutor's alone, the defendant could represent himself as the passive victim of litigation and therefore deserving of pity. Athenians believed that the powerless and helpless deserved pity: children and women, the old and the poor, the generally unfortunate.[8] Part of the spirit of the city of Athens, Demosthenes said, consisted in pity for the helpless.[9] Pity was the emotion felt for those without control over their circumstances, such as defendants: "I am driven by unyielding necessity," said one, "and have fled for refuge, men of the jury, to your pity."[10] The defendant had not transformed the quarrel into a legal case; instead, the prosecutor, seizing the initiative, had unilaterally imposed this decision on him. Defendants represented themselves, therefore, as the victims of the legal system; the appeal for pity was an effect of the decision to seek legal redress.

Defendants claimed pity also because a verdict against them had very different consequences than for prosecutors. A defendant could argue that almost any penalty a jury might inflict would bring himself and his *oikos* to ruin. Those who evoked or even paraded their families, as Aeschines did, were not merely inflaming the jurors but rather dramatizing before them the social consequences of conviction.[11] As noted in Chapter 4, Athenians often valued the preservation of a household not only for its future contributions to the city but also for the social obligations within the *oikos*. Euxitheos, defending the legitimacy of his citizenship, concluded by calling to mind the different ways a verdict could affect the complex web of duties in an Athenian *oikos*:

> Men of the jury, when you conduct your preliminary examination
> of those selected to serve as the nine archons, you ask if they treat
> their parents well. I have been left by my father as an orphan,
> but for my mother I supplicate and beseech you that by your ver-
> dict in this trial you allow me to bury her in our family's tomb.
> Don't take this away from me. Don't rob me of my homeland.
> Don't separate me from my many relatives and completely destroy
> me. If their intervention cannot save me, I would kill myself before
> abandoning them. At least that way they could bury me in my
> country.[12]

The distinct position of defendants, whose bodies, wealth, and families were at risk in ways that prosecutors' were not, created a unique rhetorical resource with which they could attempt to persuade the jury.[13]

Defendants' pleas for pity also suggest that the jurors themselves must have felt a lingering ambivalence about litigation.[14] In forensic oratory, most of those who claimed pity did so because they were the victims of litigation, not of crime. "It would be just," said one defendant concluding his speech, "that I be pitied by you and by everyone else as well, not only if I suffer the fate that [the prosecutor] Simon wishes but also because I have been compelled to stand trial as a result of such affairs."[15] The possibility of conviction at trial evoked at least as much sympathy as being the victim of a crime, so that defendants claimed compassion for simply being subject to indictment, whether innocent or guilty.

Defendants' entreaties for pity put prosecutors in a dilemma: Although they did not want the jurors to feel obliged to pity the defendant, prosecutors were reluctant to assert that pity was itself bad or that the jurors should not, as a rule, show it. Athenians often said that pity was part of their national character and one of their great civic virtues.[16] In the agora in the fifth century, they erected an altar of Pity.[17] Prosecutors did not usually argue, therefore, that the jury did not have the right to demonstrate compassion (in fact, they usually implicitly conceded that it did) but that it was inappropriate in the particular case at hand.[18]

Prosecutors frequently claimed that because the defendant had shown no pity, he deserved none, as one speaker did who charged his stepmother with poisoning his father: "How is it right that she be shown pity or be given any respect from you or anyone else? She showed no pity to her own husband; she killed him without piety or shame."[19] Demosthenes put the argument more positively when prosecuting Meidias:

> I believe that during their entire lives, all men make contributions to their own funds of credit, not only the funds that are actually collected and in which they are vested but metaphorical ones as well. For example, you are moderate and benevolent and show pity to many. You would justly receive back the same from everyone, if you ever fall into poverty or are put on trial.[20]

In a similar way, prosecutors sometimes said that their opponent's life offered no excuse or reason to pardon him.[21]

In instances where prosecutors sought to make more comprehensive the prohibition against the jury showing pity, they opposed pity to other public values. The obligation most frequently invoked to overbalance pity was the law. The prosecutor who brought the case against the younger Alcibiades for desertion told the jury that "if any of you thinks the penalty a heavy one and the law too severe, he should remember that you have come here not to legislate on these affairs but to vote according to the established laws; not to pity the guilty but much rather to be angry with them and to be protectors of the whole state." Prosecutors most frequently denied the role of pity in public cases[22] where their emphasis on the law corresponded to the public interest rather than to the need to redress a private wrong.[23] "Remembering the charges," Lycurgos concluded his prosecution speech, "make an example of Leokrates, that pity and tears are not stronger with you than the salvation of the laws and of the polis."[24]

In three public cases, the prosecutors admitted, it is true that pity was in accord with the spirit of the laws and the polis, but they contended that the defendant by his pitiless actions had forfeited his claim to this. Diodoros said that Androtion had hubristically treated citizens worse than slaves in collecting debts.

But the laws do not speak in this way, nor do the customs of our *politeia,* which it is your duty to guard. Rather, in these we find pity, pardon, and everything that is fitting for free men. This man naturally has no share either by nature or by upbringing in any of these things.[25]

In his later prosecution of Timokrates, Diodoros said that the spirit of the polis included pity for the poor and did not permit hubris by the strong and powerful.[26] Similarly, Demosthenes declared that the nature of all the dikasts included pity, pardon, and benevolence, feelings the defendant Aristogeiton should not benefit from because he had shown none of them to those he wrongly brought to trial.[27] In each of these three public prosecutions against a prominent politician, the prosecutor contrasted the pity inherent in the Athenians' character to the defendant's outrageous arrogance, his hubris. In the first two instances, the passages cited made the contrast between pity and hubris; in the third, the attribution of hubris to the defendant occurred elsewhere in the speech.[28] Demosthenes pursued a similar strategy at one point in his prosecution of Meidias, asking him:

> Will you demand that the jurors pity you or your children . . . ? Are you the only person in the world whose lifestyle is full of such arrogance toward everyone else that even those who have nothing to do with you are sickened by the spectacle of your audacious language, your manner, your entourage and wealth and insolence [ὕβριν]; and then when you're put on trial, suddenly you're supposed to be pitied?[29]

In each case the prosecutor could remind the dikasts of their compassion because he was attempting to portray the defendant as hubristic; and just as pity was a public, political virtue, so hubris, its opposite, was a public vice.[30]

DRAMATIZED APPEALS FOR PITY: WEEPING AND SUPPLICATION

Defendants not only verbally requested pity, they frequently enacted their appeal. Aristotle's *Rhetoric* confirms that litigants used gesture, voice, dress, and other aspects of delivery to increase pity.[31] Antiphon's

TABLE 5. Speakers Who Worried Their Opponent Would Weep

	Prosecution	Defense	*Diadikasia*	*Paragraphe*	Total
Private	3/26 [12%]	0/10 [0%]	0/9 [0%]	4/9 [44%]	7/54 [13%]
Public	8/29 [28%]	0/15 [0%]			8/44 [18%]
Total	11/55 [20%]	0/25 [0%]			15/98 [15%]

Prosecution vs. Defense p = .02

remark that "he begged you to have no pity on me because he feared that I would try to convince you by tears and supplications (δάκρυσι καὶ ἱκετείαις)"[32] shows the association between the evocation of pity and the dramatized means of achieving it, weeping and the ritual of supplication.

At the conclusion of their speeches, defendants sometimes enacted their appeal for pity by weeping.[33] The evidence for this practice of defendants is indirect but telling: one-fifth of prosecutors alluded to the possibility of their opponent weeping, but no defendant suggested his accuser would.[34] (See Table 5.) "I wouldn't be surprised," one prosecutor noted, "if they try to weep and make themselves seem worthy of pity."[35] The defendant's supporters, his relatives, friends, and neighbors, might cry as well.[36] Most crucially, a defendant might parade his children as he wept.[37] Demosthenes imagined that Meidias would "make his children stand up, and he will cry and will beg himself off for their sakes."[38] One speaker remarked that juries often take pity on a defendant who presents his children as he himself weeps and sobs.[39]

By bringing before the eyes of the jurors his friends, neighbors, and family, a defendant was able to dramatize the social effects of his conviction and punishment. The presence of the defendant's children was especially powerful because they depended on him entirely. More than that, however, they also represented the future survival of the *oikos*. "When you convict someone who has transgressed against you," Demosthenes said, "you don't take away all of their property. Instead, because you pity their wives and children, you leave some even to these men."[40]

Litigants also dramatized their appeal for pity through a second ritual, supplication. Speakers frequently said they were "supplicating" the jurors: "I beg all of you, men of the jury," one man said defending his father-in-law on charges of perjury, "and beseech and supplicate you to pity me and to acquit this witness here."[41] Despite this language, how-ever, John Gould claims that in the courts of the fifth and fourth cen-turies, "'figurative' supplication [that is, the language of supplication without the ritual actions] was becoming more or less emptily metaphor-ical."[42] It is true that litigants sometimes used the language of supplica-tion in attenuated and metaphorical ways, as when a litigant "suppli-cates" a jury to listen in silence or simply hear his case.[43] Nevertheless, though formalized, the language of supplication was itself powerful and was linked, furthermore, to socially meaningful practices.[44]

Athenian litigants supplicated the dikasts both as a corporate body and as individuals. Supplicating a group was like supplicating a god. Gould notes that "the ritual [efficacious] nature of the act [of supplication] de-pends essentially upon physical contact with parts of the body which . . . are regarded as having a peculiar sanctity." Those parts were the knees, the chin, and the hands.[45] When such contact was impossible, however (as with a god in the everyday world), an object, usually an altar or a hearth, stood for that god. By extension, the supplication of a group did not depend upon contact with its members but with the sacred object that stood for them.

Forms of corporate supplication were recognized and institutionalized parts of Athenian government.[46] People made requests of both the As-sembly and the Boule by supplicating them. For example, at one Assem-bly meeting each month (as Aristotle notes), "anyone who wishes, after placing a suppliant branch, may speak to the people about any matter he may wish whether public or private."[47] In such cases, as P. J. Rhodes says, the "petitioner places a suppliant branch . . . on the altar, as a sign that he is not claiming a right but asking a favour, and then [he] sets forth his plea."[48] The one who held the suppliant olive branch, therefore, pub-licly acknowledged the discretionary power of the body he petitioned.

Some evidence suggests that litigants supplicated jurors collectively. One of Aristophanes' characters imagines another going before a court surrounded by his wife and children and holding an olive branch (ἱκε-τηρία) as a symbol of supplication.[49] It is impossible to know how often speakers may have used such props, because we would not expect ex-plicit reference to them in the speeches as they are preserved. One speaker in an inheritance case, however, seems to refer to it:

> Consider, men of the jury, that this boy here has been set before
> you as the suppliant branch on behalf of Hagnias and Eubulides,
> who are dead, and the other descendants of Hagnias. They are

supplicating you jurors so that their *oikos* is not made desolate by these horrible beasts [the opponents].[50]

Litigants supplicated the dikasts not only as a group but also individually. The layout of the court, where a single speaker faced hundreds of jurors across a railing, impeded personal contact during the trial. But before the trial began, as jurors were being allocated to the courts and filing in, litigants jostled and shouted for their attention. One speaker envisioned the possibility that during this time his opponent might have used a herald to dare him to torture a slave; another reported that his opponent actually had issued a dare in the midst of the turmoil.[51] In his speech against Meidias, Demosthenes alluded to his opponent annoying the jurors and going about addressing them "just now in front of the courts."[52] Similarly, when prosecuting Aeschines, he referred to those who accosted and canvassed the jurors as they were being allotted; Aeschines, in turn, alluded to Demosthenes preparing for his case by "begging up and down the agora," around which the court venues were located.[53] Amidst the announcements and begging, litigants also apparently supplicated the jurors individually. In the *Constitution of the Athenians,* the Old Oligarch mentions that under the empire the allies had to come to Athens to conduct court cases:

> As it is now, each one of the allies is compelled to flatter the
> Athenian demos because he knows that no one but the demos has
> the power over cases for those who come to Athens. . . . He is
> compelled to entreat (ἀντιβολῆσαι) them in the courts and to
> grasp the hand of whoever comes in. Because of this, the allies
> have become more and more the slaves of the Athenian demos.[54]

By grasping their hands, litigants were supplicating the jurors. Likewise, Aristophanes' character Philokleon, when arguing that no more powerful man exists than an Athenian juror like himself, notes that "when I first come from bed to the court railings great men (even six feet tall) are looking for me. As soon as I approach, he puts his soft hand (which has stolen from the public treasury) into mine, and he supplicates me, bowing down, and says with a pitiful voice: 'Pity me, sir, I beg you.'"[55] Both the Old Oligarch and Aristophanes stress the abasement of the litigant: He "flatters" (κολακεύειν) and "entreats" (ἀντιβολῆσαι) in the first and "supplicates" (ἰκετεύσιν) and "entreats" in the second.[56]

Like general appeals for pity, we might reasonably expect that defen-

TABLE 6. Speakers Who Supplicated the Jury

	Prosecution	Defense	*Diadikasia*	*Paragraphe*	Total
Private	6/26 [23%]	3/10 [30%]	4/9 [44%]	1/9 [11%]	14/54 [26%]
Public	1/29 [3%]	4/15 [27%]			5/44 [11%]
Total	7/55 [13%]	7/25 [28%]			19/98 [19%]

Prosecution vs. Defense p = .1

dants more than prosecutors would supplicate the jury. Certainly, contemporaries expected it.[57] When litigants alluded to previous cases of supplication, they were all by defendants.[58] Only prosecutors alerted the jury to the potential supplications of their opponents.[59] Nevertheless, in the body of extant speeches, although more defendants than prosecutors used the language of supplication (28% vs. 13%), a notable number of prosecutors did as well. (See Table 6.)

The focus of this discrepancy seems to have been in private cases, since only once did a public prosecutor supplicate.[60] Yet among these private prosecutors who verbally supplicated the jurors, there was a pattern: Of the six who supplicated, five were bringing inheritance or guardianship cases,[61] just as it was with three of the four *diadikasia* speakers who supplicated the jury.[62] Likewise, most of the prosecutors who requested pity were orphans[63] suing their guardians.[64] Thus a pattern emerges: Prosecutors did not generally supplicate or request pity, except in cases concerning the transmission of the property that made up an *oikos*.

This exception proves important in interpreting the general tendency of defendants to appeal for pity and to supplicate. Prosecutors who appealed for pity or who supplicated were usually orphans and could thus more easily represent themselves as helpless.[65] More than that, however, they presented themselves as the emissary of an imperiled *oikos*. As Demosthenes concluded his speech against his guardian Aphobos, he asked for pity as the most miserable of men because he lacked the money to give a dowry to his sister, maintain his own *oikos*, and pay taxes to the state.[66] For the most part, prosecutors who begged for pity asked for this not because of their own suffering but because of the consequences this had had for their families. Jurors dispensed pity not so much to individuals as to households represented by individuals.

Appeals for pity were prominent at one other stage of the trial. Although the penalty for conviction was set before the trial began in some cases (ἀγῶνες ἀτίμητοι), in many others (ἀγῶνες τιμητοί) it was assessed in a separate hearing immediately following conviction: Each side proposed a penalty, and the jurors chose one or the other.[67] (The distinction did not correspond to that between private and public cases, both of which, depending on the specific crime charged, might be either τιμητός or ἀτίμητος.) We do not have any speeches from these penalty-assessment procedures, so our evidence is indirect and anecdotal.[68] Nevertheless, it seems that convicted defendants often appealed for pity and supplicated. Two points about the begging during this later stage of the trial stand out. First, in the few cases mentioned, it was more frequent that supporters were said to beg than the defendant himself. Second, at this stage defendants begged and supplicated not only the jury (as in the earlier stage), but the prosecutor as well.

Conviction clearly altered the relative positions of the litigants, and they would have been able to gauge this quite accurately from the numbers of votes to convict. This new dispensation gave additional and urgent reasons for a defendant to consider a compromise solution arranged directly with the prosecutor.[69] Begging and supplicating the prosecutor was a way of signaling a willingness to give in; the defendant traded a public avowal of the prosecutor's superiority for a break on the penalty he might propose. When Theokrines secured the conviction of Epichares' father, Epichares begged for a light penalty, going so far as to supplicate him by clasping his knees.[70] Such a move must have been the decisive surrender in the game of honor. Though now negotiating from positions of quite divergent power, it may still have been to the advantage of both to arrange an agreed solution, as a compromise may well have been a more enduring settlement than a decisive judicial judgment.[71] It is true that we know of instances where a compromised penalty nevertheless resulted in the successful prosecutor initiating another legal case because, so he claimed, he had not been able to get everything promised.[72] In these cases, however, I see no reason that the prosecutors would have found it easier to collect an even greater penalty just because a jury had sanctioned it. There is, however, evidence that failure to compromise on a penalty could exacerbate the dispute and lead to further litigation. In two prosecution speeches, the prosecutors specifically said that they brought their present case not merely out of revenge for losing a previous one but because once they had lost, the opponent would not acknowledge their supplications and moderate his penalty.[73]

We might expect that a conviction would give a prosecutor additional leverage to insist the defendant concede everything he wanted and would make him less likely to compromise anything. In addition to finding the solution more enduring if there were some element of compromise, however, there also seems to have been some sentiment that a prosecutor ought to show leniency to a defendant who begged. Theomnestos, who with his brother-in-law Apollodoros prosecuted Neaira, Stephanos' wife, for passing herself off as a citizen, referred to an earlier suit in which Stephanos, through allegedly slanderous allegations, had convicted Apollodoros of proposing an illegal law:

> Regarding the conviction, if this is what he really thought he should do, we don't take it badly. But when the jurors were voting about the penalty, although we begged him to compromise, he wouldn't. Instead, he proposed a penalty of fifteen talents in order to disenfranchise Apollodoros and his children and to put my sister and all of us in the greatest poverty and want.[74]

Epichares made a similar argument in his prosecution of Theokrines.[75] In both cases, the prosecutor wanted to show that the defendant deserved no pity because he had failed to show any in circumstances that called for it. These prosecutors' claims about when compromise was appropriate were, of course, self-interested and cannot be taken as reflecting a consensus. Certainly, although a jury rejected Stephanos' proposed huge penalty, another upheld Theokrines', so all large penalties cannot have seemed unreasonable to the majority of jurors at the time. Nevertheless, the failure of successful prosecutors to compromise the penalty when begged could be held against them.

THE COGNITIVE CONTENT OF RITUAL

In the Athenian courts, the effect of appeals for pity was primarily cognitive, not emotional. I am not saying that such appeals did not have an emotional aspect but that we can understand them only through their cognitive effects. Indeed, when Athenian litigants attributed pity to the jurors (or, as other references show, the demos sitting in the Assembly), there was no obvious emotional content: The Athenians showed pity when through a collective political action (arrived at through speeches and voting), they granted an explicit request of an agent that, in its request, had openly avowed (through words or actions) the superiority of the Athenians. Although there may have been an emotional aspect to such appeals, the concept of "emotion" is of only secondary importance in understanding pity in the Athenian judicial context. In fact, it has often been a major impediment to understanding it.

The idea of "emotion" does not itself explain how appeals for pity motivated the jurors' collective action. The commonplace opposing of "reason" to "emotion" fails to comprehend the complex relationships between them.[76] More than this, "reason" and "emotion" have often been more evaluative than analytic terms, used respectively to exalt and to denigrate the knowledge arrived at in different social institutions; they are thus suspect from the beginning. It is not helpful to say that juries became emotional, because the attribution of emotion to a group does less to explain collective action than mystify it by personifying the group. Collectivities as collectivities do not feel emotions: Juries no more feel pity than bureaucracies love, except metaphorically. The only meaningful way in which a group can be said to feel an emotion is if this is predicated of its individual members, but even this cannot explain the relationship between speakers' arguments and jurors' decisions. In this model, emotional appeals "move" individual jurors, who then collectively vote for acquittal. But this understanding depends on a psychology that is far too simple: It suggests that Athenian jurors were not agents but merely responded without thinking to an overpowering stimulus, language.[77] Whatever the effect of emotion on reasoning, it was much more subtle than this.

The contemporary institution of Athenian tragic theater provides no basis for understanding pity in the courts. Some scholars have recently tried to understand the operation of the courts by an analogy with the tragic theater. Though this comparison offers some insights,[78] the theater (and Aristotle's idiosyncratic analysis of it) is in many ways an inappropriate comparison for the courts.[79] Except for a few *parabaseis* in Aristophanes (when the chorus spoke directly to the audience), drama did not explicitly address the decision before the dramatic judges. Unlike litigants, playwrights did not give "reasons" for deciding that their play deserved the prize.[80] The comparison is especially inappropriate for understanding pity, which in the courts described a collective political act initiated by the petitioner's symbolic acknowledgment of his dependence on the superior power of the demos. Although drama often presented piteous spectacles, the playwright did not proclaim his inferiority to the

Athenians and his need for their help. For Aristotle, fear and pity were individual psychological states, not descriptions of collective action. The comparison would require that applauding a drama and awarding the prize be construed as acts of pity.[81] Any attempt by playwrights to motivate collective action seems to have been incidental or indirect. Whatever the audience felt when it watched a drama, it was not pity in the sense litigants sought to evoke.

Pity was not primarily or even necessarily an emotion. Kenneth Dover has noted that

> words denoting pity (*eleos*, verb *eleein*, and *oiktos*, verb *oiktīrein*, together with their cognates) do not always or necessarily denote a feeling or state of mind; the stronger 'pities' the weaker, i.e., shows pity, behaves as if compassionate, when he does what the weaker has asked him to do—rather as *thaumazein*, 'admire', or *philein*, 'love', can be used of outward manifestations without regard to inward feelings.[82]

In the courts, when litigants said "pity," they often meant "acquit"; and as such, pity was the outcome of a process of reasoning. As one defendant said: "If what we have said seems probable and the proofs we have provided sufficient, men of the jury, by every means in your power pity us."[83]

Speakers' appeals for pity should be analyzed less as arousals of unreasoning emotion and more as implicit cognitive claims. In construing them this way, I follow the lead of many recent cultural anthropologists and historians who have sought to understand how cultural activities, like ritual, give meaning to those involved. In the case of these rituals of the courts, the meaning was fundamentally political and democratic.

THE DEMOCRATIC EFFECTS
OF APPEALS FOR PITY

Through appeals for pity and the associated rituals, litigants represented and constructed their relationships to the dikasts. Most significantly, appeals for pity required that litigants subordinate themselves to the jurors to whom they appealed and that they honor the demos through their own submission to it. This was especially significant since ordinary Athenians staffed the juries, while litigants tended more often to be elites. As Athenians understood, appeals for pity dramatized democracy in the most fundamental way.

Both supplicating the jury and requesting its pity required the litigant to humble himself before the dikasts. To supplicate was to declare one's powerlessness publicly; the suppliant assumed an attitude of inferiority. "In a supplication situation . . . ," writes Gould,

> consciousness of the great imbalance of status and honour brings into play feelings of constraint and a less self-confident pattern of demeanour and behaviour, accompanied at times by an atmosphere of strain and embarrassment: hence the association in Greek sensibility between the behaviour of suppliants and that of women and children.[84]

Women were often represented as making requests by supplication, often with tears.[85] The weak had no alternative.[86] The suppliant renounced his honor and engaged in what Gould calls a "ritualized act of self-humiliation."[87] To supplicate was to declare one's powerlessness publicly, to surrender one's honor,[88] to put one's body in the posture of a woman or defeated enemy.[89] Weeping, too, although it was not shameful in all circumstances,[90] seems to have been strongly associated with unmanly behavior,[91] and the weeping in the court was part of a strategy of self-abasement and humiliation.[92]

Critics of Athenian democracy understood the potency of this ritual. For an aristocratic Greek male, supplication, whether begging for his life on the battlefield or imploring the favors of a lover, involved at least an uncomfortable compromise of honor.[93] The rituals of the court, because they too undermined a person's autonomy, could be thought of as a degrading supplication. So Plato has Socrates condemn any who had "begged and supplicated the jurors with many tears and brought forward his children to arouse pity, and many of his relatives and friends as well."[94] Such men "bring disgrace on the state" and "are no different from women."[95]

To beg for pity, a speaker cast himself as dependent upon the jury. To some extent, this was due to the decline in his own fortunes. Many appeals for pity show that this could depend in varying degrees on the merit of the man who had suffered and on his degree of wretchedness.[96] But appealing to the jury's pity also required the speaker to acknowledge the

jurors' power and collective superiority. In contrast to his own humiliation, Gould notes that "the suppliant exaggerates the τιμή [honor] of the
person to whom his supplication is addressed." [97] In the *Wasps* the juror
Philokleon repeatedly mentions the supplications of the parties as evidence of his great power. He boasts that a man undergoing an audit before the jury for his term in office "trembles and beseeches me as a god
to acquit him." [98] In the language and rituals of such appeals, the litigant
acknowledged and deferred to the power of the popular jury. "For who,"
as Isocrates wrote, "would venture to ask supplication of those weaker
than himself?" [99]

ENACTING DEMOCRACY

Appeals for pity reveal how the decision to litigate fundamentally transformed a dispute as well as the consequences of this transformation. Two
aspects of this transformation stand out as essential. First, the decision
to litigate differentiated the parties within the discourse of the law. The
roles of prosecutor and defendant were both defined in part by their different relationships to the decision to litigate. Prosecutors' stories and
arguments asserted the propriety of this decision, while defendants contested it. A defendant's appeals for pity drew the jurors' attention to the
more dire consequences for the defendant should he lose his case, consequences not only for himself but for his family, friends, and, indeed, for
the whole city. They also depended upon an understanding that the decision had been forced upon the defendant so that it bound him at the
same time as it empowered the prosecutor. Under the compulsion of necessity, the defendant appealed to the jury as someone needing its aid.

The second important aspect of the transformation of a quarrel into a
legal case was the insinuation of a powerful third party, the jurors. While
disputants related primarily to each other, litigants' relationships to each
other were mediated by their relationship to the jury. That primary relationship, the one between speaker and audience, was, in the courts,
unstable. The search for a solid ground beyond rhetorical language led
speakers to use language that was not representational or propositional
but performative. Performative language did not attempt to create a relationship with the audience through what it referred to; it did not, for
example, attempt to relate the litigant to the audience through a knowledge of past events. Instead, verbal requests for pity bypassed the indeterminacy of representation for constitutive utterances, which attempted
to bring into existence the pity they claimed. [100]

Even without accompanying actions, litigants abased themselves and avowed the jurors' collective superiority in requesting pity. Yet many speakers sought to intensify the effect and warrant their words with actions: They wept, they supplicated, they paraded those most affected by the verdict. Such spectacles seemed to offer a way around the slipperiness of language: Aeschines referred to his children in the court as a proof (τε-κμήριον) for the jury.[101] Of course, prosecutors pointed out that defendants could feign such professions and behavior: When Dinarchos prosecuted Demosthenes, he equated Demosthenes' weeping and his pleas for pity with deceptive tricks (φενακισμοί).[102] However sincere the motivations of speakers may have been, the effects of appeals for pity were clear and irreversible.

Such pleas reinforced and reproduced Athenian democracy both by leveling individuals and by highlighting the collective power of the people. As critics of Athenian democracy like Plato and the Old Oligarch recognized, supplication, weeping, and begging for pity subordinated the independence and honor of the man who proclaimed and enacted his and his household's subservience to the Athenian people. By casting himself as the suppliant of the jurors, a litigant sought to motivate collective action by instilling a collective identity, an identity constituted reciprocally with the speaker's own. One of the ways the people acquired and became aware of their own power was through the subservience of litigants. In this way, the reproduction of Athenian democracy was an unintended consequence of a system in which the uncertainty of speakers' relationship to their audience caused them to seek out more palpable grounds for authority. In appeals for pity, the speaker's authority derived precisely from the effectiveness with which he conjured his audience, conferring on them both power over him and consciousness of this power. In the dynamics of speaker and audience in litigation, Athenian democracy endured.

Six

LITIGATION AND
ATHENIAN CULTURE

The relationship between litigation and Athenian culture was complex, reciprocal, and fluid. There was an added order of both entanglement and uncertainty because the status of the relationship itself was often at stake within litigation. On the one hand, then, the boundaries of the law seem contestable and insecure. On the other, the debate on the status of those boundaries took place in specifically legal ways. For a defendant to persuade a jury that the law in its narrow sense was not the appropriate framework with which to understand a dispute was, paradoxically, an essentially legal act. Because "the law" was inseparable from its rhetorical context, the debate over the status of law was also a debate over the appropriateness of rhetorical language and of the institution in which this developed, namely, litigation. The ways litigation formalized this second-order debate about its own scope provides an additional measure of the degree of its autonomy.

Litigation at Athens constituted a semiautonomous field.[1] Although theorists disagree about how to understand the autonomy of modern legal fields,[2] and although the Athenian situation differed substantially from modern ones, the idea of semiautonomy is, nevertheless, a useful tool. It avoids the extremes of positing an institution responsive only to its own internal dynamics and entirely unaffected by the larger society or of seeing the law purely as a reflection of the larger social world. Instead, it encourages the articulation of the specific influences of culture on litigation, the institutionally unique ways these were incorporated into litigation, and, in turn, the effects of litigation on society.

Many scholars have criticized formalist views of Athenian law, rightly noting that social values other than the law played a significant role in Athenian litigation, that there was no body of specialized, professional legal experts, and that (because of this) there was neither sustained, self-reflexive analysis of the legal system by the legal system nor a group of professionals whose interests corresponded with the promotion of the institution itself. Yet it would go too far to claim that the law had no autonomy; rather, its relative autonomy took different forms than in modern legal systems. It is found in the specific practices of litigation.[3]

The decision to litigate imposed a uniquely legal shape on conflict, a shape that created prosecutors, defendants, witnesses, supporters, and "third parties" out of an undifferentiated collection of disputants. The law consistently suppressed some parties: As argued in Chapter 2, a legal narrative could express the interests of neither slaves nor women. But even within the group of citizens, the law's bifurcating stories failed to portray the complexity of many disputes. The law made decisions possible by simplifying, sometimes radically, the complexity of social life.[4] However many parties may have had a stake in a dispute, the law dichotomized conflict: It insisted on only two parties at odds.

The specifically legal roles and resources of prosecutors and defendants were distinct. Though disputants may have differed in status, wealth, social influence, political power, and many other social factors, with litigants, although these factors remained important, others came to the fore. Some factors remained equally important for both litigants, such as the ability to speak before a large audience or to mobilize others as witnesses and supporters, while others diverged. Prosecutors had a ready-made story to tell: the tale of a crime. This meant they did not face the defendant's problem of inventing a competing story, but it also constricted them more. Prosecutors had to tell the story of a crime, even if this did not correspond very well to their understanding of the conflict. Ariston's prosecution of Konon for assault (Dem. 54), with his ambivalence about who to charge and for what, reflects this problem. Here, the parties carried over into the courts their struggle about how to define the dispute. In part, the roles of prosecutor and defendant embodied the difference between legal and nonlegal definitions, though even prosecutors felt this tension, as their speeches show. The legal setting left its mark on even the nonlegal stories told in the courts, as they retrojected the law as the actors' sole motivation and the prime standard of judgment.

The degree to which the litigant's personal character mattered further distinguished the roles of prosecutor and defendant. The defendant's character and social standing were, as argued in Chapters 4 and 5, generally more at issue than the prosecutor's. Defendants invoked their services to the city, while prosecutors generally did not. This differentiation was especially pronounced in public cases, where multiple speakers often conducted the prosecution so that the emphasis on the person of the prosecutor was less likely, where prosecutors told a story in which the harmed party was the jurors or the city, and where, perhaps because of their own more abstract role, prosecutors more vehemently denied the legitimacy of defendants' personal appeals. Defendants also more frequently asked for the jury's pity. This seems to have been the result of the prosecutor's unilateral decision to transform the dispute into a legal case. This was another way in which disputants carried over into the courts the contest about how to define the dispute. The prosecutor's definition, however authoritative, was contestable. In most cases, then, trials were not symmetrical contests: Defendants' reputations, though more imperiled, were also more of a benefit.[5]

The Athenian courts were differentiated not only from the forms of conflict in everyday life but from other public, political institutions. The courts were quite distinct from the theater, but they differed significantly from the Assembly as well, a fact with important implications. For example, speakers' characters were not an explicit issue in the Assembly.[6] In preserved Assembly speeches, speakers referred to many hypothetical or unnamed opponents, and in a number of instances, speakers suggested these had been bribed. Only once, however, did a speaker name his opponent and attack his personal character, and this in a speech of dubious authenticity.[7] Thus speakers' characters, both as a basis for accepting their words and as a means of attacking them, were an explicit part not of Athenian politics and political rhetoric but of the Athenian courts and legal rhetoric. This entails important consequences for how we understand politics and the law in Athens. Ober, for example, though he recognizes that character was more of an issue in the courts than in the Assembly,[8] often conflates the two institutions. He claims, then, that "the demos judged a politician's policy at least in part by reference to his character, to his worth as a citizen."[9] This fails to recognize, however, first that the forms discussions of policy took in the courts included references to character but those in the Assembly did not and second that court cases that had policy implications were not conducted markedly differently from those that did not.[10] This is not to deny that citizens in the Assembly may have judged politicians by their character, but it undercuts Ober's explanation of the presence of questions of character as due to the relatively low "role differentiation" of politicians in Athens. In fact, questions of character, confined as they were to the courts, focused on the defendant much more than on the prosecutor, and often formulated in terms of orientation to the law,[11] indicate the relatively marked differentiation of the courts from social life in general and from other public, political institutions.

Specifying the forms of the autonomy of the law at Athens is made even more complex because litigants themselves disagreed about the proper extent of this. This debate about the law, however, was not merely the outcome of differences in personal opinions but was structured into Athenian litigation itself: The formalized roles of prosecutor and defendant represented conflicting views about the place of law in understanding social life. For the prosecutor, the decision to litigate was simultaneously and necessarily a decision to tell a legal story: to dichotomize conflict, to recognize only a legally competent opponent, and to focus on an isolated event that could be interpreted as a violation of the law.[12] Thus, a prosecutor's decision to transform a dispute into a legal case asserted a relatively higher degree of autonomy for the law, depending as it did on the assumption that social life should be interpreted primarily in light of these legal provisions. Prosecutors similarly contested the relevance and propriety of nonlegal perspectives, claiming, for example, that the jurors' oath ruled out defendants' counternarratives. Because the prosecutor alone decided to make a dispute into a legal case, the defendant's role was necessarily defined in opposition to it and challenged the validity of a narrowly legal perspective. Though defendants did not explicitly deny the relevance of the law, many of their arguments implicitly called the prosecutor's use of it into question. Their counternarratives impugned the prosecutor's motives by suggesting dark conspiracy or unjust sykophancy behind the charges. They appealed for pity as the victims of litigation. They urged the jurors to evaluate not their action in a single instance but their actions and characters throughout their lives. In these ways they challenged the narrow view of the law that was the basis of the prosecutor's story and promoted a view of litigation more open to nonlegal considerations. Both the prosecutor's assertion of the primacy of the law and the defendant's invocation of a nonlegal perspective were self-interested, strategic, and contestable. In Athens that contest took the form of litigation. Thus Athenian legal discourse and practice should be understood neither as a completely autonomous field of the law (although this is what prosecutors advocated), nor simply as an unbounded and undifferentiated corner of social life (although defendants tended to treat it as such); instead, the institutional autonomy of litigation depended on the ways it incorporated (often implicitly) this second-order debate about the proper degree of its own boundedness.

Athenians remained ambivalent about the proper degree of the autonomy of the law, an ambivalence that provided the basis for conflicting claims by litigants. Athenian law was procedurally complex and litigants' deployment of and arguments about legal procedures reveal both an aspect of the relationship of the law to society and popular attitudes toward this.[13] In certain kinds of cases, for example, Athenian law specified that the right to prosecute expired after a certain time, a statute of limitations. One litigant used this to make a straightforward defense: His accusers' case was invalid because he had not prosecuted within five years as specified by the law.[14] Against this procedural claim, however, some speakers argued that it was not the time lag that mattered but the justice of the case and that anyone who had remained unpunished for many years should not complain that they had been able to do so for so long.[15] The prosecutor of Agoratos went further. In 399 the relatives of one of the victims of the Thirty prosecuted Agoratos, who had been an informer under the oligarchs. They charged him with murder. Through the procedure of *endeixis* (a public case) they had the Eleven arrest him for trial. The Eleven, in conformity with the requirements for such a procedure, insisted that the charge indicate Agoratos had been taken "in the act." The speaker expected Agoratos to mount a defense that included a number of procedural points: that the covenant of the amnesty and its oaths made such a prosecution invalid, that the statute of limitations had expired, and that he had not been taken "in the act." Anticipating these arguments, the prosecutor tried to refute each one at length (Lys. 13.83–90). He summarized his position:

> If he makes these kinds of arguments, he's practically admitting
> he's a murderer. He throws out these impediments—the oaths,
> the agreements, the time lapse, or the words "in the act"—but he
> doesn't trust in the facts to decide the case. But it's your duty,
> men of the jury, to reject these arguments. Order him to make his
> defense on these questions: Didn't he turn informer? Aren't the
> men dead?[16]

Since prosecutors seem to have been able to argue that defendants' reliance on procedures or "technicalities" (as we might call them) thwarted justice, defendants often invoked procedures in qualified ways. One offered a lengthy justification of the statute of limitations.[17] Another speaker, alleged to have agreed to be surety for a man who had lost a suit, used the statute of limitations to support his substantive claim that he had never agreed to provide security.

> Please pick up the law that orders that securities are valid for
> a year only. I am not relying on this law so that I am not held
> legally responsible if I did become a surety. I am suggesting, rather,
> that the law is my witness that I did not become a surety at all—
> and my opponent is a witness to this as well because if I had
> become a surety he would have taken me to court over the secu-
> rity within the time written in the law.
> LAW.[18]

The ability of the speakers to rely on and contest technical procedural aspects of the law betrays a larger ambivalence about litigation. This ambivalence, however, was given an institutionally specific form both in the kinds of arguments used (e.g., arguments from probability[19]) and in the separation of the conflicting views into the roles of defendant and prosecutor.

THE CONSTRUCTION
OF ATHENIAN IDENTITY

One of the most crucial differences between litigation and a dispute was the presence of the jury. Just as the decision to litigate transformed disputants into specifically defined legal roles, it also invoked this powerful group. This meant that the central problem for each litigant became defining their relationship to this group, a process made difficult because the litigant and the jurors were unknown to each other so that the relationship was constituted entirely through the litigant's speech. The result of the struggle between prosecutor and defendant over the definition of the jurors was a verdict in any particular case, but the aggregate effect of continual trials was to create and reproduce the identities of jurors as men, as citizens, as Athenians.

The anxiety over language was an anxiety over the relationship constituted by that language. Through their various appeals, speakers were establishing relationships with their audience. Establishing these relationships did not just depend upon the identity of the audience; reciprocally, it constituted it. Litigation did not merely play upon or reflect group identities in Athenian society (though it did this as well); it also created, reinforced, and reproduced them—an important consequence of litigation.

Litigation affected the structure of Athenian society in ways the speakers themselves did not explicitly address. Litigation distinguished adult male citizens from all others. For the most part, only citizens could engage in litigation. As argued in Chapter 2, there was more at stake here than merely the legal incapacity of the majority of people in Athens. Rather, because legal stories could not be told with excluded people as their subjects, litigation required the systematic transformation of disputes into conflict between citizens.[20] This, in turn, profoundly affected the lives of both noncitizens and citizens. It is unclear, for example, how much women were caught up in male competition for honor[21] or how much they pursued other kinds of virtues,[22] but as the story of Neaira shows, however competitive they were, they could not be competitive in the same ways as men.

The exclusion of noncitizens from most litigating was important, but so was the prohibition from serving as jurors, which was even more absolute. In the courts, male citizens learned and shared certain kinds of knowledge, creating a commonalty of interests and abilities. One of these was the ability to interpret laws in an authoritative manner. The laws themselves did not indicate how to do this; rather, proper interpretive skills were learned and handed down in the culture of the courts among an interpretive community. Thus the practices of litigation perpetuated distinctions within Athenian society even without the conscious intentions of those involved.

Speakers often explicitly sought to induce the audience to identify themselves in certain ways; here, litigation affected the identity of the Athenians less by opposing them to other groups than by disposing them to define their interests in ways that favored a particular speaker. Prosecutors, especially those in public cases, induced the jurors to think of themselves as "the Athenians" or "the polis" and so to take an interest in the defendant's crime not merely as a third party but as those whom it had injured. Prosecutors sought to make the jurors identify their interests with "the laws" and, by extension, the entire democratic constitution, and they invoked the jurors' oath to support this. Defendants, for their part, tried to get the jurors to think of their interests as "Athenians" differently. They tried to portray their liturgies and services to the state as part of an economy of gratitude in which the jurors, as Athenians, were in their debt. In supplicating the jurors and seeking their pity, they similarly sought to invoke the ideology of the Athenians' mildness. The rituals associated with such appeals (weeping, the grasping of the hand, the suppliant's branch) again attempted to circumvent the vagaries of rhetorical language.

By identifying the jurors as Athenians in these cases, defendants voluntarily submitted themselves to the jurors and reminded them of their power. The effect was to undercut (though not abolish) hierarchy within the citizen body: Rich defendants commonly abased themselves to the jurors, publicly demonstrating that all citizens were responsible to the whole of the citizenry. In litigation, both in rhetorical language and in the attempts to tame this, Athenians enacted their democracy.

Appendix

THE USE OF

STATISTICS

In this book I have included a few statistical analyses of general patterns in Athenian legal speeches. This appendix offers some insight into what these figures mean and how they were compiled.

DESCRIPTIVE AND

INFERENTIAL STATISTICS

This study uses statistical procedures in two distinct ways. In the first place, it presents statistics that describe the body of speeches we have; in Table 4 (p. 111), for example, the percentage of different kinds of litigants who asked for pity. These simply describe patterns in the body of extant speeches.

A second statistical procedure offers a measure of the probability that such a pattern in the body of preserved speeches (the sample) corresponds to a pattern in all the speeches that were given, including the vast majority that have not been preserved. The measure of this probability is "p," which describes the likelihood that the differences between categories in the sample are accidental and not indicative of differences in the original population. (Thus a smaller "p" indicates a greater degree of confidence.)

Two important issues arise in using inferential statistics: the size of the sample and whether or not it is representative of the whole population. Generally, the larger the sample size, the greater the confidence that can be placed in the results.[1] A sample of one or ten or even twenty is often not large enough to make meaningful statistical generalizations. Since there are about 100 speeches preserved from the Athenian courts, even when whittled down, this remains a large enough sample to constitute a meaningful basis for statistical inference. "P" takes into account the size of the sample; generally, the larger the sample, the smaller "p" will be.

Inferential statistics also depend on the sample being representative of the whole population. This is usually achieved through the use of a random sample. There is no way to prove that the preserved speeches are a random sample of the original population; indeed, there are reasons to suspect that they are not.[2] Nevertheless, for purposes of generalization I have assumed that they are. Although such an enabling assumption is unwarranted from the standpoint of statistics, it corresponds closely to the assumptions that historians and literary critics make in drawing generalizations from texts. For example, when critics talk about "Aeschylus," they generalize from specific texts to "the author." But "the author" in this case exists only because of the enabling assumptions—that, for example, the seven tragedies preserved from Aeschylus can be meaningfully said to represent his larger work, his technique, or even the state of tragedy during his lifetime. Similarly, any account of the changes in the techniques and forms of history or philosophy in ancient Greece requires an assumption that the preserved examples allow for inferences about the many lost examples of these genres. Such assumptions, then, do not concern only the use of statistics. Without such enabling assumptions there is only the solipsism of the text, and history itself would not be possible.[3]

Enabling assumptions may be challenged and debated, and I believe it is one of the virtues, in this case, of using such statistical analyses that the assumptions that go into making history are made explicit. The generalized claims I present here should be understood as dependent upon this enabling assumption. Descriptive statistics about the preserved sample of speeches, however, do not depend on this assumption.

The use of this enabling assumption and of procedures of statistical inference in this study is a substantially conservative procedure. Statistical descriptions of the extant speeches reveal many patterns, but the question is which of these are meaningful, which, that is, reflect a real difference in the original population of all speeches. The procedures of statistical inference require (as it turns out) the rejection of most differences in the extant sample as meaningless in terms of the whole population. That is, rather than a means of constructing patterns, it is rather a criteria by which the majority of patterns in the sample have been rejected. It has not been a license for speculation, but a way of disciplining it.

HOW TO READ THESE STATISTICS

This book includes a number of tables that contain descriptive and inferential statistics. This study seeks to analyze the differences between public and private cases and between prosecution and defense speeches; thus in the tables the results of significance are the totals. (The differences between private and public speeches are reported in the right-hand column; the differences between prosecution and defense speeches are reported in the bottom row.) For completeness, all results have been recorded in the table. (Thus it is obvious, for example, in Table 4, that although there was a dramatic difference in the proportion of prosecutors and defendants who asked for pity, there was virtually no difference between public and private cases.) There were, however, two kinds of private actions in which the categories of prosecution and defense were clouded. In the *diadikasia* all parties were on equal terms and there were neither prosecutors nor defendants. In the *paragraphe,* a counterprosecution by a defendant challenging the legality of the case against him, defendant and prosecutor in the original suit traded places. In most of these, arguments about the original suit and about the *paragraphe* were mixed together by speakers on both sides, blurring the differences between prosecutor and defendant. Neither of these private actions had a counterpart among public suits. They are included, then, in the statistics distinguishing private from public cases but not in those illustrating the differences between prosecution and defense speeches. (For comprehensiveness, however, they appear in all tables.)

Each table includes "p" (based on a chi-square test), a measure of the likelihood that the difference in the sample reflects a difference in the whole original population. "P" does not apply to the whole table but only to the difference either between total prosecution speeches and total defense speeches or between total private cases and total public cases. (Each table clearly states which.) In Table 4, for example, "p < .001" means that the differences found in the sample between the total prosecution and total defense speeches would appear less than once in a thousand randomly drawn samples from an original population in which there were no differences in proportions between the categories. I have not reported as significant results where "p" is greater than .05.

STATISTICAL PROCEDURES

I have used Pandora software to search the orations, using the texts as they are presented in the *Thesaurus Linguae Graecae: Canon of Greek Authors and Works* (*TLG*). The data has been processed using the spreadsheet program Microsoft Excel.

From the body of all preserved speeches, I have excluded a number from consideration. I have excluded those delivered before the Assembly or the Boule or in a non-Athenian court. As noted in the Introduction, I have not distinguished between speeches rightly or wrongly attributed to a particular author, so long as they are genuine court speeches. A few have been excluded as later compositions; absent a decisive scholarly consensus against a speech's authenticity, however, I have included it.

The categories into which I have divided the speeches have involved a certain amount of compromise. Within private cases I have included trials held before the Council of the Areopagos, even though this was a different court from the regular *dikasteria* before which other private cases were tried. There are not enough of these speeches, moreover, to constitute an independent category capable of generating meaningful statistical results. The category of public cases includes a wide variety of procedures. Some compromises were necessary to keep the size of each category large enough to provide a reliable foundation for generalizations.

NOTES

INTRODUCTION

1. Ober 1989, 31–33; Hunter 1994, 97–98.
2. Humphreys 1983 and 1985b.
3. Plato, *Laws* 948d–e.
4. Giddens 1990.
5. Money constitutes a similar abstract system and demands trust in all manner of anonymous relationships. The Athenians seem to have felt considerable anxiety about the influence of money on society, especially the way that it constituted relationships.
6. Ober 1989, 174–177.
7. This contrasts, obviously, with sophists whose success depended on the degree to which they could highlight their language as language.
8. Such processes did not take place only in the courts, but given the preserved evidence, they are perhaps best seen there.
9. This Introduction presents a genealogy of the kinds of questions I have asked of the evidence, questions often inspired by the work of other theorists. Both the work of social theorists and comparative historical accounts should be used not to fill "gaps" in the evidence but to inspire new lines of inquiry, problematizing the past in innovative ways, or, as Paul Veyne (1984) says, lengthening the historical questionnaire. What follows, then, is not a comprehensive account of my historical methodology; rather it is a discussion of the kinds of historical problems I had in mind as I read the sources and wrote my narrative and a map that locates this book on a terrain of contiguous scholarship.
10. It is also true that litigation does not invariably involve disputes. (Trubek 1980–1981, 729–730, cites the example of an uncontested divorce.) However, although there is some slight evidence for cooperation or collusion between litigants at Athens (Osborne 1985, 45; Dem. 48.43; 58.39–40), most cases seem to have arisen from disputes.

11. The study of these other ways of pursuing disputes is the subject of a literature on "social control": Ellickson 1991; Black 1984.

12. Yngvesson and Mather 1983, 64. Cf. Mather and Yngvesson 1980–1981, 777 and 818.

13. These characteristics pertain to litigation in other societies as well, though an Athenian jury is a structurally different third party than the juries, judges, and lawyers introduced in American litigation. The specialized roles differed as well, especially, in an Athenian private case, for the person claiming to be the victim. He became not a witness for the prosecution (as in an American criminal case) nor a plaintiff (as in a civil case) but the prosecutor himself.

14. Mather and Yngvesson 1980–1981.

15. D. Cohen 1991, 49–69; Hunter 1994, 96–119.

16. Brenneis 1988, 282–285, contrasts gossip and mediation discourse in Bhatgaon, a rural Fiji Indian community, to make the point that the context of narrative telling in part determines the content of the narrative and the social judgments of its value.

17. Because of the essential role of the jury, litigation cannot be construed simply as a bilateral competition or as a form of feuding.

18. These people might still have had an effect as witnesses or supporters (as Humphreys 1985b argues), but that is to say again that litigation transformed their roles.

19. Luhmann 1982, 135. Cf. Mather and Yngvesson 1980–1981, 783–797, on the process of "narrowing" a dispute.

20. Of course, defendants contested these simplifications by arguing that the dispute should not be understood as a legal case. Yet, as I note, these attacks on a judicial narrative, articulated within the courts, took on characteristics of that institution.

21. Even in American society, most conflict (much of which could be litigated) never comes within the reach of the law. Of that which does, the majority is settled without formal adjudication.

22. Luhmann 1982, 124–125, argues this is true even of legal systems that did not rely on private prosecution.

23. For a long time in American law, conflict between a husband and a wife, for example, even when it involved physical violence against the woman, has been largely defined as nonlegal. The privilege of the male position was marked by men (within the legal system and without) not defining as a crime a husband's violence against his wife and often enough by women themselves not seeing this as criminal. Current political conflicts over issues like spousal abuse and harassment show that many still do not view the relationships between men and women as subject to the same degree of legal interpretation as relationships between men and men. In general, most people see litigation as an even less appropriate form for conflict between parents and children.

24. Yngvesson 1984.

25. This was precisely what was at stake in Dem. 54, as I argue below in Chapter 2.

26. Osborne 1985.

27. In cases of murder, the victim's kin held this right.

28. A private case was called a *dike;* there was a variety of public procedures,

the most common of which was a *graphe*. (Todd 1993, 370–371 and 378, briefly discusses these categories.) Throughout this study I have grouped together all public procedures. In treating these different kinds of cases as alike, I have undoubtedly smoothed over some differences, but I believe the kinship among them is much greater than the differences between them. Moreover, as noted in the Appendix, when categories are divided too finely so that there are only a few examples in each group, there can be little confidence in comparisons between them.

29. It also reflects that much of the professional literature is written from the perspective of third parties (judges, lawyers, mediators, or therapists) whose positions are legitimated precisely because they claim to be uniquely qualified to eliminate conflict. D. Cohen 1995, ch. 1, criticizes this functionalist perspective in detail.

30. Starr and Collier 1989, 3–5. Cf. Rosen 1989, 4.

31. Athenian litigation did settle cases, and they could not be reopened once a verdict was given. But because disputes were not cases, a verdict did not necessarily end a dispute; a dispute could, and sometimes did, continue and reappear in the form of a different case. (Some authors [e.g., Ober 1989, 144–145, following Osborne 1985] claim that cases could be and were reopened, but this confuses a dispute with a specifically legal form it might take, a case.) D. Cohen 1995, however, goes too far in suggesting that the courts never settled a dispute.

32. E. Harris 1994, 133, it is true, objects that the Athenian courts aimed to uphold the laws, not settle disputes. I do not see these as necessarily incompatible, though I would say that Athenian courts were venues for pursuing disputes (whether to "settlement" or not) by attempting to transform them into legal cases.

33. Todd 1993; Todd and Millett 1990; Hunter 1994; D. Cohen 1991; and D. Cohen 1995. It has long been present in the anthropologically informed work of Humphreys.

34. Comaroff and Roberts 1981; Felstiner et al. 1980–1981; Mather and Yngvesson 1980–1981. (This entire issue of *Law and Society Review* is devoted to the idea of the dispute.) Yngvesson and Mather 1983 follow their earlier article.

35. Rosen 1989; Starr and Collier 1989; Merry 1990.

36. As D. Cohen (1991), E. Cohen (1992), and Hunter (1994) argue.

37. Giddens 1984, 25.

38. Giddens 1984, 1–40, offers a useful brief introduction to his theory of "structuration." Pierre Bourdieu (1977 and 1990) and Marshall Sahlins (1985) both offer useful insights on the problem of structure and agency.

39. Giddens 1984, 2.

40. Bourdieu 1990, 23–141, is a good introduction to his theory. For Bourdieu the *habitus* explains why people in certain groups (e.g., classes) behave and think in similar ways. Rather than understanding patterns in culture on the model of rules, Bourdieu posits the *habitus,* a set of inculcated dispositions and habits that correlate to living conditions of the group. Because people in the same group share the same *habitus,* they tend, unconsciously, to make the same choices, even in new situations, thus reproducing both the *habitus* and the group itself.

41. "All forms of dependence offer some resources whereby those who are subordinate can influence the activities of their superiors" (Giddens 1984, 16).

42. E.g., Butler 1990; Law 1994; Turner 1990. In his final two works (1985 and 1986), both of which, incidentally, concerned the ancient world, Foucault himself moved towards recuperating a sense of agency, which had been absent in earlier writings (e.g., 1977).

43. Hunt 1989.

44. This is a reaction against the structural Marxism of Althusser, for whom individuals are "interpolated" as subjects by "ideological state apparatuses," leaving them, as Thompson saw it, with no agency. E. P. Thompson 1978 develops these points at length.

45. Sewell 1990; Scott 1991.

46. E. P. Thompson 1993, 185–258. The structure of the argument is similar in his most influential book (E. P. Thompson 1963).

47. The idea of a struggle over symbolic meanings is central to Darnton 1984.

48. Ober 1989.

49. Scott 1988.

50. It may be debated whether this exclusion and subordination of others was necessary for the historical emergence of the ideological equality of the citizens (Wood 1988). But any account of Athenian democracy that considers only the relations between citizens is less an account of power in that society than a recapitulation of an interested ideology of power.

51. Foucault's work (1978, 1985) historicized the notion of "sexuality"; for the Greek period, Winkler (1990) and Halperin (1990) have followed his initiative. Similarly, a prominent strand of feminism treats gender as culturally constructed (Scott 1988, ch. 2).

52. Giddens 1991.

53. Gouldner 1965, ch. 3; Foucault 1985. Johnstone 1994 argues that a specific class used the strategies Foucault describes as part of an attempt to differentiate itself and maintain its social superiority.

54. E.g., Loraux 1986; Wolpert 1996. Hunter 1992 concerns slaves.

55. Ober 1989, ch. 5, distinguishes two classes based on objective economic criteria and then deduces opposing interests. For example: "The poorer Athenian was not functionally the equal of his rich compatriot, despite constitutional limits on the political privileges of the rich. This functional inequality inevitably generated resentment of the wealth elite" (Ober 1989, 205).

56. Johnstone 1994.

57. Cf. Bourdieu 1991.

58. Cartledge, Millett, and Todd 1990; D. Cohen 1991 and 1995; Foxhall and Lewis 1996; Humphreys 1983, 1985a, 1985b, 1986; Todd 1993; Ober 1989.

59. Moore 1973 argues for seeing fields as semiautonomous. Chapter 6 treats this subject more fully.

60. Hansen (1989b and 1990) and Ober (1989) disagree on the place of institutions in analyzing the Athenian democracy. With Ober I agree that the important point is how institutions operated in practice, though Hansen seems right that Ober has not allowed for sufficient institutional specificity. There may be more middle ground than either argument initially allows: As this book argues, practice is part of what makes an institution distinct.

61. So, for example, as I argue in Chapter 5, I do not find the Athenian theater a particularly useful model for understanding the Athenian courts.

62. Humphreys 1985b emphasizes three stages: the initial circulation of a written text in Athens, later export to Alexandria, and finally, inclusion in a collection of speeches attributed to one of the most famous orators.

63. Ober 1989, 49 n. 113. Todd 1990c, 166–167, expresses greater doubt. Worthington 1991 argues that there were substantial revisions, because some speeches are too long to have been delivered in the allotted time, and many show a structural complexity that is more appropriate to a text intended to be read. The first claim is suggestive, but, at least as it stands in his article, entirely impressionistic. As to the second, I am unconvinced that elaborate care in composition, even if jurors could not have appreciated it (and I am not so sure of that), is a clear sign of revision for a reading audience. Worthington does not show that a complex overall structure would have worked against persuading an audience, only that they might not have perceived it. This hardly merits the assumption of a second stage of composition in which the entire speech was revised in detail to conform to the more elaborate organization. He argues further that long and complex sentences "could have created problems for the jurors in following arguments" (Worthington 1991, 63), but the fact that Dinarchos may have written some awkwardly complex sentences is fairly weak proof that he added these in revision. I also doubt Worthington's hypothesis because it requires that the revisions were not merely additions or subtractions of arguments or sections but the complete recomposition of the speech down to the rearrangement and rewriting of individual sentences. (Even with a computer, I am hesitant to imagine an author doing that much work.) All this also neglects that even most subsequent readings of a speech would have been oral. Finally, insofar as they are valid, Worthington's claims apply to only the dozen or so public speeches he treats.

64. Interestingly, the most skeptical readers tend to believe consistently that the opponent (whose speech we do not have) must have had a better case: Wyse 1904; Gagarin 1989; Carey and Reid 1985.

65. Dover 1974, 13–14; E. Cohen 1992, 37–38; Ober 1989, 43–49; Todd 1990c, 171–175.

66. Those who want even more information on Athenian society and politics should consult Sinclair 1988, Ober 1989, or Hansen 1991. Harrison 1971, MacDowell 1978, and Todd 1993 provide fuller accounts of the courts.

67. Strauss 1987 claims that conflict killed off proportionately more of the poorer Athenians. In this case, however, I do not believe the sources will bear the weight of quantification he tries to show. Nor do I see clear evidence for Athens becoming more "conservative" in the fourth century.

68. I have distinguished citizens, who were all males above 18, from those with citizen status, meaning women and children who enjoyed some of the privileges accorded citizens but in very limited ways.

69. The way liturgies were allocated changed at least twice in the fourth century, which also changed the number of people eligible (Sinclair 1988, 61–62).

70. Ober 1989, 128, catalogues the disagreements over this number.

71. Johnstone 1994.

72. Hansen, 1990, 355–356, who champions the "middle class" theory, admits it was less of a presence as the fourth century progressed.

73. As many slaves and metics as citizens probably held such "manufacturing" jobs. Even craftsmen were also often part-time farmers.

74. Ober 1989.

75. At Athens, though only citizens could own land, land ownership was not a prerequisite of citizenship.

76. Since we, too, believe that children should be excluded from the political arena, this aspect of Athenian democracy is never noted as at all problematic.

77. The Athenians called the person who initiated and prosecuted a legal case ὁ διώκων, literally, "the pursuer." I have translated this as "accuser" or "prosecutor." The Athenian διώκων, however, was not a public official who initiated criminal cases on behalf of the state, a prosecuting attorney, but a private individual who initiated and argued a case himself. Because the distinction between Athenian public and private cases does not correspond to ours between criminal and civil cases, I have not used (as some scholars do) "prosecutor" and "plaintiff" to distinguish those who initiate each kind respectively. When necessary to make this distinction, I have referred to "public prosecutors" and "private prosecutors."

78. For a more detailed account of the courts, see MacDowell 1978, chs. 2, 4, and 16.

79. Todd 1990a refers to the earlier literature. I find the debates on this subject frustrating. Sometimes, authors seem to disagree mostly about terminology: Todd's "middle class" looks to me like the same people as Markle's "poor Athenians" (Markle 1985). I am, moreover, highly suspicious of the most common way of determining the social composition of Athenian juries: by deducing it from the values speakers used in trying to persuade jurors. This requires an assumption of a mechanical relationship between objective status and recognition of interests. It also makes it impossible (because of circularity) to ask how in the courts groups were mobilized and made to recognize certain interests as their own, since that relationship has to be assumed in the first place.

80. Arist., *Ath. Pol.* 53.2–3.

81. Harrison 1971, 66, 92–94.

82. The speakers of Isoc. 20 and Lys. 24 both claim to be humble.

83. There has been considerable debate about the date, content, and sometimes even the existence of many of the changes I outline in this paragraph. Since this development is not the point of this book, I have presented a brief, consensus account.

84. Humphreys 1983 characterizes the evolution of the system as a series of attempts to balance the need for impartiality with the requirement that judges have specific knowledge of the case. Sealey 1987 sees the desire for fairness and efficiency motivating the many changes in Athenian political institutions, including the courts. Though Aristotle's *Constitution of Athens* makes this development the outcome of the democratizing intentions of reformers, it is much better to see democratization as the unintended consequence of a series of historically specific innovations.

85. From this decade are preserved the first complete texts of comedy and forensic oratory as well as the valuable, if problematic, *Constitution of the Athenians*. (The author of this work is unknown, though he is sometimes called "the Old Oligarch." Because it has traditionally been attributed to Xenophon, it is cited as [Xen.], *Ath. Pol.*) Though earlier tragedies (like Aeschylus' *Eumenides*) may provide hints, without verification from actual court speeches, it is difficult to say how much he may have changed his material.

86. Todd 1993, 57–58, and 1996 argues that the codification largely failed.

87. Hansen 1985. See further Chapter 1.

1. AUTHORITATIVE READINGS

1. I have left the Greek γραμματεύς untranslated. To call this official a "clerk," "secretary," or "notary" threatens to obscure his extensive duties as a reader as well as a writer. It is a measure of how different the Athenians were that we have no word to describe a single person who deals with the alphabet by both writing and reading aloud.

2. In most cases, the manuscripts of the speeches do not preserve the document the *grammateus* read. Instead, they merely include a lemma, in this case, "Laws."

3. Dem. 54.24–25.

4. Meyer-Laurin 1965; Meinecke 1971; E. Harris 1994.

5. Todd 1993, 61–62.

6. Todd 1993, 59.

7. D. Cohen 1995, 178.

8. Fish 1994, 141–199, notes the important differences between the practice of law and an account of the practice of law. "The law . . . is not philosophy [or history]; it is law, although, like everything else it can become the object of philosophical [or historical] analysis, in which case it becomes something different from what it is in its own terms" (Fish 1994, 177). Cf. Bourdieu 1977.

9. Todd 1993, 258–262, discusses this case. Cf. White 1990, 239–241, 247.

10. Lys. 10.6–8, 11–12.

11. MacDowell 1978, 128, for example, claims that "the law did not say explicitly that other expressions having the same meaning were also banned, though no doubt the speaker was right to maintain that this was its intention."

12. Hillgruber 1988, 11–21.

13. Todd 1993, 260, specifies only one interpretive strategy here, the first, though he includes in this the third. It seems to me too simple to say that "Lysias differentiates between the spirit of the law and its written version, and gives the former the deciding voice" (Steiner 1994, 233).

14. Solon, as the alleged founder of Athenian democracy, played an important role in democratic mythology of the fourth century and in constitutional debates. Hansen 1989a gives details and references to earlier scholarship.

15. E.g., Dem. 20.93; Hyp. 3.22.

16. Carter 1994, 69–71, 78–83, argues that the complexities of making law in the United States make the idea of "legislative intent" problematic, if not historically fraudulent.

17. Hillgruber 1988, 107–119. He believes Athenian litigants used three strategies of (mis)interpretation: they took words out of context, they used the lawgiver's intentions to overturn what a law actually said, and they used this intention to invent laws on subjects where there were none. Thomas 1994, 124, likewise asserts that "appeal to a lawgiver's intentions is, effectively, or at least potentially, going beyond the law itself, it is an extralegal argument which seeks to appeal to the source of law rather than to the law."

18. Historical context and literalism are not universally privileged. Many traditions of exegesis of the Christian scriptures, for example, have discovered their true interpretations with protocols which were neither literal nor historical.

19. E.g., Hansen 1989a, 81; Rhodes 1981b, 133.

20. Hansen 1989a, 82; Thomas 1994, 124.

21. Hansen 1989a suggests it promotes a moderate democracy, while Thomas 1994 sees it as reflecting a conservative criticism of and disillusionment with contemporary institutions.

22. It is not my claim that Athenians were incapable of discriminating the authentic laws of Solon from those that were not; it is rather that historical accuracy was not the point in such ascriptions. Aeschines (1.25) referred to the dignified posture of a sculpture of Solon on Salamis to show the restrained manner of speaking in olden times. Demosthenes' retort (19.251), that the image was made two centuries after Solon lived, proves that Athenians could historically evaluate his statue, if not his statutes.

23. Thomas 1994, 131, worries that "the idea of the lawgiver circumvents the neat legal rules of the fourth century." Yet legal reasoning involves the "extralegal." First, laws are never comprehensive or unambiguous. Second, because people can always disagree about what a text means, every reading of a law, even a strict or literal one, is an interpretation. Third, interpretive protocols, even if everyone agrees on them, are outside the law; laws themselves do not describe procedures through which they ought to be interpreted.

24. Now and again speakers used other procedures to read the laws: they interpreted the law in light of what would benefit the city the most (Lys. 14.4; cf. Dem. 18.210), or on the basis of the common usage of language. (Aesch. 1.160–165 and Ant. 5.9–10 both argued against interpreting laws by ordinary language.)

25. Lyc. 1.9. Cf. Lys. 31.27.

26. Dem. 22.8–11.

27. Aeschines (3.16) made the same claim.

28. Cf. Dem. 36.27; 58.11.

29. Isae. 2.13.

30. Isae. 2.10–12, 36–37.

31. Modern scholars usually see in this law the desire to perpetuate the *oikos* through a male heir. Such a move, however persuasive, also requires the fiction of an author, in this functionalist reading, "society."

32. Dem. 44. 57–58.

33. E.g., Dem. 21.56–57; 23.50; 54.17–19; Isae. 1.29–30; Lys. 6.14–15.

34. MacDowell 1975.

35. Aesch. 3.38; Dem. 20.90–91.

36. The lawgiver was not, however, merely an interpretive fiction, albeit a powerful one. On two occasions in the late fifth century when the Athenians had made a comprehensive review of their laws, they described these as "the laws of Solon," so that "Solon" had been intimately connected with a process which imposed a degree of coherence. These revisions took place in 410 BC (Lys. 30.2, assuming this accurately reproduces the language of the enabling legislation) and again in 403 (Andoc. 1.83, the "Decree of Teisamenos").

37. Hyp. 3.13; cf. Dem. 47.77.

38. Hyp. 3.13–20.

39. The Greek of this paraphrase of the law is not completely clear in its details; the exact meaning also depends on whether you restore ἀ[ναλώμ]ατα or ἀ[δικήμ]ατα. (See Harrison 1968, 173 n. 2.) What is clear is that the law holds the owner at the time financially responsible for the actions of a slave.

40. Hyp. 3.21–22.

41. Epikrates mentioned "the lawgiver" in §16.

42. Other examples: Aesch. 3.26; Dem. 20.90, 102–103, 104; 21.42–45; 22.25; 23.30; 24.103–106, 113–115; 43.53–67; 44.67–68; Isoc. 20.2–3; Lyc. 1.65–67; Lys. 1.31–32; 3.42–43. One speaker related that when Solon had been prosecuting someone, he, too, had used this form of reasoning (Dem. 24.212–214).

43. Dem. 22.25. Osborne 1985 discusses this passage in detail. He concludes that "the capacity to fit actions to men was a primary quality of Athenian legal procedure" (48). Todd 1993 builds on Osborne in suggesting that the primary component of the "shape" of Athenian law was procedure, especially the procedural choices it allowed the prosecutor (esp. pp. 160–163, 268–271).

44. Dem. 22.25–29. Cf. Dem. 21.25–28.

45. Dem. 44.57–59; Hyp. 1, frag. 4b, col. 10; Hyp. 4.1–10; Isae. 11.13–14, 32–35.

46. Gagarin 1989, 17–29, discusses Euxitheos' procedural arguments in detail.

47. Ant. 5.10.

48. Because I am analyzing how litigants made arguments, I am not evaluating how correctly they were describing the character of the laws in general or as they applied in specific cases.

49. The law could be equated with democracy: e.g., Dem. 24.75–76. See, too, below on the meaning of the jurors' oath.

50. Dem. 20.93; 22.25–27; 57.30–32.

51. Dem. 22.31–32. Aeschines similarly interpreted the debarment by the law of those who had prostituted themselves, mistreated their parents, shirked military service, and squandered their inheritance as aimed not at the reform of morals, but the protection of the political life of the city (Aesch. 1.28–31). Cf. Dem. 21.45–46 on the meaning of hubris. My point here, of course, is not to say what the "real" purpose of this law was but to point out how the assumption of a democratically motivated lawgiver aided in making arguments about what the law meant.

52. Arist., *Ath. Pol.* 9.1.

53. Aesch. 1.11.

54. D. Cohen 1991, ch. 7.

55. Aeschines' interpretation is not objectively wrong, though we might call it bad history. Historians' interpretations of Athenian laws would be similarly bad, if presented to an Athenian court, since they would work against the sense of unity Athenians were constantly trying to see in their laws. Thomas, for example, objects to Aeschines' interpretive method: "Yet when Aeschines, in *Against Timarchus* I, expatiates on the wise intentions of the ancient lawgiver, he is effectively claiming the authority and proper legality of the written laws, but actually inserting the completely extralegal authority of Solon's personality in his speculations about Solon's intentions—and it is these intentions that bear much of the burden of Aeschines' argument" (Thomas 1996, 131–132). Any interpretation of a law, however, even a literal one, involves the intervention of interpretive protocols not specified by the law. Aeschines' interpretation gained its authority not by borrowing Solon's charisma but by situating his interpretation of one law in a field of other, consonant laws.

56. Aesch. 1.160; Dem. 19.7; 44.64; Hyp. 3.16; Isae. 11.12.

57. Lys. 10.30. On the other hand, interpreting the laws as a system, Diodoros (Dem. 22.57) claimed that in them and in the customs of the *politeia* are to be found "pity, pardon, everything fitting for free citizens."

58. Aristotle, *Rhet.* 1374b, says that it is equitable (ἐπιεικές) "to look not to the law but to the lawgiver and not to the language but to the intention (διάνοιαν) of the lawgiver." Although this seems like a reasonable claim for how the figure of the lawgiver might be used, it bears little relationship to the actual discussion in the courts where the lawgiver stood not for fairness as opposed to the strict law but for the real meaning of the law itself. This shows why it is dangerous to take Aristotle's statements as descriptive. Cf. Carey 1996.

59. Dem. 19.255, responding to the argument of Aesch. 1.25–26.

60. Arist., *Ath. Pol.* 5, 7.

61. Athenians, too, placed great emphasis on this oath not only because of its sacred character but because, since jurors were not subject to formal review for their conduct in their office (unlike all other office holders), it was sometimes said to be the only check on their judgments.

62. Dem. 24.149–151.

63. Despite admitted uncertainty, recent treatments of the oath present no arguments for their claims of what it may have said: Plescia (1970, 26–27), Harrison (1971, 48), MacDowell (1978, 44), and Todd (1993, 54–55) offer only cursory reviews. Bonner and Smith 1938, 152–156, give a good summary of the various earlier and more detailed attempts, especially German, to restore the "authentic" oath.

64. Bonner and Smith 1938, 155, italics added.

65. *SEG* XII.87. In fact the Thirty remained an important reference point throughout the fourth century: Diodoros said to a jury in 353 that the rule of the Thirty was the most terrible misfortune imaginable (Dem. 24.57; cf. 90). Isocrates, too, in 354, still thought it appropriate that he should disassociate himself from the Thirty (*Areop.* 62–70).

66. Fish 1984, 1327, argues that "a so-called 'disciplining rule' cannot be said to act as a constraint on interpretation because it is (in whatever form has been specified for it) the product of an interpretation."

67. Though my count may miss a few instances, it does give a general sense of what the oath could be thought to concern. In the many cases where the oath was linked with more than one theme, I counted each of them.

68. Aesch. 3.6–7. Andocides' direct quotation of the jurors' oath in 399 BC, however, strongly suggests that this was not the first clause at that time (1.91).

69. E. Harris 1994, 136.

70. E. Harris 1994, 138.

71. Meyer-Laurin 1965, 29.

72. Lys. 22.5. Todd 1993, 316–320, treats this speech and its obscurities. Carawan 1983 discusses the procedure of cross-examining the opposing litigant in Athenian courts.

73. Lys. 22.6–7; cf. §10.

74. Todd 1993, 318. The grain merchants' admission that they had bought up more than fifty measures shows that they believed the prosecutor's interpretation of the oath was contestable.

75. For a detailed explanation of the tables, see the Appendix.

76. Speakers in public cases had more time for their presentations than speakers in private ones, but this alone will not account for their more frequent references to the oath. Litigants in private cases apparently found other arguments more relevant. Although about the same proportion of defendants in both kinds of cases supplicated, wept, and cited their liturgies (as I note in subsequent chapters), the use of the oath was concentrated in public cases. Besides, time was not so tight that prosecutors in private cases could not spare even a few seconds to remind the jurors of their oath. (Most references to the oath, even in public cases, were brief.) This suggests that it was less a question of time as of appropriateness.

77. The *graphe nomon me epitedeion thenai* ("indictment of an inexpedient law"), used to indict laws, was closely related to the *graphe paranomon*, the procedure for decrees. In what follows, I treat them both together. Dem. 20 and 24 are the two preserved examples of the former procedure. Hansen 1974, 44–48, discusses the relationship.

78. Aesch. 3.6–7.

79. It is potentially misleading to refer to the citation of contradicted laws as "legal" arguments (as both E. Harris 1994 and Yunis 1988 do). They were claims of fact (that two texts were contradictory) not of law.

80. Dem. 20.118.

81. Demosthenes claimed that because jurors were sworn to vote in accord with the laws, the laws should be quoted in full and in context for their proper interpretation (Dem. 18.121). Even in this case, however, as in other *graphai paranomon*, the question of meaning concerned the decree whose legality was at stake, not the meaning of the law under which the case had been brought. In all the preserved speeches, there is no discussion of what it might mean for a decree to be drafted "against the laws."

82. Aesch. 3.31; Dem. 18.121; 22.43, 45; 23.101; 24.188. Of extant cases Hyp. 2 is the only one that did not do this.

83. The use of the plural "laws" instead of the singular certainly aided this broader interpretation of the meaning of the clause.

84. Dem. 19.1, 132, 239, 297; 21.177; 59.115.

85. Hansen 1974, 62. Of six other decrees in his catalogue, the content is unknown.

86. Hansen 1974, 63–65.

87. The only speaker in a private suit who linked the dikastic oath to the preservation of the democracy (Isoc. 18.34) did so because the procedure he was using (*paragraphe*) had just been instituted as a way of reinforcing the amnesty that was part of the restoration of the democracy in 403 after the reign of the Thirty.

88. Most of the fifth century is beyond the scope of this study, but it is striking how prominently the jury courts figured in Athens' controlling its empire. Ancient critics and modern scholars alike have noted the importance of the spread of Athenian jurisdiction throughout the empire as a means of control ([Xen.], *Ath. Pol.*; Meiggs 1972). On more than one occasion when the Athenians sealed an alliance with an oath, the jurors took the oath for the Athenians as a whole (*IG* I³ 40). I have avoided here the debate about where "sovereignty" lay in ancient Athens, not only because I agree with Ober that the concept itself is not entirely appropriate but also because the question implies an answer which is entirely too simple and therefore not informative enough. Cf. Shaw 1991, 194–214, esp. 201.

89. I am convinced by the arguments of Hansen 1985 that all boards of lawgivers were staffed by jurors in the fourth century. MacDowell 1975, argues, however, that the laws governing the duties and membership of boards of *nomothetai* changed significantly at least twice in the fourth century, but even by his account, as late as 370 a board of jurors was responsible for reviewing proposed laws; even after this date a similar board of jurors annually reviewed the laws.

90. Din. 3.16. Cf. Aesch. 1.7; Dem. 22.57; 24.36, 37; 25.6.

91. Dem. 58.61. Cf. Lys. 15.8.

92. Andoc. 1.31.

93. Arist., *Rhet.* 1375a. Cf. Todd 1993, 54.

94. Ruschenbusch 1957, and Sealey 1994, 51–58. Ruschenbusch uses the theory of gaps to explain the power of the Athenian juries, whereas Sealey uses it to develop a historical account of the development of Greek justice.

95. Sealey 1994, 51. Cf. Todd 1993, 58.

96. Isae. 2.47. Cf. Isae. 4.31; 8.46; 11.18.

97. The actual practice of litigants seems to have very little to do with Aristotle's advice to litigants (*Rhet.* 1375a–b) that when the law is against them, they should appeal to justice and use the oath to legitimate this claim. As I noted before, however plausible Aristotle's advice may seem, it corresponds more to questions debated by philosophers, sophists, and tragedians than to actual arguments made in the courts. (Aristotle quotes Sophocles here to show how to argue against the written law.) Carey 1996 makes this point at length.

98. Dover 1974, 306–309, shows that though litigants sometimes said things that might logically imply that the laws could be called unjust, they never explicitly made this claim. Cf. Christ 1998, ch. 6.

99. Hyp. 3.13, which was discussed in more detail earlier in this chapter.

100. Meyer-Laurin 1965; Meinecke 1971.

101. I understand this to mean that each juror should decide on the basis of *his own* most just judgment. Sealey 1994, 51, construes the phrase to mean that they should vote for the most just opinion offered to them by the two litigants. It does not seem to me that the choice affects my argument, though I favor the former because I might expect the comparative to be used instead of the superlative in the second case. Cf., e.g., Dem. 43.34: "Whichever of the parties will seem to speak more justly and more in accord with the laws, to him, clearly, you jurors will give your votes."

102. Dem. 20.118 and 39.40 added this limiting clause. Dem. 23.96 did not. Athenians did not necessarily construe this to mean that the jurors' most just judgment was appropriate only in the absence of laws. Euthykles' argument (Dem. 23.95–97) implies that the jurors' most just judgment applied in all cases. Other evidence hints at this: Aristotle, too (*Rhet.* 1375a–b), if in fact he was referring to Athens, could interpret the clause this way, despite being able also to read it more narrowly (*Rhet.* 1354a). In comparison, the deme oath paraphrased at Dem. 57.63 does not seem to have limited the application of the deme members' most just judgment to only those instances in which there were no laws.

103. It is not clear when the oath included such a clause. The speeches that mention this clause cluster in an eight-year period: 355, 353, and 347 respectively. A similar phrase is attested in a deme oath from 345 (Dem. 57.63). (Fränkel 1878, 457, merely assumes that this was the dikastic oath.) Since the explicit evidence for this clause comes from only an eight-year period, and since the oath was revised over the century, it is risky to assume this clause to be part of the "essential" oath throughout the period. Ruschenbusch 1957, 265, uses an inscription from Delphi to establish this clause at least as early as 380 BC, but this evidence from a different city has no bearing on the question. Insofar as this inscription may be applicable to Athens, however, it calls into question most reconstructions of the Athenian oath since it began: "I will judge cases with my most just opinion, those where there are written laws according to the laws, and those where there are no laws according to my opinion." In this oath, the juror's use of his most just opinion was applied to all cases and was thought entirely consonant with judging according to the laws.

104. Surely when Max Fränkel 1878, 454, calls this "a repeatedly quoted passage" he is teasing.

105. The full name in dispute was "Mantitheos son of Mantias of the deme of Thorikos."

106. Dem. 39.39.

107. Dem. 39.40: . . . εἰ μηδεὶς ἦν περὶ τούτων κείμενος νόμος, κἂν οὕτω δικαίως πρὸς ἐμοῦ τὴν ψῆφον ἔθεσθε.

108. Ruschenbusch 1957, 263–264; Sealey 1994, 52.

109. Whether the theory of gaps is a useful description of how Athenian law functioned does not depend, of course, on the actors it describes affirming it in their own words, but it is equally true that a hypothetical (if plausible) interpretation of the oath, one that finds no confirmation in the oath's actual use, is not strong evidence for how the Athenian courts functioned. In fact, Sealey seems to

change his argument half-way through. After claiming that the gaps in the laws were to be filled by the juror's discretion, he says that parties used "legal reasoning" (arguments, for example, by analogy with laws) to fill these gaps. They remained gaps, however, because, in the absence of a professional judiciary, such reasoning had no value as precedent, that is, it was not binding law on future cases (1994, 53–54). But this, it seems to me, is to essentially admit that the Athenians thought that the law, not the jurors' discretion, covered all cases.

110. Lyc. 1.8–9. No law covered the crime, Lycurgos claimed, because the lawgivers could not imagine anyone committing such a heinous offense. Cf. Lys. 31.27.

111. Todd 1993, 54.

112. Dem. 54.19.

113. Dem. 54.1, 24.

114. As I note in the next chapter, at least as far as Dem. 54 is concerned, this view can be pressed too far. In fact, there were substantive differences between assault and hubris, and the weakness of Ariston's case, not (or not only) his youth and moderation, influenced his choice of procedure.

115. Dem. 19.132.

116. Aesch. 3.6–7.

117. Stock 1990, 37.

118. Cf. Stock 1990, 23.

2. LAW AND NARRATIVE

1. Dem. 55.1–2, 31–35.

2. Millett 1991, 139–140, and Christ 1998, ch. 5, explore the sense of neighborliness on which the son of Teisias' narrative depends.

3. Although some facts were contested (e.g., the natural course of the arroyo), both speakers seem to have agreed on many of them (e.g., that Teisias had dammed off the road, that there had been a flood, that Kallikles had suffered some damage).

4. Davis 1987, 17–23.

5. Conley and O'Barr 1990, 172; more generally pp. 12–19. Cf. Scheppele 1990, 65.

6. Conley and O'Barr 1990, 172.

7. Merry 1990, ch. 5.

8. The one party who might fit this role is the professional speechwriters, who wrote most of the speeches preserved for us. Dover 1968 has claimed that the clients made substantial contributions to the orations. Usher 1976, however, argues (persuasively, I think) that they must be considered almost entirely the product of the speechwriter. Despite this, and despite arguments that these speechwriters' acquaintance with rhetorical theory influenced their craft (Mirhady 1996, 130–131), the substantial divergences between the preserved rhetorical handbooks and the actual practice of litigants (Carey 1996) suggests that theory affected practice only indirectly and in limited ways.

9. E.g., Dem. 54, discussed just below.

10. To a certain degree, any prosecutor was externally constrained to include these elements. The officials who accepted cases exercised some minimal discretion to make sure they fit the law's requirements (e.g., Lys. 13.86). More importantly, however, the prosecutor's decision to litigate was simultaneously the decision to tell a legal story. If he did not choose to tell such a story, he did not have to initiate a case.

11. I have enclosed "crime" in quotation marks because I mean it much more broadly than our notion, which includes only violations of criminal (not civil) law. I have used it to denote any act that could lead to litigation, including acts (like breaking a contract) for which we would allow civil remedies. Athenian law did not make the same distinction we do between criminal and civil law. As I pointed out in Chapter 1, prosecutors almost invariably based their claim on law.

12. There was at Athens, however, one kind of private case, the *diadikasia,* which merely adjudicated competing claims and therefore did not require any allegation that a law had been violated. This procedure, which was used especially in evaluating rival inheritance claims, did not have prosecutors or defendants but claimants (Todd 1993, 119–121). Interestingly, though, speakers in such claims often relied on the same discourses about the law as in other cases.

13. E.g. Aesch. 1.3; Ant. 1.2; Dem. 19.221–224; Lys. 32.1.

14. Dem. 44.1.

15. Cf. Chapter 1.

16. D. Cohen 1995.

17. Dem. 54.3–6.

18. Other prosecutors' speeches reveal a tension between the requirements of a legal narrative and the speaker's nonlegal understanding of the conflict: e.g., Dem. 53.

19. My retelling of Chrysippos' story streamlines it by omitting many details not relevant to my point.

20. It is almost certain that Phormio did not attempt to defraud anyone by doing this (Isager and Hansen 1975, 161–162). Chrysippos' accusation, however, conforms to his picture that Phormio alone wronged him.

21. Isager and Hansen 1975, 156–169.

22. Chrysippos twice referred to Lampis as a slave (§§5, 10). If he was, his ability to act as a potential litigant or witness in this dispute must have depended on what some scholars believe were special rules for commercial cases that suspended the usual legal incapacity of slaves (E. Cohen 1992, 96–98). Todd 1993, 192–193, however, leaves open the possibility that Lampis was no longer a slave (he adduces other instances of former slaves whom litigants still referred to as slaves) so that his legal capacity depended on his free status. Indeed, Chrysippos remarked that Lampis lent money for shipping (§6), engaged in the grain trade himself (§36), and had a wife and children in Athens (§37), all of which sound more like the actions of a free man than a slave. Chrysippos, in fact, creates the uncertainty over Lampis' status because, as Seager (1966, 181 n. 82) remarks, he wanted both "to call him a slave and to criticise him as an independent agent." Whatever Lampis' status and the legal rules governing it, however, Lampis was an equal party in a three-way dispute.

23. Isager and Hansen 1975, 168.

24. Similarly, Ariston's prosecution of Konon (Dem. 54) radically simplified this dispute by dichotomizing it as a case between prosecutor and defendant, though his narrative contains indications of a much broader conflict. Ariston was beaten not only by Konon but by his sons and by the son of Andromenes (§8), though he charged only Konon. The earlier troubles on the frontier while in the army did not involve Konon but only his sons, yet Ariston seems to have considered these incidents integrally related to the assault. Finally, though Ariston alluded to his brothers explicitly only once (§14), he anticipated that Konon would consider them as prime parties to the dispute. His own use of the first person plural, especially in his description of the incidents in the army (§§3–6) and in his concluding remarks (§44), may well indicate that he, too, recognized them as part of the conflict.

25. "Polis": 6.8 times per 1,000 words in public prosecution speeches, 2.2 times per 1,000 words in all other kinds of speeches. "You" (plural): 14.5 times per 1,000 words in public prosecution speeches, 7.9 times per 1,000 words in all other kinds of speeches.

26. In speeches to the Assembly, second-person plural verbs were used 13.7 times per 1,000 words (variance = 28.5), about the same as public prosecution speeches.

27. Use of first-person singular pronouns: 5.9 times per 1,000 words in public prosecution speeches, 17.2 times per 1,000 words in all other kinds of speeches. Dem. 21 and 53, however, are exceptional in the degree to which they emphasize the prosecutor as the victim. Chapter 4 further considers the anomalies of Dem. 21.

28. The frequency of first-person pronouns in public prosecution speeches, 5.9 per 1,000 words, is about the same as the frequency in Demosthenes' Assembly speeches, 5.4 per 1,000 words.

29. Osborne 1985. Some prosecutors did admit that their private interests were at stake as well as the public good: Dem. 22.1–3; 24.6–10; 58.1–4, 58–60; 59.1–9; Lys. 12.2; 13.1–2; 14.1–3.

30. With the exception of certain kinds of mercantile cases (e.g., Dem. 34, referred to above), only adult male citizens could prosecute cases. Although noncitizens could be defendants, this seems not to have frequently happened. In the preserved speeches, there are only two female defendants (Ant. 1 and Dem. 59). Todd 1993, 187, argues that slaves could not be sued.

31. Although Euphiletos was a defendant in this case, his rhetorical strategy was to represent himself as though he were prosecuting Eratosthenes for seduction. As I note below, one counternarrative used by defendants was to tell a legal story in which the prosecutor was the criminal.

32. Lys. 1.16.

33. Lys. 1.27.

34. D. Cohen 1990.

35. D. Cohen 1990, 164.

36. Lys. 1.12.

37. Johnstone 1998.

38. Bennet and Feldman 1981, 94–95, 98–107, analyze defense narrative strategies in American criminal trials. Antinarrative closely corresponds to their challenge strategy; the two varieties of counternarratives roughly match their redefinition and reconstruction strategies.

39. We cannot be sure that the defendant has accurately represented or fully responded to his accuser's speech. Even so, however, he put forth an antinarrative that attempted to persuade the jurors that the prosecutor's case was incoherent and without foundation.

40. Though Bennet and Feldman 1981, 94, construe the requirement of proof beyond a reasonable doubt as a constraint on the prosecutor, it seems to have operated as much as permission for defenses to mount antinarratives alone. The absence of this stipulation in Athenian law and the need for the defendant to persuade a majority of the jurors seems to have made Athenian defendants more likely to present counternarratives than defendants in American criminal trials.

41. Ant. 5.64–66. Gagarin 1989, 99–102, considers this passage.

42. Ferguson 1996, 85; Dershowitz 1996; Nerhot 1990; Jackson 1990; Bennet and Feldman 1981, 33, 65, and 83–84.

43. Carey 1989, 87.

44. Lys. 3.21–26.

45. Also Lys. 4 and Dem. 47. As I noted above, Euphiletos' defense on a charge of murder (Lys. 1) represented Eratosthenes' death as his own responsibility because he had broken the law. Cf. Andoc. 1.110–116.

46. Dem. 36.3, 12, 54, 60; Hyp. 1.1–2; Isoc. 16.1–2; Lys. 7.39; 25.1–3. Christ 1998, ch. 3, presents a complex discussion of sykophancy.

47. Ant. 6.33–50; Dem. 18.12–16; 55.1–2, 31–34; 57.6–8, 63–65; Hyp. 4.18; Lys. 7.39. Cf. Dem. 22.42; 58.22–23.

48. Lys. 9.13–18.

49. Prosecutors anticipated such stories, either claiming that there was no hostility between themselves and the defendant or, more often, coopting such a narrative and claiming that such animosity, in addition to the illegal act of the defendant, justified the prosecution. The need for a narrative to set against the story of the "crime" motivated defendants to tell stories about enmity, whereas prosecutors, who relied on a legal narrative, discussed their hostility to the defendant more to supplement their own and to vitiate the defendant's story. The adversarial context may well have prompted prosecutors, anticipating defendants' counternarratives that explained the trial as the outcome purely of private enmity (not of a crime), to introduce accounts of enmity that supplemented and supported their judicial narratives.

50. The first name suggests fertility rituals and unrestrained sexuality, the second, the moral license of mock poverty (Carey and Reid 1985, 86–87). Ariston intends both to shock.

51. Dem. 54.13–14.

52. The defendant in Lys. 3, on a charge of attempted murder, not only blamed Simon for the attack but also suggested that litigation was an inappropriate response to a brawl in a lovers' quarrel (Lys. 3.40–43). Ariston's insistence on the multifold illegality of Konon's actions (the question I addressed in Chap-

ter 1) also anticipates that Konon, even if he denied the facts, would object to understanding the incident in the context of the laws.

53. Ant. 6.35–36, 49–50; Lys. 9.13–14; Dem. 57.63.

54. Eligibility for citizenship was determined in the local neighborhood (deme) both for routine scrutinies of those coming of age (18) and for extraordinary reviews of the citizenship roles (as gave rise to this case). This Euxitheos was not the same man charged with the murder of Herodes, discussed earlier in this chapter.

55. Dem. 57.59.

56. Dem. 18.201–204, 213–214; 22.42–43.

57. Dem. 58.22–23. Cf. §36.

58. Aesch. 1.166–170. He referred to Demosthenes' political arguments as τὰς ἔξωθεν τοῦ πράγματος ἀπολογίας.

59. Chapter 1 treats the dikastic oath in considerable detail, especially in its relationship to the law.

60. Aesch. 1.154; Dem. 23.19; 44.14; 45.50. Cf. Dem. 18.2; 29.13. Only Apollodoros (Dem. 45.50) explicitly claimed that the oath required the jurors to vote only on the prosecutor's charge.

61. Aesch. 1.154.

62. Aesch. 1.170; Dem. 22.20, 43, 45–46; 23.194; 36.61; 58.36; Lyc. 1.13; Lys. 22.7. In one case as prosecutor, however, Demosthenes used the oath to strengthen an argument that was, from a legal perspective, irrelevant (Dem. 19.284).

63. Dem. 58.36.

64. Aesch. 3.6–7, 196–198, 257; Dem. 19.239; 21.4, 188, 208–212; Din. 1.17.

65. Dem. 21.188; 45.88.

66. Aesch. 3.233; Dem. 19.1, 239; 21.208–212; Din. 1.14; 3.17; Isoc. 18.34; Lys. 14.22, 40; 15.8–11. Although it is an argument from silence, I doubt that the dikastic oath explicitly negated *charis,* because no prosecutor ever made that claim. It is true that the deme oath quoted at Dem. 57.63 explicitly required the deme members to vote without *charis,* but the institutional differences make this inapplicable to the courts of the whole polis. At the deme level, most voters would have known the people they were voting on so that *charis,* in the traditional sense of an obligation within a personal relationship, could well have been a factor. At the polis level, however, the size of the citizen body and the randomizing procedures in allocating jurors to courts meant that no more than a few jurors, if any, would have had a personal relationship with any litigant. In unequivocally overriding *charis* and hatred, the deme oath was concerned with personal motives that were much less important at the polis level. (Chapter 4 considers the important differences between personal *charis* and the collective *charis* litigants sought to invoke.)

67. Lys. 14.40.

68. Aesch. 2.1; Dem. 18.2, 6–7; Hyp. 1, frag. 1, col. 41; Dem. 29.4. Cf. Isoc. 15.21–22.

69. Andoc. 1.9; Dem. 18.2, 6–7; Lys. 19.11.

70. Lys. 19.11.
71. Dem. 27.3; 34.1; 58.3; Isae. 8.5.
72. Andoc. 1.6; Dem. 18.7; 21.7; 57.1; Lys. 19.3; cf. Isoc. 15.21–22.
73. Lys. 19.3. Note the defendant's counternarrative about the prosecutor's motives.
74. Cf. Carey 1996, 44–45.
75. E.g., Dem. 47.19–25 (the speaker was a prosecutor in this false-witness suit but had lost as defendant in a previous suit); Lys. 3.5–20.
76. Lys. 1.26–27. Cf. [Arist.], *Rhet. ad Alex.* 1444b.
77. Lys. 1.34–35.
78. Dem. 25.17.
79. Along with Isae. 6, some of the most outstanding examples of this strategy of representation include Aesch. 1; Dem. 34.36–37; 39.39–41; 40.45–49; 43.68–72; Hyp. 3.28–36; Isoc. 18.51–57.
80. Dem. 48.52–54.
81. Dem. 48.55.
82. Kallistratos' statement that this did not constitute slander (διαβολή) because it was true conforms to the commonly used meaning of διαβολή in the orators.
83. Dem. 48.56.
84. Dem. 46.14; Rhodes 1981b, 443–444.
85. His use of the lawgiver Solon to argue for this interpretation conforms to the common practice of Athenian litigants of interpreting a law by the lawgiver's intentions.
86. Kennedy 1963, 30–32, discusses arguments from probability.
87. Dem. 21.114–115; 46.24–25; Isae. 3.63–71; 12.4; Lys. 7.17.
88. Isae. 11.20–26.
89. Isae. 11.24–25. (I have followed W. Thompson 1976, 36, in omitting ἄν in this last sentence.)
90. Wyse 1904, 675–676; W. Thompson 1976, 33–37.
91. "It is the fragmentation and contending multiplicities of narrative, regulated by special rules of narrative form and shaping, that mark the central distinctiveness of narratives at trial . . ." (Gewirtz 1996a, 8).
92. Merry 1990; Gewirtz 1996b; Bourdieu 1987, 834.
93. I treat this more fully in Johnstone 1998.
94. This episode (Dem. 59.30–40, 45–48) was recounted in a suit almost thirty years later against Neaira on a charge of passing herself off as married to a citizen (Stephanos). This case, in which Neaira was the defendant, is discussed in Chapter 3. Apollodoros, the prosecutor in the later case, claimed the suit was an attempt to get back at Stephanos for verdicts Stephanos had previously won against him (§1). Of course Neaira, who risked being returned to slavery if she lost, may well have understood the case differently. The episode was only marginally relevant to the legal charge and seems to have been included (full of slanderous details I have omitted) to prejudice the jury against Neaira.

3. DARE, OR TRUTH

1. Apollodoros' speech in this trial is our source of information for the dispute between Phrynion and Neaira some two decades earlier (recounted in Chapter 2).

2. The dispute between Apollodoros and Stephanos had a history that was both personal and political. As Theomnestos told it when he opened the prosecution, Stephanos had previously prosecuted and convicted Apollodoros in a *graphe paranomon* (and attempted to ruin him with a monstrous fine of fifteen talents, which, however, the jury did not accept) and had also tried, but failed, to secure his conviction for murder. The decree that Apollodoros had proposed and that Stephanos indicted as illegal had attempted to divert Athenian funds to the military to pursue a more aggressive policy against Philip of Macedon. That trial had posed Apollodoros and Stephanos against each other as representatives of different policies and of different factions of politicians. As I noted in Chapter 2, however, from the perspective of Neaira, who risked being sold into slavery if she lost her case, the dispute behind the present case probably looked very different. For all parties, the legal case imposed a particular shape on the conflict.

3. Dem. 59.120.

4. The document seems to be genuine: Trevett 1992, 190–191; Carey 1992, 149–150.

5. Dem. 59.124 (Carey 1992 trans., revised).

6. Dem. 59.125.

7. Headlam 1893 and 1894 and Mirhady 1991b and 1996 argue the former position; Soubie 1973, Thür 1977, Todd 1990b, and Gagarin 1996, the latter.

8. Athenians often conflated these two phases of the process, speaking indiscriminately of the dare and the dared procedure (Gagarin 1996, 13). Yet it is important for us to distinguish them analytically to understand how the Athenians' fusion of the phases allowed disputants to use dares to conduct their quarrels and allowed litigants to reinterpret the functioning of dares before the jurors.

9. Gagarin 1996, 2–3. Citizens also unilaterally tortured (or threatened to torture) their slaves, either as punishment or to extract information (e.g., Ant. 5.30; 6.23; Lys. 1.18–19).

10. The sources occasionally show other forms of dares, but these were rare compared to these three primary kinds. Contrary to scholarly opinion, Athenians do not seem to have used challenges to compel the production either of witnesses or, for the most part, of documents. Though on a couple occasions speakers represented a challenge to refer to a sealed document as an attempt to bring its contents before the jury (Dem. 36.4, 7 [cf. Dem. 45]; 48.48; 49.43–44), this, too, may be a retrospective effect of litigation, not an entirely accurate description of the original use of the dare. Rather, it is possible that such a dare was not, in the first place, a means of opening the document but of inventing a different secondary contingency for the dare. Instead of deciding the case by an arbitrator or an oath, they agreed to let it rest on the wording of an absent document (as at Dem. 32.18). We know of no documents introduced as evidence before the courts that were furnished through dares. Finally, it is not clear how important such a

procedure could have been, even if it was occasionally used, given the low value attached to documents in the Athenian courts.

Isager and Hansen 1975, 114, following Lipsius 1905–1915, 885, suggest there were dares "to produce witnesses whom the challenger cannot himself produce." Nothing, however, prevented the speaker of Ant. 6.23, the evidence for their claim, from interrogating these witnesses himself; indeed, some of them probably testified for him at §15. In fact there seems to have been no real way to make a witness appear, as Todd 1990b, 24–25, argues.

11. Scafuro 1997, ch. 3, offers a detailed account of forms of arbitration at Athens. Hunter 1994, 55–67, gives a briefer description. I have followed Scafuro in calling the mandatory form of arbitration "official arbitration" instead of the usual "public arbitration," which risks confusion with private and public suits. (In fact, official arbitration was used only in private suits.)

12. Dem. 42.19 is one of the unusual cases where the offer of a straight settlement was called a dare. Though one could certainly demand that someone do something they were required to, there does not seem to me to be a class of dares to fulfill or accept fulfillment of an obligation, despite what Harrison 1971, 153, says. In most of his examples (153, nn. 2 and 3), the demand to do something was coupled with a dare to perform a customary procedure: Isoc. 17.51 and Lys., frag. 16 Th. were challenges to arbitration. Nikobulos seems to call the offer at Dem. 37.12 a dare because he was offered a choice of actions. Dem. 56.40 describes a dare to produce a ship (as a contract required), but Carey and Reid 1985, 219 and 229, take this as part of the arbitration dare at §17. (In Dareios' narrative [§§11–18], only the offer of arbitration was called a dare; the straightforward offers of settlement were not.) Apollodoros called his settlement offer at Dem. 50.31 a dare because it included an oath challenge to settle disputed expenses. Dem. 48.50 (which Harrison must mean for 48.34, a dare too cryptic to be classified at all) does seem to be a straightforward demand to do something with no secondary contingency.

13. Although dares took the form of an offer of settlement, this does not mean (as Mirhady 1996, 122, argues) that they were "all *meant* to lead to resolution" (my emphasis). As I point out, in some cases the formal offer of a settlement (through its specific terms) was nothing less than incendiary. Completed dares settled legal claims but not necessarily disputes. Dares gave a specific definition to the dispute. Usually they defined it as a legal claim, though (as I noted in the Introduction), a legal case does not necessarily correspond to a dispute. Thus, though a dare may have taken the form of an offer to settle a legal case, it may or may not have pacified the dispute behind it.

14. Dem. 27.50; 29.38; 29.50–53, 57; 30.1; 37.40–41; 47.5, 7, 9; 48.4; 49.65; Isoc. 17.55; Lys. 7.34–37; Lys., frag. *Against Archebiades* (D. Hal., *Isae.* 10). Cf. Aesch. 2.126–128; Ant. 2.4.8; Dem. 31.9.

15. Dem. 30.1. Cf. Dem. 48.4; Lys., frag. *Against Archebiades*.

16. Headlam 1893 and 1894; Mirhady 1991b and 1996; and Hunter 1994, 93.

17. Dem. 29.2; 40.43; 52.14, 30; 55.9, 35; 56.17; Lys., frag. *Against Archebiades* (D. Hal., *Isae.* 10). Dem. 48.4 may well also refer to a dare to arbitration (see §§2 and 40) as may Isoc. 17.16–17.

18. Arbitration was frequently the result of negotiations between the parties or the mediation of others, but, as I show below, the issuance and exchange of dares was simply another way for parties to negotiate.

19. Scholars may have been reluctant to link arbitration with torture and the swearing of oaths because they believe that these were irrational, primitive ways to settle a disagreement, unlike arbitration, which they usually assume to be reasonable. Understanding challenges to oaths and torture in terms of "primitive ordeals" (e.g., Plescia 1970), however, is misleading and probably misunderstands how such ordeals worked in other societies. Brown 1982 shows how much can be learned by asking (as he does about ordeals) how something functioned in society. Rosen's account of the use of decisory oaths by the *qadi* (judge) in Moroccan justice likewise shows how much can be gained by understanding such practices in their cultural contexts (Rosen 1989, 31–37).

20. Dem. 29.53–54; 30.2; 31.9; 33.13–15; 49.42, 65; 50.31; 52.15, 17; 54.40–41; 55.35; 59.60. Mirhady 1991b treats oath challenges in detail. We know of two occasions when disputants dared a public body to allow them to swear an oath (Lys. 19.32, to the Revenue Commissioners, and Isae. 12.9, to the representatives of the deme), and one when a corporate group issued the dare (Dem. 59.60, the *gens*). Aristotle's discussion of dares to oaths (*Rhet.* 1377a–b) seems to concern only oaths the two disputants offered each other: self-judgment, in other words.

21. Cf. Isoc. 17.15; cf. Miller 1990, 284–289. Unlike the Icelandic process of self-judgment Miller documents, where one party granted to the other the right (essentially) to arbitrate the dispute at their discretion, at Athens the terms of the settlement were usually set by the dare ahead of time.

22. Dem. 29.38; 29.51–53; 37.40–41; 47.5, 7, 9; Isoc. 17.55; Lys. 7.34–37. Cf. Ant. 2.4.8; Aesch. 2.126–128.

23. It is unclear how often a dare would have specified formal release or discharge, though several did (Dem. 29.39; 47.5, 7, 9; 49.65; Isager and Hansen 1975, 228–237, discuss these two procedures). Most accounts of dares do not mention this specific provision. Apollodoros' challenge (quoted above) did not use this specific language, though his potential renunciation of his prosecution (ἀφίστασθαι τοῦ ἀγῶνος) uses the same language as other instances where a party renounced (or said they would renounce) their legal rights to claim something: Andoc. 1.122; Dem. 32.18; 59.53; Isae. 2.31; 4.24; 5.2. Dem. 32.18 uses the verb exactly parallel to Dem. 59.124: the renunciation of the legal claim as the outcome of a dare. It may be that in many cases, a formal release or discharge had been envisioned even though not explicitly mentioned. It may also be that in some instances the settlement was made without a legally binding declaration. In a litigious society like Athens, failure to secure this might seem foolhardy, but it is possible to imagine reasons it might not be included (if, for example, a settlement aimed to rebuild relations of trust). Whether a settlement included such a formal declaration, though, was an issue to be negotiated between the parties. Moreover, the absence of such a declaration would not prevent a party from arguing before a jury that the quarrel had already been settled; it would only prevent them from filing a *paragraphe* to this effect (a countersuit alleging illegal prosecution).

24. Dem. 39.3–5; 40.8–12. Though the two versions are basically the same, they differ in some details.

25. Mantitheos' narrative was, of course, a highly self-interested one. Carey and Reid 1985, 160–166, offer a plausible and persuasive reconstruction of the events behind it.

26. Although Boiotos and Plangon took care to ensure their opponent would follow through on the terms of the agreement, especially by having the thirty minae left with a third party, Mantias, naively, did not.

27. Gagarin 1996, 13. At Isae. 8.45, proof "from torture" (ἐκ βασάνων) must mean "from a dare to torture," since the dare was refused, so that the dare stands for the dared procedure.

28. Gernet 1955, 110–111, argues that before an arbitrator, the refusal to swear an oath offered by one's opponent automatically lost the suit. The three passages he cites as evidence do not support this: (1) Dem. 59.60 does not say that the refusal to take the oath was grounds for the arbitrator ruling against Phrastor, nor even that he did rule against him. (2) Dem. 52.15–16 shows that refusing to take an offered oath of self-judgment could be strong grounds for expecting an arbitrator to rule against one, but it does not prove that the arbitrator would have inevitably ("infailliblement") ruled on the basis of this (cf. Todd 1990b, 35 n. 29). (3) When Mantitheos said that "my father was compelled to abide by the arbitration because of his own dare" (Dem. 40.11), this does not mean that the dare bound the arbitrator but that the (apparently) official arbitration was binding on Mantias because this had been a condition of the dare. This episode shows (as I argue further in the text) that accepted and completed dares bound the disputants.

29. Todd 1990b, 35. In Athenian trials, however, no evidence was decisive (that is, beyond interpretation, argumentation, or refutation). There was a procedure, *diamartyria,* in which the assertion of a witness was decisive, but this was used to block litigation, so no trial resulted. (In the fourth century this was used largely by direct heirs to suspend litigation over inheritances. The *paragraphe* procedure, commonly used to block illegal prosecutions in noninheritance cases, resulted in a trial in which the jury weighed the evidence.) I agree, therefore, with Gagarin 1990, 27–29, and 1996, 6, that dared procedures could not have produced evidence that the courts treated as decisive. Nevertheless, litigants did speak as though dared procedures would have produced decisive evidence. The key to the contradiction is the way that the secondary contingency, which formalized the end of the conflict, masked the decisiveness of the primary contingency, the acceptance of the conditions of the dare by both parties. As I argue below, the particular demands of persuading a mass audience caused litigants to reuse and reinterpret dares in ways quite different from the ways they functioned in disputes.

30. There are two instances where the word "dare" is used of offers that may not have had a secondary contingency: At Isoc. 17.51–52, a challenge to an arbitration had earlier (§§ 19–20) been represented as an offer of a straight settlement. At Dem. 37.12–13, the speaker was dared to take a settlement but was still given a choice of two ways to do this. Even considering these marginal cases, it is clear that dares almost always had a secondary contingency.

31. Thür 1977 is the standard work on torture. Hunter 1994, 91–95, offers a brief overview in English.

32. Isae. 5.32.

33. Dem. 33.15; 37.42.

34. Dem. 33.13; 39.3; 40.10.

35. Isae. 5.32.

36. Apollodoros said that depositions about dares were commonly written on wax, not on whitened boards prepared ahead of time, because terms were usually added and subtracted from the dare (Dem. 46.11).

37. Dem. 59.124.

38. Speakers do not seem to have been eager to discuss dares issued by their opponents that they themselves declined, and so the incidence of their exchange was probably greater than what the evidence shows. I count 29 speakers who talked about their own dares (sometimes more than one), whereas only 11 of them revealed that their opponents had made a challenge. I see no reason to believe that the speakers of preserved speeches were more likely than their opponents to issue dares.

39. Lys. 4.15; Dem. 29.38.

40. Dem. 37.40–43; Isoc. 17.15.

41. Dem. 40.39–44.

42. Dem. 49.42–43, 65.

43. Ant. 1.11.

44. Dem. 46.11.

45. Todd 1990b, 35–36.

46. A legal conviction would have also levied a 1,000-drachma fine against Stephanos (§16). Had the prosecutor (who in this case was not technically Apollodoros but his brother-in-law Theomnestos) failed to get one-fifth of the votes, he would have himself been fined 1,000 drachmas and possibly lost the right to bring a similar case in the future. Carey 1992, 147–151, also suggests that conviction would have deprived only Phano of her citizen rights, whereas the dare specified the male children (whose children is of course the question) as well.

47. At least Demo, in his dare to Zenothemis, had offered to pay a penalty if he lost the dare (Dem. 32.18).

48. Dem. 46.21. There are no obvious signs whether the deposition that specifies that Apollodoros wanted to know whether Phormio had seduced his mother is genuine or not. The scurrilous dare is consistent, however, with Apollodoros' contemporary prosecution of his stepfather for hubris (Dem. 45.4), one of the most scandalous accusations he could have made. In fact, the challenge seems likely to have been part of the preparation for that legal case (which was compromised through the mediation of Archippe). Trevett 1992, 10–11, discusses the incompatibility of this account with Phormio's (Dem. 36).

49. So Nikobulos reported that when his opponents offered him a dare, assuming he would decline it, he accepted it on the spur of the moment, unexpectedly leading toward a settlement (Dem. 37.12–16). The ways dares functioned can be reduced neither to the intentions of a single agent nor to the form they took.

50. To the extent that arbitrators did this, insofar as they attempted primarily to restore amicable relationships and not to decide who was right, their decisions moved towards being as "irrational," that is, unconcerned with "justice" and what "truly" happened, as an outcome determined, for example, by torture.

51. Isae. 2.29–33.

52. Dem. 36.15.

53. Dem. 29.13; Lys. 4.15. Dares on marginal issues may also have been ways of escalating conflict, as I suggested with Apollodoros' dare concerning Phormio's alleged seduction of Apollodoros' mother. Cf. Ant. 1.9.

54. Torture, writes MacDowell 1978, 246, "is not even an effective way of discovering facts, since it induces the witness to say what the torturer desires rather than what is actually the truth." Arbitration, too, as I noted above, did not necessarily produce an outcome that was linked to the truth or justice of the respective claims.

55. Ant. 5.32; Dem. 37.41; 53.22–23. Aristotle's rhetorical handbook (*Rhet.* 1376b–1377a) catalogued the arguments on both sides.

56. Todd 1990b, 35–36, ties the irrationality of a dare with his view that dares were ways of producing decisive evidence but which, because of their arbitrariness, no one would formulate so as to be accepted. "The reason . . . why the challenge is always formulated so as to be rejected is that litigants are afraid of being stuck with whatever evidence comes up" (36). (Hunter 1994, 90, concurs.) Yet it was precisely this arbitrariness that encouraged people to offer and to accept dares.

57. Dem. 37.41. Though Nikobulos agreed to the challenge, at the time of the actual torture he reneged because his opponent had (so he claimed) changed the conditions.

58. Dem. 53.22–25.

59. Dem. 53.2.

60. The exact implications of his response are unclear. Headlam 1893, 3–4, and Mirhady 1996, 126, suggest that Apollodoros wanted to substitute unlimited (ἐβασάνιζον ἂν μέχρι οὗ αὐτοῖς ἐδόκει) inquisitional torture by the state for the proposed usual restricted torture as the result of a dare.

61. He did not call it a πρόκλησις, but in saying he "was ready" (ἕτοιμός εἰμι) to go to the Council, he used language sometimes used of dares (Thür 1977, 61–62).

62. Dem. 53.25. Gagarin 1996, 6, takes this to mean that the *basanos* would not have settled the case. Set next to the following clause, Apollodoros seems to mean that his opponents would argue about the exact conditions of the dare when it came time to torture the slaves (the same problem is reported at Dem. 37.42), as opposed to the situation in which public officials tortured them at their own discretion. Given Apollodoros' repeated demands for a public triumph, he also seems to have worried that they would deny his victory.

63. Dem. 33.13; 49.55–58; 29.51–53.

64. Dem. 56.14–17.

65. Langbein 1977.

66. Isoc. 17.19 and 18.10, 14 both show cases of arbitration "on stated terms," an agreement to submit a dispute to arbitrators that stipulated how they

should decide. Though neither of these arbitrations were the outcome of a dare, they show that Athenians had a ready way to treat arbitration as a purely formal process. With Mantias' dare to Plangon to swear an oath (Dem. 39.3; 40.10), the outcome was supposed to be determined ahead of time, even though the formality of the secondary contingency was maintained.

67. Dem. 29.58–60; 33.12–19; 40.44.

68. Dem. 37.42–43; Isoc. 17.15. Such cases show why guarantees might be required to ensure fulfillment of the accepted challenge.

69. This is not to claim that parties never reverted to hostility after a settlement through a dare but that, since the process of settlement through dares was not imposed but rather negotiated and accepted by the parties themselves, they were more likely to abide by it.

70. Ant. 6.25–26.

71. Ant. 6.27. Cf. Ant. 5.38; Dem. 49.58; Isoc. 17.53; Lys. 4.12; 7.36.

72. As did Apollodoros in the opening citation of this chapter.

73. duBois 1991, chs. 3, 5, and 6.

74. Athenians did torture (or threatened to torture) their slaves, sometimes to discover information, but this was largely informal: Ant. 5.29; Dem. 40.15; 48.16; Lys. 1.18.

75. Lipsius 1905–1915, MacDowell 1978, and Harrison 1971 treat challenges in their chapters on evidence. Cf. Soubie 1973. Even Mirhady 1991b, who sees oath challenges as forms of dispute settlement, not evidence gathering, still treats women's oaths as ways of introducing evidence to the court.

76. Todd 1990b.

77. Todd 1990b, 32–33.

78. Apollodoros described them this way: "I think you all know that dares were invented for those transactions that cannot be brought before you. For example, it's not possible to conduct torture in front of you; there must necessarily be a dare for this. Or, if something has been done or has happened somewhere out of the country, there must be a dare for this too, to go either by land or by sea to where the thing happened, and so on for similar sorts of events" (Dem. 45.15–16).

79. In fact, Aristotle's account of dares to take oaths in the *Rhetoric* (1377a–b) reflects this: It is not about how to make an argument from the information a fulfilled dare would introduce but how to make arguments about dares that have been refused (Mirhady 1991a, 22).

80. Todd 1990b, 36: "The reason in the consent-procedures why the challenge is always formulated so as to be rejected is that litigants are afraid of being stuck with whatever evidence comes up." This is in agreement with Thür 1977.

81. Gagarin 1996. Gagarin sets out to explain the paradox that torture was highly praised but rarely if ever used. Yet in denying that it produced truth, Gagarin effectively distorts the ancient praise, which was precisely that it did reveal truth. In other words, this theory transforms the paradox: Torture was praised for being truthful even though it had nothing to do with truth.

82. This account of the use of dares before trial is unconvincing. Gagarin argues that disputants made dares to torture mostly on trivial points they knew were

true so that the opposition would not accept them, knowing they would lose. If they did accept, he argues, the challenger could just rescind his dare. But by this reasoning, there do not seem to be any more serious consequences for the opponent to accepting a dare and having the slave speak against him (since challenges were on trivial points) than to declining it. If the opponent accepted it, there would still be the possibility that the slave would support him and if the man who made the dare backed out, this could be used against him in court. In this theory, then, there are no reasons not to accept a dare (indeed, there are strong reasons to do so), and yet there is no evidence of this happening.

83. Gagarin 1996, 13.

84. Gagarin 1996, 14.

85. E.g., Dem. 41.21–24 (the prosecutor claims his opponent's wife acknowledged her mother's seal on some documents); Dem. 47.53–59 (the prosecutor's narrative of what happened at his home was, by his own account, witnessed by only his wife, children, and some slaves); Dem. 55. 24–25; Lys. 1.11–12, 19–20 (Euphiletos recounts his wife's infidelities with Eratosthenes as he learned them from her serving girl); Lys. 32.12–18 (the speaker reports, in direct quotation, a lengthy speech by a woman).

86. Detienne 1996 and, following him, Loraux 1986 give accounts of the history of the distinction of these concepts.

87. Dem. 41.20.

88. *Logos* was not, of course, always opposed to the truth. Lloyd 1990, 46, argues that when opposed to *muthos, logos* was associated with truth.

89. Ant. 5.3, 84 (= Ant. 6.47); Dem. 26.21; 55.6, 14; Isae. 2.38; Isoc. 16.48; 18.65; Lyc. 1.29; Lys. 7.30, 43; 12.33; 19.61; 25.13.

90. Din. 2.5; Dem. 19.216–217; 58.25–26, 41, 61.

91. Ant. 5.3; 6.18; Dem. 29.1, 5, 54; 30.3; 40.20–21.

92. Dem. 31.13.

93. Dem. 19.216.

94. Aesch. 3.168. Chapter 4 treats this subject in much more detail.

95. Aesch. 1.152–154; Ant. 5.38.

96. E.g., Lys. 13.66.

97. The numbers are respectively testimony, 144 (71%); documents, 40 (20%); common knowledge, 13 (6%); arguments, 7 (3%).

98. Humphreys 1985b. Cf. Todd 1990b, 27. I have discussed this in more detail in the Introduction.

99. Cohen 1995, 107–112 (cf. 166, 186), argues that witnesses routinely lied in court because litigation was simply feuding and not about ascertaining facts. That many litigants clearly did not have witnesses to important factual claims (e.g., Aesch. 1, Dem. 47, or Dem. 54), however, suggests there was a more earnest commitment to honesty than this.

100. Detienne 1996; Lloyd 1990. Accounts of litigation as diverse as Sealey 1994, 102–103, and D. Cohen 1995 agree that truth was not the aim of the system.

101. Detienne 1996, 116–130.

102. Gorgias, frag. B3 (translated in Sprague 1972, 42–46). Cf. [Arist.], Melissus, Xenophanes, and Gorgias 979a10–980b21.

103. *Encomium of Helen* 8–14.
104. Detienne 1996.
105. The authority of his reputation was probably what allowed Gorgias to communicate the incommunicability of language. The paradox of the sophists, in this way, represented the inverse of the dissonance of litigants: the sophists' explicit theory of language, that it was effective but not truthful, was at odds with their implicit practice of giving a true account of language.
106. Loraux 1986, 243–244.
107. The extent to which the Athenian courts arrived at truth is a highly complex question. The goal of ascertaining the truth certainly figured prominently in the discourse of the courts. The procedures of the courts may have realized this goal only imperfectly (D. Cohen 1995, 104–105, points out the many factors that limited the jurors' ability to evaluate the truth of litigants' statements), but all legal systems have to balance competing goals, only one of which is truth. American criminal cases, for example, are constrained by certain rules—the state has a much higher burden of proof than a private party in a civil suit, there are many rules excluding evidence, there is a privilege against self-incrimination—which often work against discovering the truth (Scheppele 1989, 2089). We forego the truth in some cases to protect citizens against the overwhelming power of government. Although many scholars conclude that Athenian courts did not reach verdicts based on the truth, the question is, it seems to me, if answerable at all, still open. (Cole 1991, 96–97, defends arguments from probability as a reasonable way to get at the truth.)

The consensus of ancient philosophical critiques of the Athenian courts was that truth was quite alien to them. Yet no one seems to have asked what the source of this critique was. Lloyd, 1990, 85, for example, treats it as an objective fact: "It was *all too obvious* that what persuaded people in the law-courts . . . might or might not be true" (emphasis added). What made this obvious, however, was not its manifest truth but what litigants, under the sway of the discourse of truth, said about litigation at Athens. The discourse of the courts was highly self-reflexive and critical. Considering this, it is reasonable to ask to what extent the ancient philosophic critique of the Athenian courts, including its idea of truth, was parasitic on the courts' own discourse.
108. Dem. 29.12. Cf. Dem. 30.35, where Demosthenes contrasts tortures to "words alone."
109. Lyc. 1.32–33. Cf. Ant. 1.6.
110. Dem. 29.54. Cf. Isae. 12.10. Similar arguments could be made about arbitration: Dem. 41.14, 29–30; 48.40.
111. Isoc. 17.53. Cf. Lys. 7.36.
112. Aesch. 2.127; Ant. 6.23; Dem. 37.40; 42.19; 47.16–17; Dem. 48.50; Dem. 54.40; Isae. 12.9–10. Cf. Andoc. 1.25–26, 35; Ant. 2.4.8.

4. CONJURING CHARACTER

1. The speech dates to about 399. It is not certain under what procedure (or on what charge) the speaker was defending himself, but it is commonly believed that it was during a *dokimasia*.

2. Though the Greek is quite general, Adkins 1960, 202, suggests that here "misfortune" means "being a defendant in a legal case."

3. Lys. 25.12–13.

4. Defendants cited their past public services in 13 of 25 cases: Ant. 5.77; Dem. 18.267; 52.26; Isae. 2.42; 11.50; Isoc. 16.35; Lys. 3.47; 7.31–32; 18.7, 21; 19.56–63; 20.23; 21.1–10; 25.12–13. Prosecutors adduced theirs in 11 of 55 cases: Dem. 19.230; 21.151–174; 23.5; 45.78, 85; 47.23, 54; 50 (passim); 54.44; 58.66–68; Isae. 6.60–61; Isoc. 17.57–58; Lys. 12.20. Three of these prosecution cases (Dem. 21, 47, and 50) were initiated from disputes arising during or about the conduct of a specific liturgy; discounting such cases, the proportion of defendants to prosecutors citing liturgies was about three and a half to one (52% versus 15%, p = .0007). Note that defendants in private and in public cases seem to have been equally likely to cite their liturgies.

In those cases where a litigant spoke about his opponent's liturgies, actual or potential, prosecutors did so 12 times (22% of all cases), defendants only once (4% of all cases, p = .05), in keeping with the general expectation that more defendants pleaded their liturgies.

5. Ant. 2.2.12 (cf. Ant. 2.3.8); 5.75–77; Dem. 34.39–40; 52.26; Hyp. 1.14–18; Isoc. 18.58–65; Lys. 7.30–33; 19.56–63; 20.23; 21.19, 21–22; 25.13. Cf. Dem. 21.136; 25.76. Cf. Bennet and Feldman 1981, 107–114.

6. Lys. 7.30–33. As I noted in Chapter 2, this defendant's presentation consisted largely of attacks on the elements and coherence of the prosecutor's story. The appeal to character through liturgies is one more example of antinarrative.

7. Lys. 19.56.

8. Lys. 19.60–61. Cf. Isoc. 18.58.

9. D. Cohen 1995, 106–112, claims that litigants adduced their character because the procedures used in Athenian courts made true knowledge of the facts of the case almost impossible. Although this correctly represents claims litigants themselves made, it is insufficient as an analysis of litigation because litigants established their character in the same way as the "facts," that is, through rhetoric.

10. Cf. Dem. 19.216, quoted in Chapter 3.

11. Lys. 19.61–62. Cf. §9–10. A similar plea was made by the speakers of Lys. 18.20–21 and Dem. 36.58–59.

12. Lys. 14.43–45. Cf. Andoc. 1.146–150.

13. Dem. 43.75–76; Isae. 7.30.

14. Comparison of liturgies: Dem. 36.55–56, 58–59; Isae. 4.27–29; 5.41–42; 7.35; cf. Isae. 10.25.

15. The formal adjudication of an estate took place in a *diadikasia*, in which there was neither prosecutor nor defendant. Some of these cases (e.g., Isae. 5 and 6) come out of private suits related to inheritance disputes; in these, though the roles of prosecutor and defendant were distinct and important, the underlying logic of competing claimants to the property still also pervaded them.

16. Isae. 6.61. (Cf. Isae. 4.27–29; 5.36–42; 7.32, 35–42.) Part of the reason the speaker said this was to dispel the resentment against his clients' wealth, which their opponent had tried to arouse (§59).

17. Dem. 27.64.

18. Dem. 28.24.

19. As I note when discussing appeals to pity in Chapter 5, Apollodoros tried to represent himself as a defrauded orphan in Dem. 45. Though he did not explicitly link his citation of his liturgies (§§78, 85) to the preservation of his *oikos*, the larger representational strategy may partially account for why he, as a prosecutor, cites his liturgies.

20. Fisher 1990, 126.

21. It is only the consideration of the pattern of deployment of arguments in all legal cases that reveals this. The strategy of reading a single case in isolation (Dem. 21 is a favorite with scholars) runs the risk of construing the exceptional as the ordinary. D. Cohen 1995, for example, cites Dem. 21 and 54 more than any others. They are the sole basis for his claim (p. 186) that the prosecutor's character was equally at issue as the defendant's. Although they are important evidence, however, they are not typical.

22. Lys. 21.25. The whole of Lys. 21, the conclusion of what must have been a much longer defense, is devoted to arguments from the speaker's liturgies. Despite (or perhaps because of) its exceptional nature, it figures prominently in scholarly accounts on the subject.

23. Herman 1987; Blundell 1989.

24. Finley 1979; Kurke 1991; Millett 1991; Ober 1989.

25. Davies 1981, 92–105.

26. In these claims for gratitude, moreover, common social values intruded into the legal realm of the courts. Finley 1973, 152; Ober 1989, 226–230; Kurke 1991, 174–175; Millett 1991, 26, 123–124.

27. Isae. 7.38–41; Isoc. 16.35; 18.58–67; Lys. 21.25.

28. Aesch. 2.171; Lys. 21.25. Cf. Dem. 20.75–83; Isae. 10.25.

29. Andoc. 1.141–150.

30. Aesch. 2.4.

31. Isae. 7.41. Cf. Isoc. 18.58.

32. Lys. 18.23, 26, 27.

33. Andoc. 1.141–150.

34. Defendants often engaged in both strategies simultaneously, but analytically they are quite distinct.

35. Defendants explicitly claimed *charis*: Aesch. 2.171; Andoc. 1.146–150; Isoc. 16.15, 35, 38; Lys. 18.23, 26, 27; 20.30–31, 33; 21.17–19, 25; 25.11. Prosecutors asked for *charis*: Dem. 21.28; 23.93; 45.85. One speaker in a *diadikasia* (Isae. 7.41) and one speaker in a *paragraphe* (Isoc. 18.58–67) did as well.

36. Certainly this collective action was mediated through individuals' actions, some of which may have been motivated by emotional states, but the emotional preconditions of a jury's decision were much less important than the cognitive ones, specifically, as I argue below, the identification of an individual with the group and its interests. It is this identification, and the actions that followed from this, that *charis* describes.

37. Isae. 7.41. This was not the Apollodoros who has figured prominently in several cases already cited in this book.

38. E.g., Dem. 18.112–113; 20.46; 21.172.

39. Chapter 5 treats more fully the ways in which speakers made implicit cognitive claims.

40. Dem. 21.67–69; Lyc. 1.139–140.

41. Dem. 19.238 (though this is about holding office, not liturgies).

42. Although this collective was imaginary, it was still intensely real. With Loraux 1986, 336, I would designate "under the term *imaginary* all the figures in which a society apprehends its identity." As suggested in the Introduction, interests are real only when people begin to imagine them as their own.

43. Ant. 6.9–10 (where the defendant makes it clear that his prosecutor claimed it); Dem. 21.28; 23.93; cf. Ant. 5.61 (where the defendant imagines a hypothetical prosecution of unspecified kind that would gain *charis*). This accounts for three of the four anomalies of prosecutors asking for *charis* or defendants denying it. The one other prosecutor (Apollodoros) in my catalogue of those requesting *charis*, in Dem. 45.85, cited his liturgies but explicitly denied that this was so the jury would feel *charis*. (I included it, however, because the denial seems so obvious as to assert. As this goes against my claim that prosecutors did not claim *charis*, including it was the conservative decision.)

44. Ant. 6.9–10.

45. Dem. 21.28.

46. Prosecutors' responses to defendants' requests for *charis* varied. On the one hand, they frequently admitted that *charis* was an appropriate response by juries to public services (Dem. 21.148–149, 160; 25.76–78; 38.25–26; 42.24–25; Din. 1.17; Isae. 5.35–38, 43–46; Lyc. 1.139–140; Lys. 6.36, 46–47; 12.38–40; 30.1, 26–27), though, suspiciously, this was always in those cases where the defendant could not (so the prosecutor claimed) show such services, and so the admission should not be construed as an objective description of the way things really were. On the other hand, they seem to have shown no reluctance to deny, for a variety of reasons, that a defendant's supporters should get *charis* (Dem. 19.238; 21.211; Lyc. 1.139–140; Lys. 14.22; 27.13–14). Nor was it rare for a prosecutor to assert that the jury should simply not show *charis* at all.

47. Demosthenes was not referring to those who undertake liturgies or other public services here, but the conduct of politicians, himself and Aeschines especially, who look out for the interests of the city or for their own. He was suggesting that the "private" motives of individual Athenians prevent them from distinguishing between good and bad politicians.

48. Dem. 19.227–229.

49. Dem. 19.239–240.

50. Aesch. 3.233; Lys. 6.53; 15.10.

51. Lys. 10.15 is the exception.

52. Lys. 6.53.

53. Aesch. 3.233. Although implicit in this sentence, throughout the rest of the paragraph the juror (ὁ κριτής) was explicitly considered singularly.

54. Arist., *Ath. Pol.* 67, describes the system in his time. Each dikast had two "stones," one for the prosecutor (with a hole) and one for the defendant (without), each of which they placed in one of two urns, one for ballots which counted,

the other for those that did not. Boegehold 1995 describes the various voting arrangements in the courts at different times.

55. Aristoph., *Wasps* 560–561. This begging takes place person to person before the trial.

56. In Xenophon's account of a mock trial at a symposium, Kritobulos urges that the balloting be secret so that the "wealth" (here meant ironically) of his opponents will not overpower him (Xen., *Symp.* 5.8).

57. The Thirty apparently required open voting in trials (Lys. 13.37; cf. Lys. 12.91). Isocrates thought that secret voting allowed wicked men intentionally to do evil (Isoc. 15.142–143). (These words are put in the mouth of an associate but explicitly endorsed later at 15.154.) Plato, too, listed it as one of the faults of Athenian juries (Plato, *Laws* 876b) and insisted on open voting in his ideal state (Plato, *Laws* 855d).

58. Aesch. 1.35; Andoc. 1.87; Dem. 24. 45, 59; 47.42; 59.90. At least some demes used secret voting in *euthynai* for deme officials (*IG* II² 1183, 18 [dated to after 340]). Rhodes 1981a, 127.

59. Wyse 1904, 423–425, argues that Isae 5.17 (ca. 389) shows the later system of voting (the one described by Aristotle), not the one known from the late fifth century (Rhodes 1981a, 127).

60. This was in fact the master plan of Isocrates' *Areopagitikos,* an antidemocratic political tract (Johnstone 1989). Millett 1989 notes too that the economic independence of the poor, made possible by pay for service to the state (such as serving as a juror), also undercut elite patronage.

61. See, for example, Adkins 1960, 193–214; Davies 1981; Ober 1989; Kurke 1991, 171–182.

62. Giddens 1984, 185–193, discusses this term.

63. Millett 1989 gives a detailed version of this thesis that makes the effect the intentional purpose of the reform.

64. Whitehead 1983.

65. One of the greatest problems with the historical theory embedded in the *Constitution of Athens* attributed to Aristotle is that every democratic feature of fourth-century Athens was intentionally invented by an earlier lawgiver.

5. CERTAIN RITUALS

1. Aesch. 2.179.

2. Dem. 19.310. He also advanced proleptic arguments against pity at §§228, 257, 281, and 283.

3. Aristotle presents them this way in the opening of his *Rhetoric* (1354a).

4. Navarre 1900, 317–320, argues that appeals to pity are less obvious in Greek oratory (when compared to Latin) because they were enacted, not spoken, and so leave little trace in the written versions of the orations. This would suggest that they were even more common than the written evidence shows.

5. Konstan 1985.

6. More than this, because prosecutors invariably condemned the appeals of their opponents as inappropriate or illegitimate, the evidence is inherently judg-

mental. My purpose is not to resolve the contradiction between what defendants did and what prosecutors said by deciding who was right. Though scholars have usually sided with prosecutors, dismissing the defendants' pleas as misleading and irrelevant, my intention is rather to accept, elaborate, and analyze the contradiction itself. The disparity in the evidence and the accompanying bias reflect the structurally distinct positions of prosecutor and defendant.

7. Defendants explicitly requested pity at: Aesch. 2.179; Andoc. 1.67; Ant. 5.73; Isae. 2.2; Isoc. 16.48; Lys. 3.48; 4.20; 18.1; 19.53; 20.34–36; 21.25; 24.7. Additionally, two of the three defendants in Antiphon's *Tetralogies* entreat the jury for pity (Ant. 2.2.13; 3.2.2; 3.2.11).

Prosecutors requested it at: Dem. 27.67–68; 28.20; 45.88; 54.43; 58.69 (the only public prosecution in the group); Lys. 32.19. Cf. Ant. 3.1.2; 3.3.3. Pity was raised in one *paragraphe* case: Dem. 36.59. Also, prosecutors in four public cases argued that the city (or some aspect of it) deserves more pity than the defendant (Din. 1.109–110; 3.13; Lys. 22.21; 28.14).

8. Isae. 5.10, 35; Lys. 14.39; 2.73; *Dissoi Logoi* 1.14.

9. τοὺς ἀσθενεῖς ἐλεεῖν: Dem. 24.171.

10. Ant. 3.2.2.

11. More precisely, they dramatized the consequences of *severe* penalties, but defendants seem to have elided the distinction. Aware of this difference, some prosecutors argued that although begging for pity was acceptable in assessing the penalty, the question of guilt or innocence should not turn on it (Aesch. 3.197–198; Dem. 54.21).

12. Dem. 57.70. Cf. Aesch. 2.179 (quoted at the opening of this chapter); Lys. 7.41.

13. Defendants risked more in losing a case than prosecutors did. Though prosecutors exposed themselves to a fine if they failed to receive one-fifth of the votes, penalties imposed on convicted defendants were much greater. D. Cohen occasionally seems to imply (e.g., 1995, 92) that defendants risked little because they could evade penalties and awards. Though some may have evaded paying a penalty awarded to a successful prosecutor, cases based on such alleged shirking (e.g., Dem. 30; Isae. 5) provide no basis for inferring the frequency of such behavior, because only an unsuccessful attempt to collect an award would generate a legal case. The evidence, therefore, is systematically and necessarily silent about convicted defendants who paid their fines. When a fine was owed to the state, failure to pay could result in a doubling of the amount, imprisonment, or even the loss of citizen rights (MacDowell 1978, 165–167; Todd 1993, 144–145). It is true that the state usually left the enforcement of these penalties to volunteer prosecutors and that the cases in which someone prosecuted a state debtor (e.g., Dem. 25; 53) provide no basis for concluding how often this happened (for a precisely analogous reason: because the absence of a prosecutor would not result in a case). Nevertheless, the failure to pay an award or fine gave a potential advantage to an opponent, not merely grounds for another legal case (like those cited earlier in this note) but for self-help in enforcing the award. (Dem. 47.52–61 shows why a person might want to avoid such enforcement. The same speech, however, also shows the risks for the self-help enforcer [§§36–46].) This asym-

metrical distribution of risks is one more reason why (as I argued in Chapter 4) litigation cannot be viewed as a simple extension of a social contest for honor.

14. Christ 1998 discusses this ambivalence in detail.

15. Lys. 3.48. A similar sentiment, that pity is due those on trial, seems to underlie one of Demosthenes' attacks on Aristogeiton (Dem. 25.82). At another time (Dem. 27.68) Demosthenes explicitly argued against the idea that those on trial deserve pity.

16. Stevens 1944, 15–17.

17. H. Thompson 1952.

18. Prosecutors' pervasive anxiety that pity not be shown in inappropriate circumstances indirectly confirms that predominantly defendants claimed it. Of 55 prosecution speeches, 26 warned against showing pity to the opponent, whereas only one defendant (of 25) bothered to make the same argument (47% vs. 4%, p < .001). Almost half of all prosecutors warned against showing pity to their opponents, whereas only one defendant bothered to make the same argument. See Table 6.

19. Ant. 1.26. The same argument that the defendant who showed no pity deserves none was made at: Dem. 19. 283; 21.100–101, 185; 25.81–83; Din. 2.11; Lyc. 1.141. Cf. Dem. 28.20. In a few cases the prosecutor said the defendant showed no pity and left it at that: Dem. 24.111; 27.65; Isae. 5.10; Din. 1.24.

20. Dem. 21.184–185.

21. Dem. 19.57; 25.76; Isae. 5.35.

22. Dem. 21.225; Lyc. 1.150; Lys. 14.40; Lys. 15.9 (a second speech in the same trial as Lys. 14). The speaker of Isae. 10 (an inheritance *diadikasia*) said that because his opponent could not argue against the laws and justice, he would instead spend his time expressing pity for the deceased who died in battle (§22).

23. In his prosecution of Aeschines, Demosthenes argued that on questions of public interest, the polis was harmed by private motives, one of which was pity (Dem. 19.228).

24. Lyc. 1.150.

25. Dem. 22.57–58.

26. Dem. 24.171.

27. Dem. 25.81. Cf. Dem. 27.65, a case in which Demosthenes casts himself, the defrauded orphan, as meriting compassion.

28. Dem. 25.26, 50.

29. Dem. 21.195.

30. Fisher 1990.

31. Arist., *Rhet.* 1386a–b.

32. Frag. D 1. The context of this remark is not known; it may not have been a legal case (though there seem to have been competing speakers, and the plural "you" suggests it was addressed to a large audience).

33. The weeping that took place in the court seems to have been much less formalized than the mourning for the dead, at least to judge by the vocabulary used. The two common words for this ritual lament—θρῆνος and γόος—were never used to describe the behavior of litigants or their relatives. Although γόος, in particular, could refer to any kind of weeping (Alexiou 1974, 226 n. 6) it seems

to have been avoided. The common terms for the crying in the court were κλαίω and ὀδύρομαι. On one occasion, ὀλοφύρομαι was used (Lys. 20.34); this is the same word used at Thuc. 2.34 to describe the women lamenting at the public funeral of the war dead.

34. The prosecution cases were Aesch. 3.209, 210; Dem. 19.310; 21.99, 186, 194, 204; 39.35; 45.88; 53.29; 54.43; Din. 1.109, 110; Hyp. 5, frag. 9, col. 40; Lyc. 1.33, 150; Lys. 27.12. Four prosecutors in *paragraphe* cases mentioned the possibility of their opponent weeping: Dem. 36.36; 37.48; 38.19, 27; Isoc. 18.35, 37.

35. Dem. 38.27.

36. Dem. 30.32; Hyp. 5. frag. 9, col. 40; Lys. 27.13. Cf. Lys. 18.24.

37. Lys. 20.34. Cf. Dem. 19.281; 21.182; Hyp. 2.9; Lys. 21.25. Two defendants explicitly announced their intentions to bring their children up before the jurors: Aesch. 2. 179; Hyp. 4.41. Another regretted he had no children to bring up: Andoc. 1.149. The presence of piteous children was common enough that Aristophanes satirized it (*Wasps* 975–978 and *Lys.* 877–888), and Isocrates (Isoc. 15.321) and Plato (*Apol.* 34c) condemned it. Most references indicate that the children were brought into the court at the end of the speech (Aesch. 2.152 is the exception) and that they were marched up (ἀναβιβάζεσθαι) onto the speaker's platform (e.g., Dem. 19.310; Hyp. 4.41). (MacDowell 1990, 399, describes the platform. Boegehold 1995, 201–205, cites the ancient evidence for it.)

Unlike children, women seem to have rarely appeared in court, even just to weep. Against the ample evidence (from both speeches and external sources) for the presence of children, there is only one specific reference to females appearing in support of a litigant (Dem. 25.84). Given litigants' reluctance even to name their female relatives in court (Schaps 1977), it is not surprising that they so rarely attended.

38. Dem. 21.99. MacDowell 1990, 321, offers no reasons for his assertion that "the weeping ought to be done by the children; D[emosthenes] is sarcastic in suggesting that Meidias will weep himself."

39. Lys. 20.34.

40. Dem. 27.65.

41. Isae. 2.44. The combination of δέομαι, ἀντιβολῶ, and ἱκετεύω seems to have been a conventional appeal. It appears 11 times in the orations; two of the three words appear in combinations another 18 times.

42. Gould 1973, 101. Pedrick 1982 supplements Gould's standard account. Herman 1987, 54–58, shows how supplication could initiate *xenia,* a ritual relationship of friendship.

43. Dem. 21.7; 45.1; 57.1; 58.3; Isae. 2.2; 6.57. See also Aesch. 3.156; Dem. 42.19. Even these "metaphorical" uses may, however, have been meaningful. In none of Demosthenes' extant speeches to the Assembly did he ever "supplicate" the audience, even to beg their attention. I suspect this reflects a different relationship between speaker and audience in the Assembly and in the courts.

44. The frequent occurrence of supplication in tragedy suggests that the ritual had not lost its potency in the fifth century. E.g., Eur., *Hecuba* 342–345 (Odysseus hides his hands and face to prevent any supplication); *Hippolytos* 324 (the nurse compels Phaedra to confess her love by grasping her hands); *Herakles* 963–

968 (Herakles' father supplicates him by the hand). I thank Laura McClure for help on this point. Cf. Aristoph., *Lys.* 1139, where a Spartan requests Athenian aid by sitting as suppliant.

45. Gould, 1973, 77. Herman 1987, 50–54, shows the importance of grasping the right hand, *dexia*, in the *xenia* relationship. This ritual was still powerful late in the fourth century, as Aesch. 3.224 suggests.

46. Dem. 18.107 (petitions to the Assembly by aggrieved trierarchs); 24.12 (a petition to the Assembly by owners of property captured in war); Aesch. 2.15 (a petition [to the Assembly?] that the state ransom captive family members); Aesch. 1.104 (a request to the Boule by an old man to be included again on the list of the disabled eligible for aid [cf. Arist., *Ath. Pol.* 49.4]); Dem. 24.50–53 (a law limiting the ability of those convicted to supplicate for leniency); Andoc. 1.110–116 (petitioning the Boule by placing a suppliant branch on the altar in the Eleusinium, during a festival, however, when the law seems to have prohibited it). Cf. Menander, *Sykionios* 190. Foreigners making requests of the Athenians also were said to carry out supplication: Dem. 50.5; *IG* II² 218.8, 24; 276.5; 336. frag. b.16; 337.34; 502.14. (The phrase ἔννομα ἱκετεύειν is restored in *IG* II² 192.2; 211.p1; 404.4.) Rhodes 1972, 55–57, suggests that *hiketeria* gave direct access to the Assembly to citizens without them having first to go through the Boule.

47. Arist., *Ath. Pol.* 43.6.

48. Rhodes 1981b, 528. Cf. Hdt. 5.51, 7.141, where the branch similarly represents a request.

49. Aristoph., *Wealth* 382–385. This is clearly in a judicial context, since Blepsidemos has been imagining Chremylos having stolen money and being charged. The olive branch could be a comic invention here (Aristophanes taking literally the figurative language of supplication), but its extensive use in other petitions to the Athenian people would hardly make its use here so incongruous as to be funny. The humor seems, rather, to derive from Blepsidemos' overeager willingness to attribute criminality to Chremylos' plan to get rich and from his comparison of the supplicating family to a famous painting with heroic subjects.

50. Dem. 43.83. As far as I know, there is no evidence that the court venues had altars on which to place the supliant bough (Boegehold 1995 does not indicate any), a point that seems to tell against this inference. Yet the absence of an altar is not decisive: We do know that sacrifices took place in court. When witnesses refused to assent to a testimony prepared by a litigant, they took an oath λαβόντας τὰ ἱερὰ (Lyc. 1.20). (In Aristotle's day, litigants also took oaths before the trial began: *Ath. Pol.* 67.1 and the comments of Rhodes 1981b. In Aristophanes' comic idea of a home-court, the session begins with prayers and a libation: *Wasps* 859–884.) This suggests either the presence of an altar or sufficient flexibility of practice that we could imagine supplication without official provision having been made for it.

51. Dem. 47.17; Dem. 37.39–42. Din. 2.13 refers to this time.

52. Dem. 21.4.

53. Dem. 19.1; Aesch. 3.1. It is, of course, impossible to verify the accuracy of either of these claims, and some suspicion is in order as both are meant to show that the opponent has attempted to circumvent justice. But neither of them

would have made sense unless jurors understood it as a common practice. Under παραγγελία Harpocration cites these two passages and a third by Dinarchos (καὶ τὰς ἰδίᾳ παραγγελίας γεγενημένας καὶ τὰς δεήσεις, Loeb frag. A.2), which may well have referred to similar activities, but because it is only a fragment, we cannot be sure. Demosthenes seems to have suggested that Aeschines' brothers may have been involved in begging the jurors to save him at some time before the trial: καὶ γὰρ εἰ τινῶν δεδέηνται τουτονὶ σώζειν . . . (Dem. 19.239). Though the context refers to his brothers' impending advocacy at the conclusion of Aeschines' speech, the tense of the verb implies a previous action, and the plural indefinite pronoun should mean that not all jurors have been so implored. It is unclear whether παραγγελία at Dem. 19.283 refers to canvassing before the trial or not.

54. [Xen.], *Ath. Pol.* 1.18.

55. Aristoph., *Wasps* 552–556. Early in the third century the comic poet Poseidippos had one of his characters say that the courtesan Phryne, when she had been on trial, won acquittal by grasping the right hand of each juror and weeping (Athen. 591e–f).

56. [Xen.], *Ath. Pol.* 1.18; Aristoph., *Wasps* 555, 560. These two pieces of direct evidence for supplication of the jurors, the *Wasps* (422 BC) and the *Constitution of the Athenians* (after 446 but no later than 412), date before the bulk of the court speeches in the fourth century. MacDowell 1990, 292 (in line with the scholarly consensus), claims that "by this period [353–352, the date of Dem. 21] such canvassing had been made virtually impossible in ordinary courts, because the system of allotment made it impossible to know in advance which jurors would try which case." Nevertheless, the references in the speeches to canvassing all come from the mid-fourth century, including Dem. 21, the very speech on which MacDowell is commenting. (Dem. 19 dates to 343; Lavency 1964 fixes Dem. 37 in 346–345, Dem. 47 in 355–354.) Moreover, Aristotle's extremely detailed description of the allocation of jurors to courts (*Ath. Pol.* 63–65), on which MacDowell relies, a description that dates from 328–322, almost 30 years after Dem. 21, does not seem to correspond to the archeological evidence (see Rhodes 1981b on 63.2); nor does it seem to preclude, even if it is correct, the canvassing of jurors as they went into the assigned courtrooms after allotment. Boegehold 1995 gives a detailed account of the physical and spatial aspects of the courts.

57. Isoc. 15.321.

58. Aesch. 1.113; Dem. 30.32; Dem. 47.43 (before the Boule); Dem. 58.27–28 (before the Assembly); Dem. 59.81 (before the Areopagos); and Hyp. 5, frag. 6.26. All were public cases.

59. Din. 1.109; Lyc. 1.143; Lys. 6.55; 15.3; 22.21.

60. Din. 3.21. Lyc. 1.150 invoked metaphorical supplication of the jury by the country and the trees but not by the prosecutor himself. A prosecutor in a public case would be less likely to supplicate, because he usually represented himself as moved by a harm not to himself or his household but to the Athenians as a whole.

61. Dem. 27; 45; and 48. Dem. 28 and 46 were second speeches in the same trials following Dem. 27 and 45 respectively. Dem. 56.4 is the one exception. I am allowing that Dem. 45 and 46 were guardianship cases, because although

technically suits for false witness, the witness' testimony had been in an original claim against a guardian, and the speaker Apollodoros spent much of his time rehearsing his grievances against his guardian.

62. Dem. 43.83–84; Isae. 8.45; 9.37.

63. In Greek, orphan often denotes those without fathers, even if their mothers were still living.

64. Four of the prosecutors requesting pity meet this criterion: Dem. 27.67–68; 28.20; 45.88; and Lys. 32.19. Two others do not: Dem. 54.43; 58.69. In the last, however, Epichares was suing Theokrines in retaliation for his having sued, convicted, and disenfranchised Epichares' father. The massive fine imposed in that previous case had destroyed their *oikos,* and in Dem. 58, Epichares presented himself as its representative. Only one defendant, Theopompos, who was being sued for maltreating an orphan, suggested that his prosecutor might ask for pity (Isae. 11.38).

65. Apollodoros (in Dem. 45 and 46) must have stretched the appeal somewhat. Even at the time of his father's death, he had been a full adult. By the time of these speeches some twenty years later, he had become a prominent and wealthy Athenian, as evidenced by his liturgies (Trevett 1992, 14). He seems to have pursued a similar strategy of self-representation in an earlier suit he lost, because the speaker for his opponent Phormio had warned that jury that Apollodoros would weep as though he were poor, when really he was rich (Dem. 36.36).

66. Dem. 27.66–68. Cf. Dem. 45.85.

67. Todd 1993, 133–135. Harrison 1971, 80–82, describes which cases were of which kind. This procedure is like forms of arbitration used in professional sports: The requirements that each side can submit a proposal only once and that the arbitrator must choose one or the other (and not a compromise of their own devising) is intended to encourage good-faith proposals.

68. The evidence may be found at Aesch. 1.113; 3.197–198; Dem. 30.31–32; 47.42–43; 53.17–18; 54.21; 58.19; 58.70; 59.6; Isae. 5.17–18. All these refer to earlier cases. Cf. Dem. 24.50–53; 59.81; Lys. 1.25–26. Plato's fictionalized account of a penalty hearing in the *Apology* is useful only for illustrative purposes.

69. After conviction, the prosecutor could not suspend the penalty assessment, but he could still propose and advocate a mild penalty. In one case, prosecutor and defendant came to a settlement as the votes on conviction were being counted, so they had this vote stopped (Isae. 5.17–18).

70. Dem. 58.70.

71. As I suggested in Chapter 3.

72. Dem. 47.42–43; 53.17–18; Isae. 5.17–18. The failure in these instances for the compromise solution to end the dispute says nothing about other cases where it may have done exactly this, since a successfully ended dispute, precisely because it was concluded, would leave no record in the evidence of the legal speeches.

73. Dem. 58.1–2, 70; 59. 6.

74. Dem. 59.6. Theomnestos' point is that Stephanos wanted a fine so large (fifteen talents was several fortunes) that Apollodoros could not have paid it and would have lost his civic rights by defaulting.

75. Dem. 58.70.

76. De Sousa 1987 argues that emotion does not necessarily impede reason (as, for example, Aristotle suggests [*Rhet.* 1254a25]) but, rather, that without emotion, reasoning itself is impossible.

77. Gorgias, a fifth-century sophist, claimed that persuasion overwhelmed the listener like magic, drugs, or violent kidnapping (*Encomium of Helen* 8–14). Not only does this model abolish any contingency in the process or agency in the auditor (which was Gorgias' intention because he was trying to excuse Helen's flight with Paris), it fails to account for the competition of speeches in the courts. In the trial scene in Aristophanes' *Wasps,* a defendant's appeal for pity deeply affects Philokleon, but he votes to condemn anyway (967–989). E. P. Thompson 1993 shows that even in "food riots" in eighteenth-century England, crowds acted in structured, strategic ways, largely based on a sense of morality.

78. E.g., Humphreys 1983; Ober 1989. Hansen 1990, 350, expresses reservations about this comparison.

79. It is true, however, that Aristotle's claim that the sight of undeserved misfortune motivates pity (*Poetics* 1453a) conforms to many of the appeals in the courts.

80. I do not mean to suggest that Athenians reacted to drama in a purely "emotional" way but that the assimilation of legal oratory to drama obscures the degree to which the former was explicitly critical of itself and made the grounds for deciding part of the substantive debate. Though there were *agones* (competitions) in drama, there was never a debate over which play deserved the prize and what reasons were appropriate in determining this. (Aristophanes' *Frogs* dramatizes such a discussion, but it makes no argument about why this play should receive the prize over its competitors.)

81. The relationship between performers and spectators was very different from that between litigants and jurors.

82. Dover 1974, 195–196.

83. Lys. 19.53. See also Ant. 2.2.13; 5.73; Dem. 25.76; Lyc. 1.148; Lys. 6.3; 10.22; 29.8.

84. Gould 1973, 88.

85. Aesch. 1.99; Isae. 8.22; Lys. 32.11.

86. The notion is common in Isocrates' rhetoric: e.g., Isoc. 4.57, 67; 6.75; 9.14; 14.1, 6, 56; 12.169. Cf. Aesch. 3.157; Lys. 2.11, 39.

87. Gould 1973, 89.

88. Plato, *Apol.* 39a; *Symp.* 183a.

89. Athenian men were extremely anxious to differentiate the free, independent bodies of citizens from those of inferior groups (Halperin 1990, 98–99).

90. E.g., Demosthenes suggests it was proper on hearing of the misfortunes of the city (Dem. 18.291), and Isocrates sees it as appropriate when close friends part (Isoc. 15.88).

91. Alexiou 1974, 105, and Loraux 1986, 45. Such is also the presumption that Dem. ep. II.25 has to overcome.

92. Dem. 21.186.

93. Plato, *Apol.* 39a; *Symp.* 183a.

94. Plato, *Apol.* 34c. Xenophon too reports that Socrates refused "to bring

up χάρις with the jurors and flatter them and beg (κολακεύειν καὶ δεῖσθαι) contrary to the laws" (Xen., *Mem.* 4.4.4).

95. *Apol.* 35a: αἰσχύνην τῇ πόλει περιάπτειν. *Apol.* 35b: γυναικῶν οὐδὲν διαφέρουσιν. In the ideal state of the *Laws* (949b), Plato outlaws defendants using unseemly supplications or womanly lamentations (μήτε ἱκετείαις χρώμενον ἀσχήμοσιν μήτε οἴκτοις γυναικείοις).

96. E.g., Isoc. 16.48. Dover 1974, 197, comments on this passage.

97. Gould 1973, 94.

98. Aristoph., *Wasps* 571: ὥσπερ θεὸν ἀντιβολεῖ με τρέμων τῆς εὐθύνης ἀπολῦσαι. Cf. 882.

99. Isoc. 4.57. The context refers to suppliants coming to the city of Athens.

100. Cf. Connerton 1989, 58–59.

101. Aesch. 2.152.

102. Din. 1.92, 111. Cf. Dem. 21.204. Lycurgos, as I mentioned in Chapter 3, had compared the deceptiveness of tearful appeals for pity with the certainty of torturing slaves (Lyc. 1.33).

6. LITIGATION AND ATHENIAN CULTURE

1. Moore 1973 advocates looking at social fields as semiautonomous to analyze the degree of the effect of the law on them. But if "complete autonomy and complete domination are rare, if they exist at all in the world today, and semiautonomy of various kinds and degrees is an ordinary circumstance" (p. 742), then litigation itself is a semiautonomous field in its relationship to society at large.

2. Bourdieu 1987, Luhmann 1982, ch. 6, and Teubner 1983 offer three interesting but different approaches. Lempert 1988, although a critique of Luhmann's approach, nevertheless helps make clear some of his difficult concepts. Wolfe 1992 is similarly critical but useful.

3. If "the law" means the specific institutional features of a modern legal system that make it autonomous, then, almost by definition, it is hard to find any autonomy in Athenian law. Yet, as I have argued throughout this book, at Athens we should understand "the law" as essentially rhetorical, that is, as equivalent to litigation.

4. Luhmann 1982, 135.

5. As noted in Chapter 4, this was not universally the case. In a few cases (e.g., Dem. 21, 50, and, to a lesser extent, 54) where the prosecutor chose to define the "crime" as an improper honor or dishonor, he was able to call upon his social status much like the defendant normally could. When Demosthenes, although the prosecutor, said he deserved to act like and be treated as the defendant (Dem. 21.5–7), he was in fact playing on the normal structural distinction between the two litigants. Prosecutors claiming the role of defendants were exceptional, and it would be misleading to generalize from these cases.

6. Plutarch noted that personal abuse was a feature of only legal oratory at Athens: *Moralia* 810c–d (*Praecepta reipublicae gerendae*).

7. Dem. 10.70–74.

8. Ober 1989, 147.

9. Ober 1989, 126.

10. Though there were differences between public and private cases, especially with regard to the resources available to prosecutors.

11. Chapter 2.

12. Many prosecutors did not restrict themselves to only such legal narratives, but all prosecutors had to present them.

13. Christ 1998 provides a detailed account of Athenians' ambivalent attitudes toward litigation and legal procedures.

14. Dem. 38.17–18, 27.

15. Lys. 10.84. Cf. Isae. 10.18–21 and Dem. 43.67, where the speakers were attempting to ward off not an argument from a statute of limitations but a claim that a justified case would have been brought in a timely manner. Compare this too to the argument of Aristodemos' son, that whoever resorts to a *diamartyria* is showing their bad character (Dem. 44.57–59).

16. Lys. 13.88–89. This argument also suggests that defendants were vulnerable if they simply undercut the prosecutor's narrative instead of supplying one of their own (as I argued in Chapter 1).

17. Dem. 36.26–27.

18. Dem. 33.27. Cf. Ant. 5.8.

19. Three other speakers claimed that the lapse of time showed that the claim against them was groundless (Dem. 37.2; 55.3–7; Lys. 3.39). The speakers of Dem. 18.13–15 and Lys. 7.20–22 hinted at the same thing.

20. Johnstone 1998 considers this question at greater length.

21. Foxhall 1996.

22. Versnel 1987, 65–66.

APPENDIX: THE USE OF STATISTICS

1. The probable validity of statistical inferences does not depend on the size of the population about which inferences are being made, or the size of the sample relative to this, but only on the absolute size of the sample itself.

2. The preservation of speeches in ancient times for literary merit as well as the preponderance in the sample of prosecution speeches and of professionally written speeches strongly suggest that the sample is not random.

3. The reason that in most cases the use of statistical analyses are inappropriate for Athenian history, then, is not because of the need for such assumptions, but because the preserved samples will not give meaningful results even with such enabling assumptions.

BIBLIOGRAPHY

Adeleye, Gabriel. 1983. "The Purpose of the *Dokimasia*," *Greek, Roman and Byzantine Studies* 24: 295–306.

Adkins, Arthur. 1960. *Merit and Responsibility*. Oxford: Oxford Univ. Press.

Aicher-Hadler, Gabriele. 1989. "Das 'Urteil' des amtlichen Diaiteten." *Revue internationale des droits de l'Antiquité. Ser. 3*, 36: 57–73.

Alexiou, Margaret. 1974. *The Ritual Lament in Greek Tradition*. Cambridge: Cambridge Univ. Press.

Allan, D. J. 1980. "ΑΝΑΓΙΓΝΩΣΚΩ and Some Cognate Words." *Classical Quarterly* 30: 244–251.

Bennet, W. Lance, and Martha S. Feldman. 1981. *Reconstructing Reality in the Courtroom: Justice and Judgment in American Culture*. New Brunswick: Rutgers Univ. Press.

Berkowitz, Luci, and Karl A. Squitier. 1986. *Thesaurus Linguae Graecae: Canon of Greek Authors and Works*. 2nd ed. Oxford: Oxford Univ. Press.

Bers, Victor. 1985. "Dikastic *Thorobus*." *History of Political Thought* 6: 1–15.

Black, Donald. 1984. "Social Control as a Dependent Variable." Pp. 1–36 in Donald Black, ed., *Toward a General Theory of Social Control*, vol. 1. Orlando: Academic Press.

Blundell, Mary Whitlock. 1989. *Helping Friends and Harming Enemies: A Study in Sophocles and Greek Ethics*. Cambridge: Cambridge Univ. Press.

Boegehold, Alan. 1995. *The Lawcourts of Athens*. Princeton: American School of Classical Studies at Athens.

Bonner, Robert J., and Gertrude Smith. 1938. *The Administration of Justice from Homer to Aristotle*. Vol. 2. Chicago: Univ. of Chicago Press.

Bourdieu, Pierre. 1977. *Outline of a Theory of Practice*. Cambridge: Cambridge Univ. Press.

———. 1987. "The Force of Law: Toward a Sociology of the Juridical Field." *Hastings Law Journal* 38: 805–853.

————. 1990. *The Logic of Practice*. Stanford: Stanford Univ. Press.

————. 1991. *Language and Symbolic Power*. Cambridge, Mass.: Harvard Univ. Press.

Brenneis, Donald. 1988. "Telling Troubles: Narrative, Conflict and Experience." *Anthropological Linguistics* 30: 279–291.

Brown, Peter. 1982. "Society and the Supernatural: A Medieval Change." Pp. 302–332 in *Society and the Holy in Late Antiquity*. Berkeley: Univ. of California Press.

Butler, Judith. 1990. *Gender Trouble*. New York: Routledge.

Carawan, Edwin M. 1983. "*Erotesis:* Interrogation in the Courts of Fourth-Century Athens." *Greek, Roman and Byzantine Studies* 24: 209–226.

Carey, C., ed. 1989. *Lysias: Selected Speeches*. Cambridge: Cambridge Univ. Press.

————, ed. 1992. *Greek Orators*. Vol. 6. Warminster: Aris and Phillips.

————. 1996. "*NOMOS* in Attic Rhetoric and Oratory." *Journal of Hellenic Studies* 116: 33–46.

Carey, C., and R. A. Reid. 1985. *Demosthenes: Selected Private Speeches*. Cambridge: Cambridge Univ. Press.

Carter, Lief H. 1994. *Reason in Law*. 4th ed. New York: Harper Collins.

Cartledge, Paul, Paul Millett, and Stephen Todd, eds. 1990. *NOMOS: Essays in Athenian Law, Politics, and Society*. Cambridge: Cambridge Univ. Press.

Chartier, Roger. 1987. *The Cultural Uses of Print in Early Modern France*. Trans. by Lydia Cochrane. Princeton: Princeton Univ. Press.

Christ, Matthew. 1998. *The Litigious Athenian*. Baltimore: Johns Hopkins Univ. Press.

Cohen, David. 1983. *Theft in Athenian Law*. Munich: C. H. Beck'sche Verlagsbuchhandlung.

————. 1989. "Greek Law: Problems and Methods." *Zeitschrift der Savigny-Stiftung für Rechtsgeschichte. Romanistische Abteilung* 106: 81–105.

————. 1990. "The Social Context of Adultery at Athens." Pp. 147–165 in Paul Cartledge, Paul Millett, and Stephen Todd, eds., *NOMOS: Essays in Athenian Law, Politics, and Society*. Cambridge: Cambridge Univ. Press.

————. 1991. *Law, Sexuality, and Society: The Enforcement of Morals in Classical Athens*. Cambridge: Cambridge Univ. Press.

————. 1992. "Honor, Feud, and Litigation in Classical Athens." *Zeitschrift der Savigny-Stiftung für Rechtsgeschichte. Romanistische Abteilung* 109: 100–115.

————. 1995. *Law, Violence, and Community in Classical Athens*. Cambridge: Cambridge Univ. Press.

Cohen, Edward. 1992. *Athenian Economy and Society: A Banking Perspective*. Princeton: Princeton Univ. Press.

Cole, Thomas. 1991. *The Origins of Rhetoric in Ancient Greece*. Baltimore: Johns Hopkins Univ. Press.

Comaroff, John L., and Simon Roberts. 1981. *Rules and Processes*. Chicago: Univ. of Chicago Press.

Conley, John M., and William M. O'Barr. 1990. *Rules versus Relationships: The Ethnography of Legal Discourse*. Chicago: Univ. of Chicago Press.

Connerton, Paul. 1989. *How Societies Remember*. Cambridge: Cambridge Univ. Press.

Cronin, James Farley. 1936. *The Athenian Juror and His Oath* (part of a Ph.D. dissertation, submitted to the University of Chicago in 1934). Private edition, distributed by the University of Chicago Libraries.

Darnton, Robert. 1984. *The Great Cat Massacre and Other Episodes in French Cultural History*. New York: Vintage Books.

Davies, John K. 1971. *Athenian Propertied Families*. Oxford: Clarendon Press.

———. 1981. *Wealth and the Power of Wealth in Classical Athens*. New York: Arno Press.

Davis, Natalie Zemon. 1987. *Fiction in the Archives*. Stanford: Stanford Univ. Press.

De Sousa, Ronald. 1987. *The Rationality of Emotion*. Cambridge, Mass.: MIT Press.

Dershowitz, Alan M. 1996. "Life Is Not a Dramatic Narrative." Pp. 99–105 in Peter Brooks and Paul Gewirtz, eds., *Law's Stories: Narrative and Rhetoric in the Law*. New Haven: Yale Univ. Press.

Detienne, Marcel. 1996. *The Masters of Truth in Archaic Greece*. Trans. by Janet Lloyd. New York: Zone Books. First published Paris: F. Maspero, 1967.

Dover, K. J. 1968. *Lysias and the Corpus Lysiacum*. Berkeley: Univ. of California Press.

———. 1974. *Greek Popular Morality in the Time of Plato and Aristotle*. Berkeley: Univ. of California Press.

duBois, Page. 1991. *Torture and Truth*. New York: Routledge.

Ellickson, Robert C. 1991. *Order without Law: How Neighbors Settle Disputes*. Cambridge, Mass.: Harvard Univ. Press.

Felstiner, William L. F., Richard L. Able, and Austin Sarat. 1980–1981. "The Emergence and Transformation of Disputes: Naming, Blaming, Claiming . . ." *Law & Society Review* 15: 631–654.

Ferguson, Robert A. 1996. "Untold Stories in the Law." Pp. 84–98 in Peter Brooks and Paul Gewirtz, eds., *Law's Stories: Narrative and Rhetoric in the Law*. New Haven: Yale Univ. Press.

Finley, M. I. 1973. *The Ancient Economy*. Berkeley: Univ. of California Press.

———. 1979. *The World of Odysseus*. London: Penguin.

Fish, Stanley. 1984. "Fish v. Fiss." *Stanford Law Review* 36: 1325–1347.

———. 1994. *There's No Such Thing as Free Speech*. Oxford: Oxford Univ. Press.

Fisher, Nick. 1990. "The Law of *Hubris* in Athens." Pp. 123–138 in Paul Cartledge, Paul Millett, and Stephen Todd, eds., *NOMOS*. Cambridge: Cambridge Univ. Press.

Foucault, Michel. 1977. *Discipline and Punish*. New York: Vintage Books.

———. 1978. *The History of Sexuality*. New York: Vintage Books.

———. 1985. *The Use of Pleasure*. New York: Vintage Books.

———. 1986. *The Care of the Self*. New York: Vintage Books.

Foxhall, Lin. 1996. "The Law and the Lady: Women and Legal Proceedings in Classical Athens." Pp. 133–152 in L. Foxhall and A. D. E. Lewis, eds., *Greek Law in Its Political Setting: Justifications not Justice*. Oxford: Clarendon Press.

Foxhall, Lin, and A. D. E. Lewis, eds. 1996. *Greek Law in Its Political Setting: Justifications not Justice*. Oxford: Clarendon Press.

Fränkel, Max. 1878. "Der attische Heliasteneid." *Hermes* 13: 452–466.

Gagarin, Michael. 1989. *The Murder of Herodes: A Study of Antiphon 5*. Frankfurt: Verlag Peter Lang.

———. 1990. "The Nature of Proofs in Antiphon." *Classical Philology* 85: 22–32.

———. 1996. "The Torture of Slaves in Athenian Law." *Classical Philology* 91: 1–18.

———. 1997. *Antiphon: The Speeches*. Cambridge: Cambridge Univ. Press.

Gernet, Louis. 1955. *Droit et société dans la Grèce ancienne*. Paris: Recueil Sirey.

Gewirtz, Paul. 1996a. "Narrative and Rhetoric in the Law." Pp. 2–13 in Peter Brooks and Paul Gewirtz, eds., *Law's Stories: Narrative and Rhetoric in the Law*. New Haven: Yale Univ. Press.

———. 1996b. "Victims and Voyeurs: Two Narrative Problems at the Criminal Trial." Pp. 135–161 in Peter Brooks and Paul Gewirtz, eds., *Law's Stories: Narrative and Rhetoric in the Law*. New Haven: Yale Univ. Press.

Giddens, Anthony. 1984. *The Constitution of Society*. Berkeley: Univ. of California Press.

———. 1990. *The Consequences of Modernity*. Stanford: Stanford Univ. Press.

———. 1991. *Modernity and Self-Identity*. Stanford: Stanford Univ. Press.

Gould, J. 1973. "Hiketeia." *Journal of Hellenic Studies* 93: 74–103.

Gouldner, Alvin W. 1965. *Enter Plato*. New York: Basic Books.

Halperin, David. 1990. *One Hundred Years of Homosexuality*. New York: Routledge.

Hansen, Mogens Herman. 1974. *The Sovereignty of the People's Court in Athens in the Fourth Century B.C. and the Public Action against Unconstitutional Proposals*. Odense Univ. Press.

———. 1985. "Athenian *Nomothesia*." *Greek, Roman and Byzantine Studies* 26: 345–371.

———. 1989a. "Solonian Democracy in Fourth-Century Athens." *Classica et Mediaevalia* 40: 71–99.

———. 1989b. "On the Importance of Institutions in an Analysis of Athenian Democracy." *Classica et Mediaevalia* 40: 107–113.

———. 1990. Review of Ober 1989. *Classical Review* 40: 348–356.

———. 1991. *Athenian Democracy in the Age of Demosthenes*. Trans. by J. A. Crook. Cambridge, Mass.: Basil Blackwell.

Harris, Edward M. 1994. "Law and Oratory." Pp. 130–150 in Ian Worthington, ed., *Persuasion: Greek Rhetoric in Action*. New York: Routledge.

Harris, William. 1989. *Ancient Literacy*. Cambridge, Mass.: Harvard Univ. Press.

Harrison, A. R. W. 1968. *The Law of Athens*. Vol. 1. Oxford: Clarendon Press.

———. 1971. *The Law of Athens*. Vol. 2. Oxford: Clarendon Press.

Harvey, David. 1990. "The Sykophant and Sykophancy: Vexatious Redefinition?" Pp. 103–121 in Paul Cartledge, Paul Millett, and Stephen Todd, eds., *NOMOS: Essays in Athenian Law, Politics, and Society*. Cambridge: Cambridge Univ. Press.

Headlam, J. W. 1893. "On the πρόκλησις εἰς βάσονον in Attic Law." *Classical Review* 7: 1–5.

———. 1894. "Slave Torture in Athens." *Classical Review* 8: 136–137.

Herman, Gabriel. 1987. *Ritualised Friendship and the Greek City.* Cambridge: Cambridge Univ. Press.

Hillgruber, Michael. 1988. *Die zehnte Rede des Lysias.* Berlin: Walter de Gruyter.

Humphreys, Sally. 1983. "The Evolution of Legal Process in Ancient Attica." Pp. 229–256 in E. Gabba, ed., *Tria Corda: Scritti in onore di Arnaldo Momigliano.* Como: Edizioni New Press.

———. 1985a. "Law as Discourse." *History and Anthropology* 1: 241–264.

———. 1985b. "Social Relations on Stage: Witnesses in Classical Athens." *History and Anthropology* 1: 316–321.

———. 1986. "Kinship Patterns in the Athenian Courts." *Greek, Roman and Byzantine Studies* 27: 57–92.

Hunt, Lynn. 1989. "Introduction: History, Culture, and Text." Pp. 1–22 in Lynn Hunt, ed., *The New Cultural History.* Berkeley: Univ. of California Press.

Hunter, Virginia. 1989. "Women's Authority in Classical Athens: The Example of Kleoboule and Her Son (Dem. 27–29)." *Echos du Monde Classique* 8: 39–48.

———. 1992. "Constructing the Body of the Citizen: Corporal Punishment in Classical Athens." *Echos du Monde Classique* 11: 271–291.

———. 1994. *Policing Athens.* Princeton: Princeton Univ. Press.

Isager, Signe, and Mogens Herman Hansen. 1975. *Aspects of Athenian Society in the Fourth Century B.C.* Trans. by Judith Hsiang Rosenmeier. Odense: Odense Univ. Press.

Jackson, Bernard S. 1990. "Semiotics and the Problem of Interpretation." Pp. 84–103 in Patrick Nerhot, ed., *Law, Interpretation and Reality: Essays in Epistemology, Hermeneutics and Jurisprudence.* Dordrecht: Kluwer Academic Publishers.

Johnstone, Steven. 1989. "Social Relations, Rhetoric, Ideology: The People's Power and the Athenian Courts." Ph.D. thesis, Univ. of Chicago.

———. 1994. "Virtuous Toil, Vicious Work: Xenophon on Aristocratic Style." *Classical Philology* 89: 219–240.

———. 1998. "Cracking the Code of Silence: Athenian Legal Oratory and the History of Slaves and Women." Pp. 221–235 in Sandra R. Joshel and Sheila Murnaghan, eds., *Women and Slaves in Greco-Roman Culture: Differential Equations.* London and New York: Routledge.

Kennedy, George. 1963. *The Art of Persuasion in Greece.* Princeton: Princeton Univ. Press.

Knox, Bernard. 1968. "Silent Reading in Antiquity." *Greek, Roman and Byzantine Studies* 9: 421–435.

Konstan, David. 1985. "The Politics of Aristophanes' *Wasps.*" *Transactions of the American Philological Association* 115: 27–46.

Kurke, Leslie. 1991. *The Traffic in Praise: Pindar and the Poetics of Social Economy.* Ithaca: Cornell Univ. Press.

Langbein, John. 1977. *Torture and the Law of Proof.* Chicago: Univ. of Chicago Press.

Lavency, M. 1964. *Aspects de la logographie judiciaire attique.* Louvain: Bureaux du Recueil Bibliothèque de l'Université.

Law, John. 1994. *Organizing Modernity.* Oxford: Blackwell.

Lempert, Richard. 1988. "The Autonomy of Law: Two Visions Compared." Pp. 152–190 in Gunther Teubner, ed., *Autopoietic Law: A New Approach to Law and Society.* Berlin: Walter de Gruyter.

Lipsius, Justus Hermann. 1905–1915. *Das Attische Recht und Rechtsverfahren.* Leipzig: O. R. Reisland. 3 vols.

Lloyd, G. E. R. 1990. *Demystifying Mentalities.* Cambridge: Cambridge Univ. Press.

Loraux, Nicole. 1986. *The Invention of Athens.* Trans. by Alan Sheridan. Cambridge, Mass.: Harvard Univ. Press. First published Paris: Mouton, 1981.

Luhmann, Niklas. 1982. *The Differentiation of Society.* Trans. by Stephen Holms and Charles Larmore. New York: Columbia Univ. Press.

MacDowell, Douglas. 1962. *Andokides: On the Mysteries.* Oxford: Clarendon Press.

———. 1963. *Athenian Homicide Law in the Age of the Orators.* Manchester: Manchester Univ. Press.

———. 1975. "Law-Making at Athens in the Fourth Century B.C." *Journal of Hellenic Studies* 95: 62–74.

———. 1978. *The Law in Classical Athens.* Ithaca: Cornell Univ. Press.

———. 1989. "The *Oikos* in Athenian Law." *Classical Quarterly* 39: 10–21.

———. 1990. *Demosthenes: Against Meidias (Oration 21).* Oxford: Clarendon Press.

Markle, M. M. 1985. "Jury Pay and Assembly Pay at Athens." *History of Political Thought* 6: 265–297.

Mather, Lynn, and Barbara Yngvesson. 1980–1981. "Language, Audience, and the Transformation of Disputes." *Law & Society Review* 15: 775–821.

Meiggs, Russell. 1972. *The Athenian Empire.* Oxford: Oxford Univ. Press.

Meinecke, Joachim. 1971. "Gesetzesinterpretation und Gesetzesanwendung im Attischen Zivilprozess." *Revue internationale des droits de l'Antiquité.* Ser. 3, 18: 275–360.

Merry, Sally Engle. 1990. *Getting Justice and Getting Even: Legal Consciousness among Working-Class Americans.* Chicago: Univ. of Chicago Press.

Meyer-Laurin, Harald. 1965. *Gesetz und Billigkeit im attischen Prozess.* Weimar: Hermann Böhlaus Nachfolger.

Miller, William Ian. 1990. *Bloodtaking and Peacemaking: Feud, Law, and Society in Saga Iceland.* Chicago: Univ. of Chicago Press.

Millett, Paul. 1989. "Patronage and Its Avoidance in Classical Athens." Pp. 15–47 in Andrew Wallace-Hadrill, ed., *Patronage in Ancient Society.* London: Routledge.

———. 1991. *Lending and Borrowing in Ancient Athens.* Cambridge: Cambridge Univ. Press.

Mirhady, David C. 1991a. "Non-Technical *Pisteis* in Aristotle and Anaximenes," *American Journal of Philology* 112: 5–28.

———. 1991b. "The Oath-Challenge in Athens." *Classical Quarterly* 41: 78–83.

———. 1996. "Torture and Rhetoric in Athens." *Journal of Hellenic Studies* 116: 119–131.

Missiou, Anna. 1992. *The Subversive Oratory of Andokides.* Cambridge: Cambridge Univ. Press.

Moore, Sally Falk. 1973. "Law and Social Change: The Semi-Autonomous Social Field as an Appropriate Subject of Study." *Law & Society Review* 7: 719–746.

Nader, Laura, and Harry F. Todd, Jr., eds. 1978. *The Disputing Process: Law in Ten Societies.* New York: Columbia Univ. Press.

Navarre, Octave. 1900. *Essai sur la rhétorique grecque avant Aristote.* Paris: Librairie Hachette.

Nerhot, Patrick. 1990. "Interpretation in Legal Science: The Notion of Narrative Coherence." Pp. 192–225 in Patrick Nerhot, ed., *Law, Interpretation and Reality: Essays in Epistemology, Hermeneutics and Jurisprudence.* Dordrecht: Kluwer Academic Publishers.

Ober, Josiah. 1989. *Mass and Elite in Democratic Athens.* Princeton: Princeton Univ. Press.

Osborne, Robin. 1985. "Law in Action in Classical Athens." *Journal of Hellenic Studies* 105: 40–58.

———. 1990. "Vexatious Litigation in Classical Athens: Sykophancy and the Sykophant." Pp. 83–102 in Paul Cartledge, Paul Millett, and Stephen Todd, eds., *NOMOS: Essays in Athenian Law, Politics, and Society.* Cambridge: Cambridge Univ. Press.

Ostwald, Martin. 1955. "The Athenian Legislation against Tyranny and Subversion." *Transactions of the American Philological Association* 86: 103–128.

Ott, Ludwig. 1896. *Beiträge zur Kenntnis des Griechischen Eides.* Leipzig: Gustav Fock.

Pearson, Lionel. 1972. *Demosthenes: Six Private Speeches.* Atlanta: Scholars Press.

Pedrick, Victoria. 1982. "Supplication in the *Iliad* and *Odyssey*." *Transactions of the American Philological Association* 112: 125–141.

Plescia, Joseph. 1970. *The Oath and Perjury in Ancient Greece.* Tallahassee: Florida State Univ. Press.

Pomeroy, Sarah B. 1975. *Goddesses, Whores, Wives, and Slaves.* New York: Schocken Books.

———. 1994. *Xenophon, "Oeconomicus."* Oxford: Oxford Univ. Press.

Rhodes, P. J. 1972. *The Athenian Boule.* Oxford: Clarendon Press.

———. 1981a. "Notes on Voting in Athens," *Greek, Roman and Byzantine Studies* 22: 125–132.

———. 1981b. *A Commentary on the Aristotelian* Athenaion Politeia. Oxford: Clarendon Press.

Rosen, Lawrence. 1989. *The Anthropology of Justice: Law as Culture in Islamic Society.* Cambridge: Cambridge Univ. Press.

Ruschenbusch, Eberhard. 1957. "ΔΙΚΑΣΤΗΡΙΟΝ ΠΑΝΤΩΝ ΚΥΡΙΟΝ." *Historia* 6: 257–274.

Sahlins, Marshall. 1985. *Islands of History.* Chicago: Univ. of Chicago Press.

Sandys, J. E. 1896. *Select Private Speeches of Demosthenes.* Vol. 2, 3rd ed. Cambridge: Cambridge Univ. Press.

Schaps, D. M. 1977. "The Woman Least Mentioned: Etiquette and Women's Names." *Classical Quarterly* 27: 323–331.

Scheppele, Kim Lane. 1989. "Forward: Telling Stories." *Michigan Law Review* 87: 2073–2098.

———. 1990. "Facing Facts in Legal Interpretation." *Representations* 30: 42–77.

Scott, Joan W. 1988. *Gender and the Politics of History.* New York: Columbia Univ. Press.

———. 1991. "The Evidence of Experience." *Critical Inquiry* 17: 773–797.

Seager, Robin. 1966. "Lysias against the Corndealers." *Historia* 15: 172–184.

Sealey, Raphael. 1987. *The Athenian Republic.* University Park: Pennsylvania State Univ. Press.

———. 1994. *The Justice of the Greeks.* Ann Arbor: Univ. of Michigan Press.

Sewell, William H., Jr. 1990. "How Classes Are Made: Critical Reflections on E. P. Thompson's Theory of Working-class Formation." Pp. 50–77 in Harvey J. Kaye and Keith McClelland, eds., *E. P. Thompson: Critical Perspectives.* Philadelphia: Temple Univ. Press.

Shaw, Brent. 1991. "The Paradoxes of People Power." *Helios* 18: 194–214.

Sinclair, Robert K. 1988. *Democracy and Participation in Athens.* Cambridge: Cambridge Univ. Press.

Soubie, André. 1973. "Les preuves dans les plaidoyers des orateurs attiques." *Revue internationale des droits de l'Antiquité.* Ser. 3, 20: 171–253.

Sprague, Rosamond K., ed. *The Older Sophists.* Columbia: Univ. of South Carolina Press.

Starr, June, and Jane F. Collier, eds. 1989. *History and Power in the Study of Law.* Ithaca: Cornell Univ. Press.

Steiner, Deborah Tarn. 1994. *The Tyrant's Writ: Myths and Images of Writing in Ancient Greece.* Princeton: Princeton Univ. Press.

Stevens, Edward B. 1944. "Some Attic Commonplaces of Pity." *American Journal of Philology* 65: 15–19.

Stock, Brian. 1990. *Listening for the Text.* Baltimore: Johns Hopkins Univ. Press.

Strauss, Barry S. 1987. *Athens after the Peloponnesian War.* Ithaca: Cornell Univ. Press.

Svenbro, Jesper. 1993. *Phrasikleia: An Anthropology of Reading in Ancient Greece.* Ithaca: Cornell Univ. Press. (French original 1988.)

Teubner, Gunther. 1983. "Substantive and Reflexive Elements in Modern Law." *Law & Society Review* 17: 239–285.

Thomas, Rosalind. 1994. "Law and the Lawgiver in the Athenian Democracy." Pp. 119–133 in Robin Osborne and Simon Hornblower, eds., *Ritual, Finance, Politics: Athenian Democratic Accounts Presented to David Lewis.* Oxford: Clarendon Press.

Thompson, E. P. 1963. *The Making of the English Working Class.* New York: Vintage Books.

———. 1978. *The Poverty of Theory and Other Essays.* London: Monthly Review Press.

————. 1993. "The Moral Economy of the English Crowd in the Eighteenth Century." Ch. 4 in E. P. Thompson, *Customs in Common.* New York: The New Press. First published in *Past and Present* 50 (1971).

Thompson, H. A. 1952. "The Altar of Pity in the Athenian Agora." *Hesperia* 21: 47–82.

Thompson, Wesley E. 1976. *De Hagniae Hereditate: An Athenian Inheritance Case.* Leiden: E. J. Brill.

Thür, Gerhard. 1977. *Beweisführung vor den Schwurgerichtshöfen Athens: die Proklesis zur Basanos.* Vienna.

Todd, S. C. 1990a. "*Lady Chatterley's Lover* and the Attic Orators: The Social Composition of the Athenian Jury." *Journal of Hellenic Studies* 110: 146–173.

————. 1990b. "The Purpose of Evidence in Athenian Courts." Pp. 19–39 in Paul Cartledge, Paul Millett, and Stephen Todd, eds., *NOMOS: Essays in Athenian Law, Politics, and Society.* Cambridge: Cambridge Univ. Press.

————. 1990c. "The Use and Abuse of the Attic Orators." *Greece and Rome* 37: 159–178.

————. 1993. *The Shape of Athenian Law.* Oxford: Oxford Univ. Press.

————. 1996. "Lysias against Nikomachos: The Fate of the Expert in Athenian Law." Pp. 101–131 in L. Foxhall and A. D. E. Lewis, eds., *Greek Law in Its Political Setting: Justifications not Justice.* Oxford: Clarendon Press.

Todd, Stephen, and Paul Millett. 1990. "Law, Society and Athens." Pp. 1–18 in Paul Cartledge, Paul Millett, and Stephen Todd, eds., *NOMOS: Essays in Athenian Law, Politics, and Society.* Cambridge: Cambridge Univ. Press.

Trevett, Jeremy. 1992. *Apollodoros the Son of Pasion.* Oxford: Clarendon Press.

Trubek, David M. 1980–1981. "The Construction and Deconstruction of a Disputes-Focused Approach: An Afterword." *Law and Society Review* 15: 727–747.

Turner, Bryan. 1984. *The Body and Society.* New York: Basil Blackwell.

Usher, Stephen. 1976. "Lysias and His Clients." *Greek, Roman and Byzantine Studies* 17: 31–40.

Usher, Stephen, and Dietmar Najock. 1982. "A Statistical Study of Authorship in the Corpus Lysiacum." *Computers and the Humanities* 16: 85–105.

Versnel, H. S. 1987. "Wife and Helpmate: Women of Ancient Athens in Anthropological Perspective." Pp. 59–86 in Josine Blok and Peter Mason, eds., *Sexual Asymmetry.* Amsterdam: J. C. Gieben.

Veyne, Paul. 1984. *Writing History.* Middletown, Connecticut: Wesleyan Univ. Press.

White, James Boyd. 1990. *Justice as Translation: An Essay in Cultural and Legal Criticism.* Chicago: Univ. of Chicago Press.

Whitehead, David. 1983. "Competitive Outlay and Community Profit: φιλοτιμία in Democratic Athens." *Classica et Mediaevalia* 34: 55–74.

Winkler, John. 1990. *The Constraints of Desire.* London: Routledge.

Wolfe, Alan. 1992. "Sociological Theory in the Absence of People: The Limits of Luhmann's Systems Theory." *Cardozo Law Review* 13: 1729–1743.

Wolff, Hans Julius. 1966. *Die attische Paragraphe.* Weimar: Hermann Böhlaus Nachfolger.

Wolff, Hans Julius. 1970. *"Normenkontrolle" und Gesetzesbegriff in der attischen Demokratie: Untersuchen zur γραφή παρανόμων.* Heidelberg: Carl Winter.

Wolpert, Andrew. 1996. "Rebuilding the Walls of Athens: Democratic Ideology, Civic Discourse, and the Reconciliation of 403 B.C." Ph.D. thesis, Univ. of Chicago.

Wood, Ellen Meiksins. 1988. *Peasant-Citizen and Slave.* New York: Verso.

Worthington, Ian. 1991. "Greek Oratory, Revision of Speeches and the Problem of Historical Reliability." *Classica et Mediaevalia* 42: 55–74.

———. 1992. *A Historical Commentary on Dinarchus.* Ann Arbor: Univ. of Michigan Press.

———. 1994. "The Canon of the Ten Attic Orators." Pp. 244–263 in Ian Worthington, ed., *Persuasion: Greek Rhetoric in Action.* New York: Routledge.

Wyse, William. 1904. *The Speeches of Isaeus.* Cambridge: Cambridge Univ. Press (reprint: New York: Arno, 1979).

Yngvesson, Barbara. 1984. "What Is a Dispute About? The Political Interpretation of Social Control." Pp. 235–259 in Donald Black, ed., *Toward a General Theory of Social Control,* vol. 2. Orlando: Academic Press, Inc.

Yngvesson, Barbara, and Lynn Mather. 1983. "Courts, Moots, and the Disputing Process." Pp. 51–83 in Keith O. Boyum and Lynn Mather, eds., *Empirical Theories about Courts.* New York: Longman.

Yunis, Harvey. 1988. "Law, Politics, and the *Graphe Paranomon* in Fourth-Century Athens." *Greek, Roman and Byzantine Studies* 29: 361–382.

INDEX

INDEX OF PASSAGES CITED

Printed and bound by CPI Group (UK) Ltd, Croydon, CR0 4YY

09/06/2025

14685839-0002